THE 15:17 TO PARIS

A TRUE STORY
THE REAL HEROES

THE 15:17 TO PARIS

ANTHONY SADLER, ALEK SKARLATOS,
SPENCER STONE AND JEFFREY E. STERN

HarperCollins*Publishers*

HarperCollins*Publishers*
1 London Bridge Street
London SE1 9GF

www.harpercollins.co.uk

First published by PublicAffairs, an imprint of Perseus Books, LLC,
a subsidiary of Hachette Book Group, Inc. 2016
This edition published by HarperCollins*Publishers* 2018

1 3 5 7 9 10 8 6 4 2

Book design by Jane Raese

A catalogue record of this book is
available from the British Library

ISBN 978-0-00-829229-4

Printed and bound in Great Britain by
CPI Group (UK) Ltd, Croydon, CR0 4YY

To my family —S.S.

To Zoe —A.A.S.

To my family —A.S.

CONTENTS

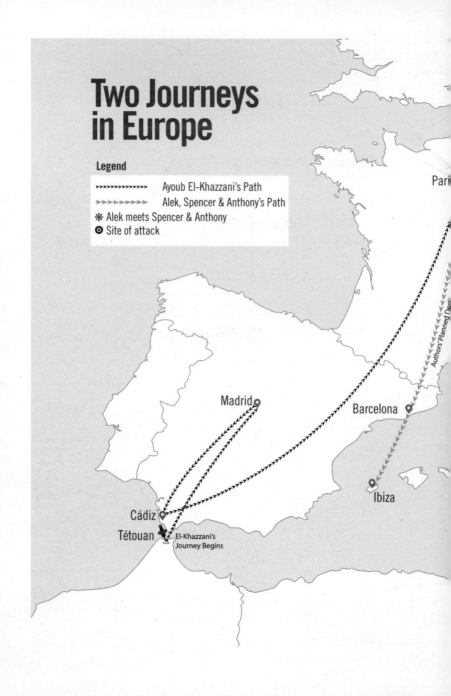

Two Journeys in Europe

Legend

▸▸▸▸▸▸▸▸▸▸▸▸▸ Ayoub El-Khazzani's Path
▸▸▸▸▸▸▸▸▸ Alek, Spencer & Anthony's Path
✳ Alek meets Spencer & Anthony
◉ Site of attack

Paris

Authors' Planned Departure

Madrid

Barcelona

Ibiza

Cádiz

Tétouan
El-Khazzani's Journey Begins

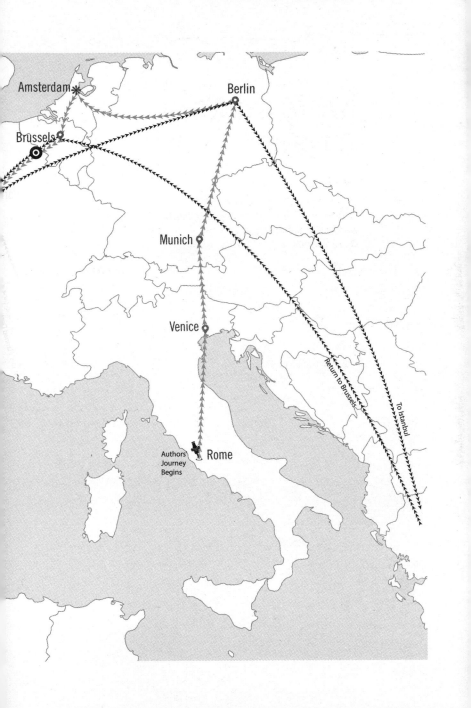

Amsterdam

Berlin

Brussels

Munich

Venice

Return to Brussels

To Istanbul

Authors'
Journey
Begins

Rome

Chance is perhaps the pseudonym of God
when he does not want to sign.

— Théophile Gautier

PROLOGUE

ANTHONY SADLER, KNIGHT OF THE LEGION OF HONOR

Anthony Sadler:
Still alive dad we're in Amsterdam and staying at the A&O hostel. We will be here till Friday

Pastor Sadler:
Okay Son—how are you doing?

Anthony Sadler:
I'm great leaving wifi, talk to you in a bit

Pastor Sadler:
Okay

Anthony Sadler:
Hi dad so it's 8am on Friday here
right now. We head out of Amsterdam
to Paris today at 3pm and will get
around 6pm. I'll text you hotel info
when I receive it

Pastor Sadler:
Okay son

FRI AUG 21, 4:43 PM

Anthony Sadler:
Call me dad

THALYS TRAIN #9364

Somewhere in northern France.

Five hundred fifty-four passengers on board.

Spencer is holding two fingers against a pulsing wound in Mark's neck. As the train races through the countryside at over 150 miles per hour, he's trying to plug the carotid artery because if he doesn't, Mark dies.

Anthony watches from above.

If there are screams, Anthony doesn't hear them; if the sound of wind rushing by the windows is loud, he doesn't register it. He is totally focused. The terrorist is bound, hog-tied on the floor. Mark groans. Anthony feels as if the people lying there below him are the only other people in the world.

The carpet is covered in blood. There is so much blood. It is astoundingly quiet.

The bell that signals the train doors opening and closing is the only other noise, an eerie, antiseptic chirp. Anthony might as well be in the hushed corridors of a hospital. None of it feels real. *Did we just do that?*

The train moves along quickly, smoothly—normally—as if they've imagined everything that just happened. The motion is almost soothing. No one seems afraid. No one seems *here*. There are no extraneous people around Anthony except the ones who took part in the drama that just played out. No one except the ones he's immediately concerned with. He seems to have blocked the rest from his mind.

He's blocked a lot of things from his mind. Including some important things, like the notion that the terrorist might not have been acting alone—that there might be two more, or five, hiding somewhere on board, about to attack. There's no good reason to think there's only one. Still, as far as Anthony's concerned, there's only one. He's become wholly absorbed with only this man, solving the problem that is immediately in front of him, and at the moment it is impossible for him to think about anything he cannot immediately see. His brain has walled itself off like a vault, only occasionally letting light in through the cracks and seams in the metal.

Alek is back—where did Alek go? He disappeared with the machine gun, but he's back now, collecting ammunition and putting weapons in a bag.

Did that all really just happen?

Alek tried to kill a man. While Spencer was trying to choke him. Alek held the machine gun right up to the terrorist's temple so that the bullet would have opened his head up and passed right into Spencer. Anthony had been trying to help subdue the terrorist when one of his friends almost killed the other. But the gun didn't go off. Anthony doesn't know why.

No one will believe it. Anthony's not sure *he* believes it. It doesn't feel real; it feels like he slipped into a video game character, his own thoughts not wholly relevant here, as if he were mostly a spectator of even his own actions. It is so quiet, and so calm, it is not yet possible to comprehend the fact that his life has just changed forever.

He takes out his phone and begins filming. He needs proof. For his friends; for himself.

He is not thinking about evidence. What he's doing doesn't feel like thinking at all really, it's more like reacting.

He'd been reacting a moment ago when they were all tying the terrorist up and he heard a noise behind him. A groan? He turned, registered three distinct things all at once—a man in a soaked shirt, blood geysering across the aisle, and the man's eyes moving toward the ceiling as if something important had gotten stuck up there.

Then the neck slackened, the chin collapsed into the chest, and the man rotated forward out of the seat.

Anthony watched it in high resolution and perfect detail, as if he were able to slow down motion just by observing it. He had a superpower.

Then this: a pool of blood crept from under the man toward the chairs.

Look at the blood. It was bright and pulsing, and a lesson from his human anatomy class bubbled up and presented itself to Anthony—*bright because it's oxygenated, so that's arterial blood*—blood meant for the man's brain was seeping into the carpet instead, which meant he was even worse off than he looked.

Anthony took off running. He crashed through the train door into the first car and yelled. Too loud? His body was charged through with a new force he couldn't wholly control. "Do any of you speak English?"

"Me," "I do," "Yes," ten people responded, a dozen, all different accents.

"Do any of you have a towel?"

Silence, confusion. *Fuck you guys,* at the same moment he decided a towel wasn't enough anyway. Back to the train car, back to Spencer on the ground, Spencer still tightening knots, and telling him there was a man bleeding out right behind him. Spencer wiped the blood from his face, crawled over to Mark, took off his shirt to use as a bandage. "I'm just gonna—I'll just try to plug the hole." Spencer reached forward to Mark's neck, and just like that, the bleeding stopped.

Spencer hasn't moved since. Anthony stands above him, standing guard, looking down as Spencer remains unmoving, on his hands and knees, shirtless, bloodied, fingers in a man's neck, the image so absurd it's almost humorous.

When did that all happen? A minute ago? An hour?

Anthony isn't forming memories properly. His sense of time is distorted; the hardware in his brain that makes memory has been co-opted to dump so much adrenaline that his digestive tract has shut down; he won't sleep for four days, and his sense of time has become plastic.

And where's Alek?

To Anthony, his friend Alek seems only partially present; here, gone, back, no longer a whole person, just wisps and flashes across Anthony's vision. He's there cutting open Mark's shirt, then gone. Walking away with the machine gun, then back. Alek is like a person in an old tintype photograph who fled midway through exposure, leaving behind just a blurred, ghostly residue on Anthony's memory.

That's another reason none of this feels real: none of it makes *sense*. It doesn't make sense that it's so calm on board.

It doesn't make sense that Alek keeps disappearing.

Mostly, it doesn't make sense that Spencer got out of his seat so fast it was like he charged the terrorist before the terrorist even showed up.

Anthony has to ask Spencer about that. He feels it as an urgent, corporeal need. *Spencer, how did you know?* But Spencer is busy talking to Mark, the man with the bullet wound, who's started groaning again.

"I'm sorry, bud," Spencer says. "If I move, you die."

Mark doesn't seem concerned with the hole in his neck. The woman next to him—his wife, Anthony assumes—is getting more agitated; she thinks Mark might have another problem, maybe he was shot twice, or there's an exit wound. Alek finally decides to accommodate her.

Alek is here again.

Alek takes the scissors from the first-aid kit Anthony didn't realize he was holding.

Alek cuts the man's shirt and does a blood sweep, running his hand up and down the man's back, looking for a wound. It's strangely intimate. The three of them all try to keep a man alive with their bare hands on his body.

There is no blood on the man's back.

Alek is gone again.

Even Mark is calm. "Guys, my arm hurts," he says. He says it evenly. He has an arterial bleed, and is only alive because Spencer is plugging it with his fingers, but Mark doesn't seem to know or care all that much about the fact that he's dying.

"I can't move you," Spencer says. "I'll lose the hole."

"Just let me shift a little, my arm's really sore."

"Yeah. We're not worried about your arm right now."

No one seems to have any sense of how serious any of this is. Mark is unbothered that his head is inches from the terrorist who shot him. They're lying right next to each other, right there on the carpet. Neither of them cares. The terrorist is unconscious, and Mark is close behind.

They wait.

They ride the train for thirty more minutes.

Anthony knows police in France will want to talk to them.

He knows newspaper reporters in France will probably want to as well. Through the fog lifting in his mind he understands that they've just encountered a terrorist. *We just frigging stopped a terrorist.* Spencer and Alek are off-duty US service members. Anthony knows that will matter. Anthony knows that will make this a big story in France.

The train curls into the station, and when he presses his face up to the window he can see the French National Police standing on guard next to SWAT-type vehicles. Still, he does not know what will follow. That they will become celebrities, not just in France but in America too. That they will be on the cover of *People* magazine, that the CEO of Columbia Sportswear will give them his private jet for a week and that Anthony will ride it home, that his arrival will be captured by cameramen in helicopters overhead, that plainclothes officers will stake out his college classes, that he will sit next to a gorgeous starlet and have a conversation on TV with Jimmy Fallon, that the president of the United States will invite them over so they can see the secret catacombs of the White House, that Alek—Alek!—will be on *Dancing with the Stars* and make it to the final night, that they will ride a float through their hometown during a parade in their honor, that a glittering Megyn Kelly will win a nationwide contest for their first group interview.

That a trip Anthony only began planning a few months before, when his application for a high-limit credit card he definitely could not afford was miraculously approved, would make him an international celebrity.

All he could think about at that moment was, *I gotta talk to Dad.*

*   *   *

WHAT ANTHONY WILL UNDERSTAND later is that, at the moment he recognized the threat he was facing, his body was overtaken by a series of physiological changes that prepared him to take it on but prevented him from accurately perceiving his surroundings; that literally changed how he experienced sights, sounds, and feelings. Others called it "fight or flight" but that didn't do it justice, didn't express the power of the processes taking over their bodies. This he knew something about; he was a kinesiology major. That the moment he recognized what was happening on the train, chemicals released, arteries constricted, noncritical systems shut down. Sugar was pumped where it was needed, which is why he felt a superhuman level of energy, but also his perception changed. His body jettisoned senses that weren't mission critical. People didn't get that—their bodies actually *changed*. Everything changed, down to tiny muscles that flattened the lenses of their eyes so they could focus on objects in the middle distance. Better to see charging predators or paths of escape, but that same change stole their peripheral vision. They were looking through tunnels.[1]

But the most beguiling thing of all was that he wasn't processing information accurately, because he was blocking out things that weren't important. He did not remember any other people on that train car except the ones he interacted with. Spencer. The hog-tied terrorist. Mark moving closer to death. Were there even other people in the car? He could not honestly say he remembered them, though of course he knew that there were.

But most relevant to what he was experiencing at that moment, this disruptive, disturbing inconsistency, was that the moment he recognized the danger and this process began inside him, his perception of *time* changed. Events presented themselves to him as slower than they were actually happening, and his memory imprinted things out of order. Sometimes his memory was simply blank. There was a reason for this too: as his body was overtaken by physical changes, the hardware in his brain that formed memory was co-opted to dump chemicals. The memory-forming machinery was no longer left to simply form memories — part of what was happening to Anthony on that train was a medical condition with a commonly known name: amnesia. He couldn't form memories correctly, in effect because the video recorder in his brain was being used for something else.

Perhaps that's why Anthony never saw that pistol. Or rather, Anthony could not *remember* seeing that pistol. It's a funny thing about memory: it doesn't always feel hazy when it's wrong. Maybe it's why witnesses to violent crime swear they saw things they never did, and swear they didn't see things that happened right in front of them. It's why burglarized store clerks sometimes don't recognize what's going on in the jumpy CCTV footage of the robbery or the shoot-out: what they actually experienced felt entirely different from what they see on the screen.

Sometimes memory can feel precise, a laser-cut model of what happened, so you can see a fully detailed picture right there in front of you when you close your eyes. It can feel certain when it's wrong. How are memories formed, but through a system of sensors arranged around your body to take in sights, sounds, smells? What if those senses are off? What if they're calibrated wrong? What if the shape of your eye has changed so that, like through a fisheye lens on a camera, the image you capture is altered? What if even the way you're experiencing *time* has changed? Anthony experienced the attack differently from Alek, who experienced it differently from Spencer. The acceleration and near-freezing of time began and ended at different points for each of them. Each have large black spots over their memories of parts of the attack, extraordinary clarity over other parts.

Later Spencer would say he wished he had a video of what happened, but his older brother, Everett, a highway patrolman, disagreed. Everett knew what it was like to go through a traumatic confrontation that felt so maddeningly different from what an unfeeling security camera captured that it was actually disorienting. "It's better that you just have your memories," he said.

But that was just it. Their memories were different.

AYOUB

In 1985, European officials met in Schengen, Luxembourg, to hammer out an agreement. The purpose was free trade. European countries had similar values, and if you could ease passage between them, you could make trade easier. Easier trade was good for everyone; all economies would benefit. All countries would get richer as goods and services passed seamlessly between them, with fewer regulations, fewer taxes, fewer holdups at border crossings.

The idea was to turn the whole territory into effectively one country—once you were in, you were in. Internal borders would become almost meaningless.

For someone traveling from outside, the challenge would be getting into Europe. Once you arrived, you could move within the continent at will. If you had a Schengen visa, you usually wouldn't get ID checks. The agreement also made it easier for foreigners, like American tourists, to vacation in Europe. They didn't need visas at all, and after they arrived in one of the participating countries, they never had to show their passports again, even when they moved between countries.

Not all of Europe signed on to the Schengen Agreement immediately, but among the first seven members were three critical ones: Belgium, France, and Spain. It made Europe, or at least those countries, more appealing to American tourists. And to immigrants.

Ayoub El-Khazzani was born in Morocco, and lived in a place called Tétouan. Its name came from the Berber word for "eyes," a reference to the watersprings that littered the city; Ayoub was raised in something of a Moorish paradise. His family was not wealthy, not even middle class, but the world that surrounded him was luxuriant, suffused with souks overflowing with handicrafts, pomegranate and almond trees lining the hills. It was a North African crossroad; the clothes and crafts in shops testified to all those who had marched through and deposited part of their culture there, most prominently the Berbers, but also the Moors and Cordobas. It was mostly Muslim and, in a way, a reflection of a bygone period thirteen hundred years earlier, when the Muslim world was at its richest, a cultural and intellectual powerhouse, a place with security and civil liberties where even Christians and Jews were protected because they too were sons of Ibrahim. And although they paid extra taxes for their beliefs because they were of course still infidels, they also didn't have to fight in the army. Things were fair. Things were balanced, stable, orderly. The great Caliph Usman came along and eliminated poverty. Great scientific discoveries emerged from that place. Al-battani, the astronomer and mathematician who fine-tuned the concept of years lived then, as did the father of optics, Ibn al-Haytham, the man who proved that eyes don't emit light, but take it in. Al-Farabi, the greatest philosopher after Aristotle, studied there. It was the time of the House of Wisdom, where philosophies were translated from Greek to Arabic so they could end up in the West.

The world owed the caliphate its knowledge; the West owed Muslims.

Ayoub was well east of ancient Mesopotamia, the site of the explosion of culture that emerged where the Tigris collided with the Euphrates, and that became known as the cradle of civilization. But his city gave the cradle a run for its money. It resembled the place and the time that continue to produce such powerful yearning in its descendants.

And which also, occasionally, produces such extraordinary violence in those who believe they can return the world to that utopian period, if enough trauma can be delivered to the powers corrupting Muslims that they shrivel up and retract like severed arteries.

Despite the wealth around him, work was sparse; Ayoub was near that rich, verdant world, but not of it. His family was poor.

In 2005, Ayoub's father was forced to board a ferry for the short ride to Spain so that he might find better work. Eventually he got a job dealing in scrap metal, extracting value from the things other people discarded.

He was gone for two years, so Ayoub went through his adolescence straddling two kinds of lives. Not fatherless, but his father was absent, living in another country, living on another continent, and yet not even a hundred miles away. There, and not there. Close, but in another world.

PART I

AIRMAN SPENCER STONE

AUG 13, 11:49 AM

Joyce Eskel:
Spence how is your ankle? What
happened?

Joyce Eskel:
Hey need to post pictures!!!

1.

JOYCE ESKEL CLOSED THE COMPUTER with an uneasy feeling.

She didn't love the idea of Paris. She'd followed the story of the terrorists attacking the magazine there, *Charlie Hebdo*, a few months back. She'd been reading about Islamic extremists since 9/11, and she knew France had open borders. Paris was a big city of course (she'd been there before, but that was many years ago now) and the odds that the boys would be at any kind of risk were low. She knew that.

Still, she felt something.

Plus Anthony was there, and whenever her son got together with Anthony, things just happened. Two weeks into their trip, she couldn't quite believe they'd managed to avoid major catastrophe.

Although they'd avoided major catastrophe only barely. She knew about the two drinking just a little too much, so that Spencer stumbled over a cobblestone and nearly broke his ankle, on the very first night of their trip. Spencer told her, when he connected to the Internet, that he might need to call it off and go back to base. Call off the whole trip, done on the first day. Could you even get an X-ray there? Would his insurance cover it?

It was uncanny, how they brought the mischief out in one another. She couldn't figure out their relationship, two mostly laid-back kids who didn't seem to have much in common, but when they were together . . . She remembered once when they were in eighth grade how they'd redecorated the neighbor's house with a dozen rolls of toilet paper, then took turns ringing the doorbell and diving for cover in the hedges. When together, the two just seemed to love trouble.

So she sat down after closing the computer, and thought about the feeling. Twenty years ago she might have dismissed it; now she knew what it was. The still, small voice. She called it "intuition" to those who wouldn't understand; to those who would, she called it what she knew it was: God. Preparing her for the events that would follow, just as he'd done countless times before, once she learned to listen, warning her when her children were in danger. What mattered now was what to do with it, and so she decided to do what she always did in situations like this: she prayed. Joyce Eskel closed her eyes, bowed her head, and prayed that things would turn out okay for the boys in France.

By then, joyce had learned to leave a lot up to God. She'd learned early, when Spencer was a baby, when she first brought the kids to their new house, fresh off a traumatic divorce and a devastating custody battle. She'd taken them to her parents' first, a single mom feeling like a failure and wondering what had just happened.

For a time that was a refuge for her, but she couldn't rely on her aging parents forever. She mustered up all her strength and got a job, and with her parents' help she found a house with room for the kids to roam. The neighborhood had a swim club and a tennis club, all within walking distance. Joyce excitedly pointed it all out to the kids that first day, but when they pulled up to the house, the kids got out of the car looking deflated. To them the house was old and ugly. It was the best Joyce could do with almost no income of her own, but the carpets were worn through, the rooms stank, and the paint was faded. It was a signal to the children that their big bright lives with two loving parents and a big happy home had been blown apart, and this was what was left. An ugly old ranch-style, beckoning them into a new and uncertain world.

But Joyce had a vision. She would turn this place into a colorful home for the kids. It was a mighty burden she had: the three kids and a messy divorce, the children's father not so far away but mostly out of their lives, finally a new job but as a worker's comp adjuster for the state, which meant the kind of long days that could wreck you and leave you gasping for air. It meant constant exposure to the ugliest human qualities; the things people do to each other, the things that happen to them. The way wily people manipulated the system to get a buck; the way the system suppressed people in need. Every day she was submerged in desperation, and in greed. She hardened. She began to feel that her whole life prior to her failed marriage and her new job she'd been embarrassingly naïve. She'd always assumed the best in people. That everyone was capable of goodness; that everyone was inclined to act on it.

Not anymore. Now she read bullshit professionally, and her children were beginning to pick up the skill.

When Spencer cried in his room because it was cleaning day—what an emotional child he was!—she gave no quarter.

When she lay in her room and yelled out to Spencer and Everett, "What's all the noise?!" as long as Spencer said, "We're just having fun," even if it was in an oddly pinched, high voice, she let them be.

Of course, she didn't know that most times, outside on the floor, Everett was sitting on top of Spencer's chest, holding him by the wrists and making him punch himself, saying he'd swing harder if Spencer snitched. "Tell Mom, 'We're just having fun.' Say it!"

Even then, as far back as when Spencer was a four-year-old, he was picking up on his mother's skepticism. He had a hard time accepting rules, no matter from what height they came. Joyce took him to church with her, sat him right up front every Sunday, and when the pastor asked who'd like to receive salvation, Spencer raised his hand. Every single week; the pastor smiled every time. "I got you, buddy." Joyce tried to teach him the scripture. "You don't need to do it again and again every week!" But the rule didn't make sense to Spencer, that you only had to do it once. Who decided that? Why was it up to that person? Maybe it was insolence, maybe Spencer just wanted to eat more than his fair share of the savior, but Joyce started to see it differently, that Spencer had a tender heart; her boy wanted to be right with God every week. So she decided to stop fighting. She saved her energy for the fights that mattered.

She pinched pennies and turned the ugly old house into a warm family home, fires always burning when it dropped below fifty, shrubs well tended and grass always mowed. Saturday was cleaning day. She wanted her kids to go out into the world, when they were ready, knowing how to leave it a little better off than they found it. Having won custody, she tried to raise them herself, to keep the kids safe and fed and help them with their homework. And daily she felt she could use an assist, so she looked up and asked God for his favor. She did it in times of particular struggle, or particular need, but also when an opportunity presented itself, like when the couple next door started talking about moving out, and Joyce recognized a chance. She went around the property and found strategic places to pray, conveying upward her preferences for the next tenant. Ideally a single mother like her, please, because it'd be nice to have someone to commiserate with. Ideally one with children the ages of her own, so that the children's social lives might improve, without Joyce having to drive them more.

And he answered, proving his grace in the form of a young mother coming off her own divorce with two kids in tow and one in her arms. Spencer's sister, Kelly, took the new neighbors flowers from the yard to welcome them, and then came trotting back, bubbling over with excitement. "Mom, she's kind of like you!" Joyce invited the woman over for coffee, and the instant they began talking, Joyce's eyes widened with surprise. "You used to be a flight attendant too?" Joyce had traveled the world that way, and Heidi had as well. The country too. Heidi had worked for a bus company before that. She laughed. "Guess I've always been in the travel business," and her latest trip had brought her right here to Joyce. As they spoke, a series of uncanny coincidences revealed themselves, and the two women talked over each other.

"You adored your parents too?"

"You worry about being overprotective of your boys?"

"You also look back, a little embarrassed at how naïve you used to be?"

Joyce had been delivered a replica of herself. The only difference was Tom, a rock of a man whom Heidi had started dating, and who took to her kids like they were his own. He plied them with pizza and Chris Farley movies, had a good job, and was so obviously a strong man with a good soul. But Heidi was reluctant to take the plunge with him, she said; she didn't want to marry right away because she still didn't trust herself after what she'd just put her kids through. But he was there, a stand-in father for her kids, and soon for Joyce's too.

The two became like sisters; their two houses became two wings of the same estate. They might as well have had no doors or walls because the kids moved through them so freely. Joyce was sure the Lord had something to do with it, that it was he who deserved the credit for this new friend. Or perhaps more accurately, he deserved most of the credit and Joyce perhaps just a little bit of gratitude herself, if you please, for having thought to ask him in the first place, thank you very much.

They were two pillars leaning in on one another, doubly strong. Each was exactly what the other needed, at exactly the moment each needed the other the most. They were both strong-willed and wise, but both in desperate need of support, and for someone with whom to let her guard down, because the kids needed stability after what they'd been put through. Each woman felt guilty. Each felt the need to subdue her own feelings for the sake of the children, because what the children needed was a dependable parent, not an emotional one. It was only with each other that each could let down her guard and admit to even having feelings.

Joyce and Heidi filled a missing piece for one another, and as if that wasn't enough, their children were just the right ages. Joyce's son Everett was still the oldest, and Heidi

had Solon, the youngest of the new crew, but Heidi's son
Peter was Kelly's age, and Heidi also had a young son who,
it turned out, was born within a few months of Spencer.
A quiet child with an occasional flare for the dramatic. She'd
wanted to call him Alex, for Alexander, a good Greek name
like her first son Peter's, but when a speech therapist next to
her at Lamaze class pointed out it was hard to say the *s* in
Skarlatos after an *x*, Heidi decided to tweak it. He would be
Aleksander. People would call him Alek.

Spencer and Alek became as close as their mothers; they
were always together. Alek was usually quiet, a reserved
child, but he had a sense of humor and of self-expression
that came out in the most unexpected ways. A fleeting
obsession with Batman during which he wore a Batman
muscle costume all day, every day, for months, even out on
errands with his mom, earning compliments from cashiers
and supermarket stock boys.

He played a tin soldier in the church's Christmas produc-
tion, done up with the full French-style moustache, drawn
on with a makeup pen. When an audience member came up
to him after the show and kneeled down to congratulate
him, the six-year-old Alek looked up and considered the
man. He frowned, then he said, "So do you want my autograph?"

Alek was still water running deep, picking up and feeling
more of what went on around him than he let on. A barbeque Joyce and Heidi held ended early when the police
showed up at Heidi's door, claiming they were responding
to an emergency. Joyce looked at Heidi, who raised her
eyebrows — she didn't know of any emergency. It took half an
hour for the moms to find out that Alek, who hadn't been

getting enough attention during the festivities, had decided to call 911 and report a crime in progress. Alek explained to Spencer, who defended his friend; Alek was guilty only of laziness, not sabotage. He'd picked up the phone at Spencer's house to make the fifteen-foot phone call over to his own, but his finger slipped when typing the 916 area code. An honest mistake!

Or like how well Alek understood Spencer. Spencer's favorite topic of conversation during his first five vocal years was his own birthday. Without letting on, Alek picked up bits and scraps of things Spencer said about it, and then, when it was finally time to bake a cake for the neighbors, Alek asked Heidi if he could be in charge. He dragged her to the toy store, made her buy three plastic army men and a tiny American flag, and wedged them into the top of the cake in a loose approximation of the marines at Iwo Jima.

Spencer walked into the kitchen on his tenth birthday, saw the cake, looked over at Alek, and then smiled, overwhelmed by the feeling that never before in the whole grand course of human history had a more perfect gesture been performed by one friend for another.

ALEK SITS NEXT TO HIM, looking out the window. Spencer is slumped in his seat, feeling himself beginning to fade. He takes a photo of the laptop on the tray table, the half-sized bottle of red wine, and posts a picture: "First Class Baby!"

Then his eyelids go heavy, and he leans back to bask in the wonderful, heavy swaying, slipping in and out of much-needed sleep.

Soft, reassuring motion, R&B on the noise-canceling head-phones. He does not know how long he's been asleep when there is a moment of foggy disruption, a distant jangling behind the music. Body in uniform at full sprint across his vision, the half realization that he is waking up, tumbled headlong into a movie scene already under way. Headphones off. Eye contact across the aisle, Anthony's face screwed up in confusion.

Now he is fully awake and crouched between the seats. A gate in his brain has lifted, and a tidal wave of adrenaline is crashing in; his muscles tighten and time decelerates for him. He sees a glass door slide open, a skinny man with an angry face wearing a backpack the wrong way, strapped to his stomach, and somehow Spencer knows without having to think that the bag is full of ammunition and swung to the front because that way it's easier to reload. Spencer can hear the footfalls as clear and loud as if the man was stomping on purpose; he steps forward, reaches to the ground, and picks up a machine gun that for some reason is lying there. He lifts it up, and Spencer can hear the metal-on-metal cha-chunk of the weapon being cycled.

A beat passes. Someone has to get this guy. A sliver of frustration sparks off something in his brain. *I'm gonna die here*—then an electrical charge surges through his entire body and one more final thought tumbles home with a flood of energy, a notion stored away from a classroom at Fort Sam two years ago that his brain now accesses like a hard drive retrieving a kernel of information: *I am not going to die sitting down.* The realization verges on euphoria. Sound compresses so he no longer hears the screams, and the shattering glass he only now understands is what woke him filters into a thin and distant memory, like the noise itself has been sucked from the train into the past and now all he hears, the only noise in the entire world, is heavy, clomping footsteps. The terrorist is getting closer. He hasn't started shooting yet.

Spencer gets up and starts running. Alek's voice comes to him as encouragement from another universe, cheering him on: "Spencer, go!" and Spencer locks eyes with the terrorist; then his vision narrows, his more extraneous senses leave him. He does not register sound at all, his peripheral vision collapses, and he can see nothing but a small part of the man he is charging, a square of fabric, and he aims for that.

He realizes that he is totally exposed.

There is no cover.

There is no other distraction for the shooter because everyone else is crouching.

He is a big, easy target. He is exposed for one second, two seconds, *Here is where I die,* three seconds, four seconds—the terrorist cocks the gun back again, lowers it at Spencer, and as Spencer pumps his legs, he hears with total, focused clarity the shooter pulling the trigger and the firing pin striking a bullet.

Then everything goes dark.

2.

GUNS WERE PERHAPS the only difference between Heidi and Joyce. Spencer had free rein to play with whatever kind of toy he wanted, and his mother had given in to the fact that her boys loved guns, because—well, boys love guns. She had to laugh at Heidi who, bless her, still grasped on to her misplaced hope that Alek and his siblings would grow up in a gun-free household. *Good luck,* Joyce thought. The two new surrogate sisters established boundaries to deal with the one part of parenting that caused friction. The trash cans between their two houses marked the demilitarized zone: no guns on Heidi's side.

It was just a few years later that Joyce walked out to see Heidi, waiting in the driver's seat of her SUV, while a commando team of camouflaged teenage paintballers piled into the back. She was overrun; she'd given up. Joyce couldn't help herself. "Man, Heidi," she yelled, "looking good with all that camo!"

Heidi looked out the window, and tried to suppress a smile. Then they both exploded with laughter.

By then Alek and Spencer had formed a kind of im-promptu league of war games. They tipped over trash cans in the street and dove behind cars, they gathered neigh-borhood kids to serve as comrades, lined up on opposite ends of Woodknoll Way, and charged, pelting each other with so many airsoft pellets that the gutters ran neon yellow and green, as if the roads of northeast Sacramento had been drenched by psychedelic rain. Other kids wanted in. Soon there were five to a side, then ten, running kamikaze charges at each other from opposite ends of the street.

There was no strategy at first, then it was just that if you got hit you were out, but how could you prove someone got hit? Arguments broke out, so it grew more intense, then became refereed by a set of unwritten and eagerly disputed rules, veritable conventions at the summit of Woodknoll Way, where two dozen arguing kids hammered out the finer points of make-believe warfare, all in an attempt to even the scales and maintain some sense of fairness. This became especially necessary because Alek began bringing firepower other kids couldn't compete with. One day he came out to fight with what Spencer figured must be a $150 replica Colt 1911 gas-blowback CO2-powered pistol. Alek could fire rounds at 350 feet per second, so the other kids were diving behind cars and tumbling into hedges while Alek strafed the neighborhood like a pint-sized Tony Montana. Order had to be restored. So they started dividing up teams according to quality of equipment. Alek would be paired with whomever the new kid was who wanted to play but only had some pissant little peashooter.

Down a few streets from the Stone-Skarlatos Forward Operating Base, there was a kind of nature reserve behind the Schweitzer school, where the teachers used to teach things like Albert Schweitzer's philosophy of reverence for life and peace, but that the boys colonized for the purpose of intensifying their philosophy of reverence for imaginary war. Behind BMX bike platforms and half pipes recast as antitank obstacles blocking imaginary tanks from amphibious landings on an imaginary Omaha Beach, they put on masks and fired off paintballs by the bushel. Paintballs were expensive on an allowance, but better than airsoft because you couldn't cheat as easily. You could spend less time arguing and more time fighting.

Spencer never got tired of it, and Alek didn't either; they'd started a little insurgency in their leafy Sacramento suburb; they fought into the night. And Spencer tried to make those days stand still, because even then he had the sense that other forces were coming along to change their lives; powerful forces beyond their ability to control. Something big and hard to see and almost impossible to confront, stronger than just him, which he and Alek would try to weather together, but that would eventually drive them apart. At least for a time.

3.

Spencer charged.

He'd had enough; Everett was driving him crazy. Jerkface Everett, dumb idiot butthole Everett. Spencer's brother was in his own uneven way trying to fill the man-sized hole in the family left by their father, but had no way of knowing what that should look like. Joyce saw her oldest son driven to torment Spencer and Kelly by what was fundamentally a good, pure instinct: to be a strong man in the house, an authority figure. It was just that it came out all wrong. He lorded over Spencer and Kelly, exercising authority by showing he could control them, not just physically but also emotionally. He knew what buttons to push, how to stoke the flames of rage in Spencer just right. Everett needled and needled, and then when Spencer was near exploding, Everett put on an impassive look like he hadn't the slightest idea what poor little Spencer was so upset about. So one day when the kids were home alone and Everett was goading, Spencer finally exploded, running past the kitchen, putting his shoulder into Everett's chest, and then to his own surprise, driving Everett back four steps, off his feet and into the wall—the wall cracked and they went tumbling right through it, the two boys collapsing into a giant water tank they hadn't even known was back there.

A moment of confusion.

Oh, crap.

They scrambled to their feet and surveyed the damage to

the wall: a hole approximately the size of two adolescent boys. A water tank peering back out at them.

They snapped to action. First Spencer called Alek. "Crap, Alek, put your stepdad on, we're in so much trouble"

"He's not here, Spence. He went to the station. He's working."

Spencer called the fire station. "Is Tom there?" An impossibly long time for Tom to pick up. "Tom! Sorry to bother you, sir, but please come right over. We need your help—we really screwed up."

"Calm down, Spence. What's the problem?"

"We . . . um . . . we broke the house."

"You did what now?"

"Well, Everett mostly, he broke the house. He . . ." Everett was speaking over him, trying to litigate Spencer's assignation of blame, while Spencer waved at Everett's face with his hand. "Please, Tom, you gotta come help us! We gotta fix the wall before Mom comes home!"

"Gosh, Spence! I'm sorry, bud, I'm still at work! Anyway the stores are all closed, we wouldn't be able to get supplies."

"No, no!"

"Don't worry, just fess up to it. I'm sure it won't be that big of a deal. Just be honest."

Joyce arrived home two hours later. Everett met her out front, helped her out of her car, diverted her from the front door, and escorted her instead through the garage, into the laundry room, showing her the house like a peppy real estate agent. "And here we have the newly cleaned floor!" He showed her the whole house vacuumed, spit-polished, candles burning on the mantelpiece, ending the tour by the front door, where Spencer and his cousin were standing sentry, stately as palace guards. Chivalrous as you like . . . if a little awkwardly close to the wall.

"Well, will you just look at this house! To what do I owe this wonderful surprise?"

The candles flickered; Spencer looked at his big brother. Slowly, sheepishly, he stepped forward and revealed the hole.

The glow on her face disappeared. "Are you fricking *serious?*" She threw her hands in the air and started yelling, stormed around the house booming threats, came back— "You're gonna fix this!"—and then went to her room to calm down, leaving Spencer to wallow in the worst feeling possible: having disappointed his mom.

As EVERETT LEFT SPENCER in elementary school and moved on to junior high, his nose for trouble began to concern Joyce. She heard about him getting pushed around at school, and more frightening still, about him pushing back. It wasn't just boys being boys anymore; the boys were becoming men. Other kids were menacing Everett in the halls, drawing their thumbs across their throats when he walked by because he'd dared to shove one of them back. A gang of them came by her house one day before she got home, threatening Everett and goading Kelly, who came out of the house screaming in defense of her older brother, which only emasculated Everett and riled him up even more, pushing him closer to that place where boys do stupid things out of pride. Joyce started to worry about brawls happening at her house as much as in the halls of the school. Everett wasn't backing down.

This school was doing bad things to Everett; it was not a safe place for a kid to learn. And even if Everett could handle himself, what about Spencer? Spencer was still small, still sensitive. Joyce was sick with worry about what would happen to her youngest when he moved on to junior high.

And bullying aside, the public school wasn't handling Spencer right. Because Spencer was behind on reading, the teacher wanted to dose him up on drugs for ADD. Joyce confabbed with Heidi about it. It turned out the school was saying the same thing about Alek, because—and this was rich—Alek liked to look out the window in class. Joyce and Heidi agreed over coffee that it was unconscionable for teachers to try and medicate their kids.

When Joyce went to a parent-teacher conference and said she wasn't about to put her kid on meds (*Just because you're not very good at your job*, she'd wanted to say), Spencer's teacher told her, "Well if you don't medicate him now, he'll self-medicate later."

That just about put her through the roof.

"You know, boys with single moms," the teacher went on, "it's just statistics, Ms. Eskel. Statistically they're more likely to develop problems."

Statistics? Joyce seethed. How dare this woman look down on her just because she was a single mom and her kid was a little behind? She lit up with a million things she wanted to say to this woman. *You know what,* she thought, *my God is bigger than the world's statistics, so I don't really care what any of you say. You don't get to talk to me like that.* When she composed herself, she stood up and pronounced, matter-of-factly, "If you think I'm going to drug my child to make your job easier, you're sorely mistaken." The teacher rolled her eyes, and Joyce stormed out.

And that had been the last straw. Spencer needed a better place. He needed a place where there weren't kids in the halls who might beat him to a pulp, no teachers who wanted to fill him up with chemicals. She needed a place where the adults had more control of their kids, and where he'd be protected, looked out for, maybe a place that provided some of the mentoring Spencer and Alek missed out on from being separated most of the time from their fathers. But private school was expensive. So she prayed. And when a close friend told her about a small Christian school, she knew she'd been given another miracle. The school was nearby, a five-minute drive, not even two miles from her house. How had she not known of it before? It was like it just appeared in her backyard. The school was inexpensive enough by private school standards that she might actually be able to afford it. Best of all, they had activities all the time. Evenings after school the kids would have constructive things to do and some supervision, and weekends too. The school would be like extra parents.

So it was agreed. Spencer and Alek would go to a new school. Their prayers had been answered.

It was almost too good to be true.

4.

AT FIRST, SPENCER TRIED to get along. He ran for school president. Alek served as his de facto campaign manager. They put their heads together and came up with a progressive platform of free burritos.

They designed a campaign poster that consisted of Spencer holding an M16 replica paintball gun in front of an American flag, wearing full camouflage and an Uncle Sam–style "I want *you*" frown.

Then, to make sure they remained true to their message, the two boys went to school in full camouflage. It was important to take the campaign seriously, because Spencer had big plans to change the world. "I will switch the Coke machines to Pepsi machines," he said, "because Pepsi is more American!" But on the day the candidates were to address all the voters, his opponent read flawlessly from a beautifully written speech, and Spencer, rattled and nervous, mumbled through his campaign promises so quietly nobody heard a single thing he said. His big plans for more patriotic vending machines went unheard, whispered into his own chest, and the vote was not close. Spencer did not win.

His political ambitions crushed, Spencer's hatred for the school grew. The place rubbed him the wrong way. They were too involved. The way they enveloped every part of his life was too much; he had gone from a fatherless home to a place with a dozen new fathers and mothers. It didn't feel right, even though he didn't quite know how to explain why it felt wrong. Spencer was small and unconfident, and the teachers felt off to him; they were unlike the teachers at his old school. He didn't like going to church and school with the same people, under the same authority; it was the mixing of two worlds for which some separation felt natural. People were always watching. They were too interested in him, but seemed to be looking past him, through him, like he had some rotten thing inside he hadn't known about but they were certain was there. When he bristled and pushed back they punished him, pulled him into the principal's office and kept him there for hours, which felt like days, insulting his character, invoking God to reduce him to tears and assure him he was shaming the Lord, that he needed to conform because he was walking down a path toward sure damnation.

"They're crazy, Mom. I'm telling you, they're crazy, and you don't care!" Spencer screamed, but Joyce didn't believe it, or at least at first she didn't want to believe it. She knew Spencer needed structure, and she didn't exactly have a wealth of options. She was pinching pennies to make ends meet and keep the kids in private school; there was only one she could afford, and she couldn't stomach sending Spencer back to be eaten up and spat out by the bigger kids in public school, while teachers pumped him full of prescription pills. She chalked it up to character building and hoped his attitude would change. Surely he'd soon see the value in it, finally begin to apply himself.

But all that happened was that he hated it more, and the bond between him and Alek, his one coconspirator, grew stronger. They both bucked under the authority of this strange place to whose faults both their mothers were blind. That was the only saving grace for Spencer: that Alek saw it too.

Alek was stalwart and dedicated in his apathy toward schoolwork. Alek made Spencer certain it wasn't just him. It was those people at the school; they didn't deserve to judge him, and it definitely didn't have any right to tell him whether God was on his side or not. It felt like the two of them, Spencer and Alek, were together in the trenches of some strange kind of psychological warfare. And since it was just the two them who didn't buy into it, the two latecomers, interlopers in this world that all the other students had attended since kindergarten, it was Spencer and Alek more than anyone who earned the ire of the school administration.

Alek responded in the way that was becoming his style. He checked out. He ignored them. He did what he wanted and didn't let what they said affect him, which seemed to arouse their anger even more; but Spencer saw the way they treated Alek and seethed.

Battle lines were drawn.

5.

IF THE NEW SCHOOL WAS BECOMING a nightmare for Spencer, there was at least one silver lining. A black kid who came on a minority scholarship, brought in to pump up an anemic athletic program, because you could barely mount a team with only fifteen kids per class, unless you brought in a ringer.

Anthony Sadler would be the starting point guard on the basketball team as a freshman and the starting wide receiver on the (flag) football team, but he was the kind of kid who didn't hide his frustration on the field. He cussed, he yelled at teammates, he found himself frequenting the principal's office, which by then was a daily way station for Spencer and Alek. If the two boys from Woodknoll Way didn't have much in common with the new kid from Rancho Cordova, they were at least familiar with frequent delinquency. That, they had in common. They went home at night to different parts of the city, but during the day they spent most of their time in the same office.

And there was something else about Anthony that made it seem like destiny that he would be brought into their friendship: his last name. Sadler, which came just before Skarlatos, which came just before Stone, all of which meant that every time the students had to line up in alphabetical order, Spencer was next to both of them. Their friendship was fortified by alphabetical happenstance.

It could not have been a worse coincidence for the school

administration: the three most mischievous kids always assembled together.

For Spencer, it was exciting to have another outsider around. It was like a vestige of a bygone era, the glory days of public school. Spencer and Alek had been forced to hang out with a bunch of kids who'd fully bought into this system and knew nothing else. In Anthony, there was finally another normal person. And he knew cool stuff. He knew how to dress, what kind of sneakers to wear. How to sag your pants, how to wear your T-shirt two sizes too big. The boys from Woodknoll Way were still going to school in camouflage because they thought that was cool. From Anthony they learned that it (emphatically) was not. And Anthony cussed all the time. That's what you did in public school, he told Spencer, did you forget? He did it in sports; he did it for no reason. He said he was trying to scale back, but it was like unlearning a language, and that was refreshing as well; Spencer and Alek cussed too, and whenever an f-bomb slipped out their classmates looked like they'd been slapped in the face. With Anthony, Spencer could talk about normal stuff, in his normal way. It was a bond forged in four-letter words.

Soon, the three of them feeding off one another, they started getting called to the principal's office together. "You said *what?!* This is a Christian school!"

Spencer watched Anthony work on it though. Spencer was amazed; Anthony had an uncanny ability to adapt to his surroundings. He seemed keenly aware of his environment and always knew exactly how to fit in, while Spencer didn't care and Alek didn't seem to either.

So Anthony, once he understood that cussing didn't fly

here—and that people snitched—got his temper in check. He prided himself on always, always knowing how to act; it just took him some extra time at the school to find out what wouldn't go over. He started reining it in. Spencer watched Anthony become the prodigal son. The adults there, like adults everywhere, started to adore him. Adults *always* adored him. Or they found him quiet and polite, which Spencer was wise to. That was an act. That's what Anthony wanted them to think, but Spencer knew that in reality, Anthony was like him.

When Spencer brought him home to meet his mom, Joyce found Anthony sweet but quiet; she couldn't get a read on him. When she woke up to an angry call from a neighbor whose house had been covered in toilet paper by two boys who, in the halo from the street lamp, looked to be a chubby pasty white kid and a tall skinny black kid, Joyce was mortified. Not only had her son shamed himself to the neighbors, but what would she tell Mr. Sadler?

Spencer and Alek had been the only two people for years who didn't buy into the system, but Anthony had that same independent streak Spencer and Alek had, the same eye for mischief. It wasn't just that the school days had been so monotonous for so long; the school had its tentacles in other parts of their life. Aside from paintball and airsoft gun battles, Spencer and Alek hadn't really had lives outside of the school. Now they did.

If Anthony provided a breath of fresh air—a kid who wasn't a drone like all the others seemed to be, a freethinker like Spencer and Alek, a kid with style, and a window into culture Spencer and Alek had no other exposure too—he was obviously just as bowled over by them. The first time he

went over to Spencer's house and saw all the guns—toy
guns, airsoft guns, paintball guns, an actual shotgun in
Spencer's bedroom—his jaw dropped.

"Your parents let you have this?"

Spencer shrugged. "You've never seen one of these?"

"Nah, not a for-real one."

"You've never been hunting?"

"No, I mean . . . black people don't really hunt. It's not like
a thing we do in our leisure time."

Anthony had never seen anything like it. Spencer began
to understand that in this way too Anthony's life had been
a little different from his, that Anthony's family had real
exposure to tragic gangland violence. Anthony's father was a
delivery driver who became a pastor, a pastor who became
a fixture in the community. He was the kind of man who
counted the mayor and chief of police as personal friends,
along with whatever celebrities Sacramento could claim,
because whatever your politics were and whatever your
religion was, you respected a man who went out to talk to
gang members and put his body in front of violence. Pastor
Sadler tried to build relationships with the people at the
fringes of society, connecting his own flock with the dope
peddlers and gangbangers. He tried to pull the police into
it, build up relationships between police and those inclined
to violence in depressed parts of the city, so that the two
groups wouldn't only see each other when people started
shooting, and so that people shooting might be avoided in
the first place. Even before he was ordained, Anthony's dad
had seen guns ruin far too many lives far too close to him to
let his children have them as toys.

In this he mostly succeeded, keeping his children from

having any exposure to guns, even while they lived in a community riddled with them. It was only when Anthony went from a public school in a rough neighborhood to the small private school in a safe one that he finally was exposed to guns.

At Spencer's house, Anthony was out of Pastor Sadler's reach, and he was blown away. He saved up $30 immediately to get his own airsoft gun, upgraded to an MP5, then an airsoft shotgun, and he got lost in the epic battles Alek and Spencer staged in front of their houses and down in the woods behind Schweitzer. Whole Saturdays disappeared while the three of them charged through the woods, then left and charged up Woodknoll Way toward an awaiting army. They re-created epic battles from the movies. At school the only class the three of them found at all interesting—the one subject they couldn't even pretend not to care about—was history, because their teacher talked all the time about the world wars, and then the boys went out after class and on weekends to relive the great heroic battles: the landings at Normandy, the bombardment at Khe Sanh.

It helped that their history teacher seemed the most . . . well, normal. He was animated, and he fueled the boys' interest in wars and the sporadic acts of heroism throughout history. They studied FDR; the idea of a person like that, leading a country through its greatest challenge while he himself was in physical pain, it was energizing. The teacher went into more depth about the wars than any other teacher had: World War II, Vietnam, and especially this one man, FDR, who'd handled a frenetic world and despite it had done the right things at the right times to defuse dangerous situations at critical moments. In class the boys held on to every word.

They'd watch movies, *Saving Private Ryan, Letters from Iwo Jima,* the fascists in the movies feeling a little familiar, *Black Hawk Down, Glory, Apocalypse Now,* and by the time the credits rolled, they'd swung onto their elbows and were talking over each other, "What I'd do when I got to the beach is hide behind the boat until they were reloading." History wasn't boring, not if you pulled open the curtains just enough so you could imagine yourself on stage. Playing the part of an infantryman charging the shoreline or a pilot buzzing the treetops to skirt enemy radar. They dreamed up scenarios in which they defeated a threat against all odds and saved the day; it got their pulses beating, and then they went out and shot each other with pellets, imagining what would happen if one day, it was one of them in the line of fire.

6.

"I WANNA GO TO THE PROM," Anthony said.

Spencer laughed. "You mean like with me?"

"No, man! I mean just in general, we don't have it here. That's my point, there's no prom here, or homecoming, no— I don't know. No public school stuff." Anthony was already preparing to leave. He had a better chance to make something of himself in sports at a public school, and find a girlfriend too. Spencer couldn't argue. You weren't even supposed to *talk* to girls here. If he'd had a chance to escape, he would have taken it too.

So Anthony moved on, but the bond between them was set. They stayed in touch, Anthony still came over to play with guns and watch World War II movies. But school wasn't the same without him there. He'd brought something new and exciting to their lives, and now that he was gone this place was even harder to tolerate.

A new school year started. Again, it was a community of two. Spencer and Alek, a bunch of people they didn't understand, a bunch of people who didn't understand them.

It was then, that first year after Anthony left, that the school finally went too far.

To Spencer, it was clear. Alek was singled out; he was quiet and didn't complain, but like Spencer, everyone knew Alek didn't buy in to the whole code. The ritualistic trips to the principal's office were no longer enough; pressure mounted. A teacher nosing around the students' backpacks took out Alek's iPod, scrolled through the songs, and found one with a bad word. Another claimed to have overheard Alek talking about an argument with a classmate, and that was enough. Alek was labeled a problem child.

He was only in eighth grade, but Spencer watched him patted down every day before school like he was some kind of ex-con, and they went a step further. The school believed he needed to live with his father, and presented the new arrangement as a fait accompli to Heidi. She felt blindsided. It was dizzying; it didn't make sense, the very school that had asked her again and again to help them, to coach soccer, volunteer in the lunchroom, volunteer in the nursery, suddenly deciding someone else's home would be better for her child. She'd hardly had the chance to make sense of the absurd idea that Alek—Alek!—was being called a problem child, or the chance to speak her mind, before he was gone, first to his father's house just across town, then even farther.

Spencer thought the whole thing was bullshit. He hated the place even more for separating him from his best friend. The notion that Alek, of all people, was some kind of threat was so ridiculous it was almost funny. Spencer worried about him, although when he went to visit Alek at his dad's house, Alek seemed to be doing just fine.

"Wow," Spencer said, running a hand over a speaker box, part of an elaborate intercom system Alek's father had installed. "You're pretty spoiled now."

"Dude, I'm not spoiled." Just then, the intercom crackled to life and a woman's voice came over it. "Alek? Honey? Would you like chocolate sauce on your brownie?"

Spencer looked at Alek. "Okay," Alek said, "maybe like a little spoiled."

JOYCE WATCHED WHAT Heidi was going through with sadness. Spencer didn't think his friend was deserving of so much attention, but was happy his mother was finally getting her blood pressure up about the school. Now Spencer had a powerful ally, and it wasn't a moment too soon. Alek said his dad was going to let him go to the Del Campo school, the bigger, more normal public school, which was good for Alek, but it meant Spencer was going to be stuck here, all alone.

The truth was, Joyce by then didn't need much convincing. As much as she wanted to believe the private school was a good thing for the kids, the school community had started to rub her the wrong way. They'd have Sunday fellowship meetings, which already she didn't love because after church she liked a little time to just be with her children, but fine, she went, and hosted parties when it was her turn to host parties in the spirit of open-mindedness, or fellowship, or whatever. But the people were just—she just couldn't connect with them. They didn't mingle; they kept to themselves. They didn't seem capable of relating to anyone who wasn't part of their church. They treated anyone else with scrutiny, even mistrust, and when the school intervened in Heidi's life, as far as Joyce was concerned, that was it. She made up her mind.

"Spencer, hon, I need to talk to you."

"Okay . . ."

She came into Spencer's room with a serious look on her face and shut the door; Spencer worried that some tragedy had befallen the family. "So, listen." She sat on the bed, and considered him. "Do you want to switch schools?" He couldn't believe it. Was this a joke? Was she actually going to let him leave? The clouds parted, the future brightened; he wouldn't be left behind, all alone, while Anthony and Alek moved on to exciting new lives. Now there was just the matter of reentry into the wild, finding excuses to leave school early so they could sneak over to Del Campo for football tryouts.

Spencer and Alek had won a huge victory. The battle felt no less than existential. To an adolescent boy few things could be more devastating than the prospect of missing out on high school life. Sports, girls, parties, dances—their confinement to the tiny school was stunting an impulse that was no less than biological. Even their hormones were telling them they had to get out.

Both had been given an important two-year lesson by Anthony, who'd descended on their lives like an oracle of cool, reminding them what they were missing out on. Prom, homecoming, football, the high calling of high school jockdom. Spencer was excited for public school; for Alek it was mostly just the escape that seemed to appeal. The school had beaten him down. He didn't really care where he went afterward.

Together, they arrived at Del Campo like two orphans fleeing, with little besides Anthony's advice to tell them how to behave or what kind of clothes were okay to wear. They found a bench no one sat on, and the two of them, Spencer smiley but overweight, Alek quiet and brooding, both profoundly uncool, both happy but uncomfortable in their new surroundings, sat and ate their lunch, just the two of them, like a couple of old-timers at a neighborhood park.

They watched the other kids mingle, kids who'd established their cliques and clubs and groups and study partners, but Spencer and Alek ate their wax paper–wrapped sandwiches with just each other. Spencer didn't know precisely how to engage with normal kids, but he had a feeling that sitting just with Alek wasn't healthy. They both needed new friends. As hard as it would be to try and mingle, as much as he stood to be ridiculed, he had to branch out. So one day at lunch he decided, *Let's go. It's now or never.* He got up, and looked down at Alek. "You coming?"

Alek shook his head. So Spencer ran the gauntlet alone. Alone, to bounce around from group to group until he found a place where he could fit, for a while, and Alek remained, content, still on that bench, keeping to himself, watching teenage life pass him by while Spencer tried to mingle without a wingman. They'd both wanted to be here, but now that they had what they wanted, this was when their separation began. Spencer couldn't help but feel he was, in a way, leaving Alek behind.

He just didn't know how permanent it was going to be.

Still, as hard as Spencer tried to blend in, there were a few people who made it impossible. He himself for one; he still never knew what to wear. The small Christian school had stunted his fashion sense and he always felt off. He stuck out in the crowd. Alek didn't know anything about fashion either, but didn't seem to care that they were always dressed noticeably different from the kids who'd gone to normal schools. And at football practice, one of the coaches liked to pair Spencer and Alek for the "heads" drill, lining them up, fingers down, and then, lest anyone forget the two had come from the small Christian school, he'd yell, "Watch out, it's a holy war!" as Spencer and Alek charged each other.

And then one day Alek was gone. Off to Oregon with his dad. Spencer had to keep it a secret; Heidi didn't even know until she called Alek one day to find out if he wanted to come over for dinner, and Alek said he couldn't because he was in Oregon. Just like that. And though it felt cruel and sudden to have his friend gone so quickly, and Spencer missed him, he thought, *Oregon, yeah. It's probably better for him out there.* Something about nature, open fields. He wasn't exactly sure why, but that's how Spencer pictured Oregon, and that's what he pictured his best friend needing.

7.

As SPENCER WALKED UP to the dais to receive his high school diploma he heard what sounded like a boo.

Could it be a boo?

It couldn't be a boo, could it?

What, the—why are they . . . ?

It was. It was three people, maybe five. A jokester, a friend, he later found out, thought it'd be funny to get a few people to boo when Spencer went up to get his diploma. But the people nearby must have assumed there was a good reason, so it caught on, and soon the whole damn crowd was booing. Spencer walked across the stage squeezing his fists together, seething inside, ready to explode with anger. His whole family was out there, watching him get booed. He wanted to give everyone the finger, to scream obscenities at the crowd, but he repressed it. He took his diploma and walked off the stage, eager to close this chapter of his life for good. It was a fitting send-off for a postgraduate life that would be thoroughly undistinguished.

Spencer finished high school and started waffling. He took a job at Jamba Juice. He gained weight. He did little for exercise besides the occasional jujitsu class. His brother, Everett, had taken up the sport, and Everett was the one with the car, so Spencer followed him to whatever diversion Everett was willing to drive to. Spencer had always liked martial arts, because Spencer liked martial anything, but he'd grown frustrated with karate. He'd come home from a class and try to practice on Alek's little brother, but when his sparring partner didn't position himself according to the rigid rules of the form, Spencer couldn't show off his moves. He wanted to do moves on everyone, but it just didn't seem to work against someone who didn't know karate.

Jujitsu was different. Jujitsu wasn't like the other martial arts. Jujitsu worked on anyone. It worked if they knew jujitsu, and it worked if they didn't know jujitsu. *Especially* if they didn't know jujitsu.

That also made it practical. Not just because you could choke out your best friend's little brother no matter what form of resistance he tried to put up. You could subdue any person on the street who tried to attack you, or hurt someone else. As long as he didn't know jujitsu better than you, you could beat anyone.

At $8 an hour serving smoothies, he couldn't afford to train, so he walked into new gyms, signed up for free trial memberships, took their classes, then apologized, "You know, actually this location isn't that convenient for me," and went to find another free trial.

A dozen different fighting styles from a dozen different teachers.

He couldn't make any kind of progress, but he liked the camaraderie, and this rare combination of confidence and humility you got from it, even though those two things felt like opposites. Any skinny old man walking down the street could choke you out if he was better trained than you, and that made you respect everyone. But if you were the better-trained one, you could submit anyone, regardless of what advantages they might have over you. At least, he figured, unless they had some kind of weapon.

But mostly he spent those days hanging with Anthony, who'd started college, or texting with Alek. And he spent time around Meghan, the kind-faced girl with piercings and sleeve tattoos who worked next to him at Jamba Juice. She'd just come up from the Bay Area. Spencer helped her move and more than that; without totally realizing it at the time, he provided her a soft buffer to help ease her into a new phase in her life. She wound up doing the same for him.

The Jamba Juice was across from a recruiting center, so servicemen and -women came in all the time and Spencer, who by then was, above everything else, just bored, started quizzing them. Before he learned to tell by their uniforms, he asked what service they were in, and if they could do it all over again, which would they choose? He mined vicarious joy from it: he could see himself doing the tours they did, on the adventures they had. He pictured himself on the deck of an aircraft carrier, in a desert in Afghanistan.

He started to think that the cure for his boredom might just be to join up. But not *just* join up; he wanted to do it in a big way. He wanted to be the best of the best, make his family proud, maybe be a Navy Seal, a Green Beret. He talked to his friend Dean from Del Campo, who was training to be in the US Air Force Pararescue, and Spencer began reading about it. It harmonized with his own thoughts about how to approach life—an emerging sense that he wanted a change, wanted to go, to leave here for a while and have an adventure, to be where the bullets were flying, to be a little crazy, and take a few too many risks, but to have a good reason. And it fit with the notion that the way you could justify doing that was by helping people. So what better service than one that sent you into battle, dropped you from a helicopter while people were still shooting, to get soldiers stable, get them out, save their lives? Whose very motto was *That Others May Live*?

The more he thought about it, the more he resolved that pararescueman was the perfect job for him. Maybe the *only* job for him. More than a job, it was a calling. They were elite, the Navy Seals of the air force, but somehow almost *more* badass since their purpose was saving people.

He wanted it badly. He *had* to have it. He imagined himself flying above the battlefield in Fallujah, in Kunduz, deploying a parachute at a thousand feet or leaping off a helicopter with a harness and rappelling down to a wounded soldier, talking a man through his most frightening moments. Putting hands on him and drawing him back to life. It raised his pulse. Nothing else would do. Plus he'd end up with a paramedic license, and after his contract was up he could get a job at the local fire and rescue department. It all made perfect sense.

But he was overweight. And he hadn't ever really worked very hard at anything. Ever. Now that he thought about it, not once in his life had he ever really applied himself. Everett was the achiever, Everett who passed the California Highway Patrol test. Kelly, his talented and hilarious sister, had gone down to LA to at least give the entertainment industry a try, and what had Spencer ever done? What risks had he taken? He'd never been very motivated to study, perhaps a bad taste from the private Christian school that never went away. He'd given up football to focus on basketball, given up basketball when he couldn't get playing time.

The only thing he could really remember was once, when he was working as a bag boy for the local grocery store, a man tried to run out with $300 worth of stolen liquor. Spencer helped run him down, chased him out into the parking lot where an off-shift cashier laid him out. That was it. When else had he ever gone above and beyond the call of duty? He couldn't remember. He'd barely summoned the interest to try higher education. He'd signed up for a few classes up at American River College but couldn't stay focused, couldn't see the point.

Here he was then: he didn't have college, he didn't have a plan, he spent his days pressing, blending, cleaning, then going to the market to sweep and tidy up there, then hanging out and going to bed. The least glamorous life he could imagine was his own. Maybe the worst part of it was, he kind of liked it. He had no pressure on him and his mother had stopped pushing; she'd resigned herself to letting Spencer live his life out at his own pace. He loved his other friends. He and Meghan had a warm, if never articulated, protective instinct for each other, and Dean was a stabilizing force, loyal to Spencer and always available for a little advice. Should he really be asking for more than that? Maybe he had what was important: a steady job, the occasional bender, some good friends. In Meghan blending smoothies next to him, in Dean, in Anthony starting at Sacramento State across town, Alek just across the state line. Life was pretty good.

But without glory.

What if he grew old, never having pushed himself to accomplish anything?

He felt he could do more; he *wanted* more. Being a pararescueman felt like exactly that: something *more*.

His first big personal project was going to be trying to join one of the most elite units in the entire military.

"Hey, man, big news," he wrote to Alek. "I'm signing up for air force pararescue." He figured Alek would be thrilled for him. A minute went by, five minutes; finally, later in the day Alek replied, "That's great, good luck."

A little lukewarm for such a momentous decision, but that was Alek. Never one for words.

If Spencer was going to have it, he needed to be in peak physical form, and sporadic jujitsu classes during trial gym memberships just weren't going to cut it. But he couldn't afford to do them more regularly.

No problem; he'd set off on his own journey.

He started working out twice a day. He ran six miles, swam two thousand meters, then hit the weights, then did it all again the next day. He gave up his favorite foods, ate cleaner than he ever had. He had liquid dinners for a year. Jamba Juice was the perfect job, even if it was only $8 an hour and the work was monotonous, because when the boss wasn't around he could make his vegetable juice concoctions—and juice was freaking *expensive*.

He did his first pull-up. He'd never been able to complete one before; too much weight to carry, but now he had less. Now he was stronger.

Six months passed, then eight; he dropped fifty pounds. He convinced the manager at a swim club to let him come in early before the guests arrived, pull the pool covers back, and practice holding his breath under water. He'd need to do two whole laps to qualify, and a whole lot more if he wanted to actually make it through the program. All he talked about at Jamba Juice was the pararescuemen, which he learned to start calling para jumpers, then just PJs, like it was a club he was already part of. All he thought about, all he talked about, was what he had left to do before joining the PJs, what he'd do when he was there. Meghan smiled and shook her head.

Ten months passed; he topped out at thirteen pull-ups and still didn't feel ready. He'd built his weight back up as almost twenty-five pounds of muscle, but wouldn't enlist until he could do fifteen pull-ups and seventy pushups in two minutes.

A year passed and still he didn't join; he wouldn't risk it all being for nothing, he wouldn't screw it up, he *couldn't* screw it up, it had become his identity and even though he felt like Superman he could be better. So he would wait, and wait, and only sign up for the test when he *knew* he was ready.

Finally he heard from Dean, who'd been kicked out of pararescue training for a pulled groin, and had some advice. "Look, Spencer, you gotta pull the trigger. If you don't do it now you'll never do it. You'll get hurt, or something will come along in life and distract you from it. Sign up now."

So he did. He signed up. He'd built up too much muscle though, was thirteen pounds overweight. Within three weeks he'd lost it; within a month he was in a car with the recruiter, driving out to a Cal Fit so he could take the special operations physical test, jittery with nerves. But then something amazing happened: he passed every single fitness test. He performed better than everyone else on every test but one, and he ran his best recorded time, a mile and a half in under nine minutes. It was all almost too good to be true. He'd tried as hard as he could to prepare, and he was *prepared*. He was flying high. A few months later he spent the night at the sprawling DoubleTree hotel near the Arden Fair mall, and went out in the morning to MEPS, the Military

Entrance Processing Station, for the final step. He was about to achieve the only thing he'd wanted for a year, the thing he'd worked the hardest for in his life, something for which he had to physically transform himself, and he began to feel the fulsome contentedness of having found a purpose and then proven himself capable of achieving it.

They drew his blood. He stripped down to his boxers so the doctor could check his body for abnormalities. He had none. Everything now was routine, just formality; he could hardly contain his excitement. And the very last thing to test for was vision; the very last vision test was depth perception.

"Which circle is different?" the doctor asked. Spencer was moments from glory, already thinking about what he was going to drink that night to celebrate. He looked into the contraption. It was old, he thought. *Funny, how ancient the crap they use here is.*

But okay, focus.

"Um, let me see," he said. He saw twelve rows of black circles, all exactly the same. That was strange—or else that was the point! It was a trick to see how you responded to some kind of cognitive challenge. "They're all the same, sir." A beat passed.

"Well, pick the one you think is different." The doctor had no levity in his voice. Now Spencer wasn't sure what to do. He could swear they were all exactly the same shape, but the doctor insisted he pick one that looked different. So he guessed. "Number three is different, sir."

LATER, AFTER ALL THE TESTING, he went up to the air force liaison office to check out, and the staff sergeant handed him a list of jobs he'd qualified for. He scanned it, couldn't believe it, scanned it again.

"Sir, sorry, but the job I wanted isn't on here. I don't see pararescue." The staff sergeant took the paper back and looked at it again.

"Looks like you didn't qualify." He handed it back.

That can't be. "Sorry, sir, excuse me." Spencer sensed people in line behind him swaying with impatience. "But what do you mean by didn't qualify? I passed every fitness test and completed all the examinations. None of the doctors told me anything was wrong . . ."

"It looks like you didn't pass depth perception."

"Sorry?"

"You don't have depth perception."

"Depth perception?"

"You lack depth perception. Can't be a PJ without it. Choose another job from the list. And I'd pick quickly if I were you, or you might not get anything. Pick before you leave. We're open for another thirty minutes."

"PJs is the only thing I'm here for."

"If you leave today without picking a job, you might not get anything. Twenty-nine minutes left now. Pick fast."

And that was it. Just like that, it was over.

Later, when playing it back in his mind, he thought, *Lack depth perception? What a load of crap. Then how could I pick up a cup? How did I play basketball?* But it didn't matter; there was no way of appealing the decision. Spencer was unfit for service. He would not be an air force pararescueman, not ever. A year of punishing himself, for nothing. He'd never felt so deflated in his life. He went home, closed the door behind him, and he wept. When he was done, he felt empty, all his motivation completely depleted. He was zapped. He felt foolish for having worked so hard when such a small stupid thing was waiting all along to derail him.

Depth perception?

It was a mistake, it had to be. He was sure of it. But there wasn't anything he could do about it. It was as frustrating as it was demoralizing, that someone in some position of authority had decided that some useless old device could determine whether or not you got what you'd worked so hard for. An old piece of metal. He would have been a good pararescueman, he would have been happy, and he would have saved lives, and whoever it was up there making decisions was preventing that.

So what was the point? Why had he worked so hard? He hadn't accomplished anything in his life, but at least before he could always say it was because he hadn't really tried. Now he couldn't say that. It was almost worse.

He called Dean, who had cleared the initial medical testing to get into pararescue training but had now been forced to drop out twice after injuries, and was waiting to get in for a third try. Dean offered some encouragement. It helped for a few minutes, and then his encouragement ran out like a pill wearing off, and there was nothing Spencer could do. He'd failed. His eyes had failed.

Spencer's eyes are no longer working so he's running blind. He's entered into a gauntlet and his senses have left him. The whole world narrows to a single unprotected corridor, and everyone else is hiding. He is running straight for a man with a weapon he knows is there but can't see, because he can't see anything; tiny fibers in his eyes have tensed and pulled the lenses flat so everything next to him disappears, and he is running down a dark tunnel with a speck of light at the end. Then that's gone too, and he is simply running, waiting for bullets to tear through him. His last coherent thought is, *Maybe I will delay him enough for others*, and then he launches himself.

A blast of light and pain across his face, his mouth exploding with the taste of pepper and metal—gunpowder. Has the bullet gone through his mouth? His forehead roars with heat, he knows now he's been hurt badly but not exactly how, or if a bullet struck him, or what exactly just happened, but he is on the ground and he can move, so he begins to fight. He struggles to pin the man as he starts to lose vision again, blood curtaining his eye, which is swelling shut anyway. The man is skinny, but his power is astounding, superhuman. He must be on a drug that gives him abnormal strength. They fight in the aisle, Spencer can see almost nothing, light and shapes, he tries to control the gun but can't get it in his grip, every time he feels his fingers glance off metal it slips away again, pulling from his hand, he cannot see well enough to know he dislodged it when he hit the man, and is now trying to pull from the man's grip a weapon the man is no longer holding.

They scramble to their feet, Spencer tries to hit him but they're too close, so he grapples at the man, pulls him into a clench, holds him close to his own body, and now they're standing. Spencer works himself behind the man, remembering the staple of jujitsu, the rear naked choke, just trying to protect himself, swaying with the terrorist, so when the terrorist jerks right Spencer jerks right with him, this part is like a dance, trying to stay even so he doesn't lose balance, because if he loses his position he's exposed to whatever weapon the terrorist has ready next. He hooks his elbow under the man's neck so that their bodies are flat against one another, and then Spencer summons all his strength and launches himself backward. Flying in tandem across the seats, his own body padding the terrorist's fall, his own skull slamming against the train window so hard that sparks of light fill his vision and a head-shaped inkblot of blood smears the window behind him. The man rotates powerfully in Spencer's grasp, and Spencer tries to pull his forearm tighter under the man's neck, desperately trying to choke off blood flow to the man's brain. But the man will not stop struggling, does not even seem to weaken, and a wave of terror goes flitting through Spencer's thoughts. This man should have been out in seconds. Alek is yelling something, thank God Alek is here, and Anthony is right there next to him, if only to see what is happening, and then the gunman's fists are curling backward. 180-degree uppercuts into Spencer's face and he can feel that they're working, sapping his strength, glancing off his eye that's already swollen and bleeding, his face feeling like a raw piece of meat being beaten with a rock, the top half of his vision is blurred, like something's hanging over it. How much time has passed? What if he loses control—what if he dies and can't stop this man? Spencer is bleeding into his swollen eye and fighting half blind. The terrorist has an astounding store of strength and still does not seem to be tiring at all. Spencer is pinned against the window, doesn't know how many weapons this man has, doesn't know what happens if he loses this fight and the man takes the gun back, if the man slips from his grip he'll have all the odds in his favor and he'll find that machine gun again and then he'll really get to work—and just now Spencer hears, from some distant corner of his consciousness, a familiar voice.

"Stop, fucker!"

It's Alek, holding the machine gun up to the terrorist's head.

8.

He thought he'd recovered by the time the recruiter called. In that moment of shock after his disqualification Spencer had, in a daze, selected SERE, preparing people for getting captured behind enemy lines. At least what the acronym stood for sounded intense—survival, evasion, resistance, and escape—and he didn't have much else to go on, but it seemed like perhaps a chance to accomplish *something*. It was between that and TACP, tactical air control party, but in the moment, as cool as calling in airstrikes sounded, the short paragraph describing TACP made it sound a little too much like air traffic control. He'd be learning to do "deconfliction." He didn't want to tell pilots who were actually doing things how to avoid crashing into each other. He'd rather help them learn how to survive if they did. So he'd listed SERE in the moment of shock, then gone home and forgotten about it.

He barely knew what SERE really was, and he wasn't ready. He was still reeling from those twin emotions that held him back, the notion that there wasn't really any good reason to work hard for anything, and the impulse to question people in positions in authority.

He couldn't have been entering an environment he was more poorly suited for.

The whole *purpose* of SERE training was preventing you from having control, mimicking a situation in which you were entirely at someone else's mercy. Some of it was preparing to actually be a prisoner. It was a class set up to test your resolve, but resolve was something Spencer was running low on. He was having a hard time caring much about anything.

On the night he shipped out, Anthony came over to the hotel in Sacramento. He brought a girl with him, but was focused mostly on Spencer. They hung out for a few hours, took a picture, watched some TV. Basketball was on. Spencer was going to Texas for basic training, but from there he'd report to his assignment, wherever in the world it was, and wouldn't be back until his air force career was over. He could be sent anywhere, to war maybe. Which meant this could be goodbye for a while; the next time they saw one another, as far as they knew, could be after Spencer had returned from some foreign adventure.

They spent a little more time together, watched some more basketball, then said goodbye. Neither quite knew if it was time for a hug. They shook hands.

Spencer said, "Well, I guess I'll see you when I see you," and he turned to go back to his room.

"Listen," Anthony said, "just . . . just keep your head down."

Spencer smiled. He was touched, even though Anthony's concern felt a little much. *It's the freaking air force,* Spencer thought. *It's not like I'm going off to fight terrorists.*

And then Anthony went back to his girl.

9.

LACKLAND AIR FORCE BASE is an air education and training command. That means enlisted men come out of basic training and go there to learn specialties. As a cruel coincidence, the dorms for the SERE instructor program were directly across from all the special operations training squadrons, including pararescue. So as Spencer went into intense sleep deprivation, he got to watch pararescuemen from the next building over preparing to be battlefield airmen. He was constantly confronted with his failure. He did his physical training, running down to the SERE schoolhouse with his SERE classmates, while the pararescue trainees ran down to theirs, ran to the pool, carrying their rucksacks, looking just a little more badass, a little prouder, a little more glorious.

He managed to make it through the first week without major incident. It was all pretty straightforward: you worked hard, withstood some discomfort, picked up some skills, that was it.

But it was hard to bear suffering for something when the thing he was suffering for didn't even appeal all that much, and as the instructors became more and more involved, old instincts kicked in like muscle memory. That habit he'd inherited from his mother, to look for bullshit, to always see it when it was there, to sometimes see it when it wasn't. He had a hard time accepting authority and here authority was everywhere. SERE was a program *designed* to show him he had none. And still, of all the things he had to withstand, the one that finally did him in was sewing.

It turned out sewing was the survivalist's secret weapon, because if you ejected from a stalling fighter jet, you could make almost anything out of a parachute, provided you knew how to sew. Hammocks, tents, trip wires for perimeter defense, hunting tools. So it was sewing for a good reason; Spencer knew that. Still—sewing! He wanted to be out training to save good guys and kill bad guys, instead, he was up all night practicing to become a poorly equipped seamstress. The more tired he got, the more orders rubbed him the wrong way, regardless of what they were. Someone told him he had to sew, which automatically made sewing feel worthless. Even when he knew why he was doing it. It was just reflex.

His hands felt big and clumsy. A classmate took pity and gave him a jury-rigged hand-saver, a device he'd made with a spoon stolen from the chow hall, wrapped with tape and bent nearly in half so he could put it around his palm and pound needles through, without his hands going raw. He was doing hundreds and hundreds of stitches, but still Spencer couldn't get them tight enough. His assignment was simple: use a parachute cord to make a water bag, and a mat to keep equipment free from dirt and debris, but he couldn't keep the stitches close. He was up at four in the morning, then physical training until one, then "team-building exercises" for the remainder of the day, which was really just physical training with extra challenges and punishments. He was getting behind on his assignments, and the course was designed to snowball on you if you couldn't pick things up fast enough. He was banging a needle through hard uncooperative canvas all night; each row took four hours or more and he kept messing up, which meant he couldn't sleep, which maybe was the point.

The instructors piled on more and more homework assignments. He had to prepare lesson plans too, because the whole point was not just to survive behind enemy lines, but to teach other people how to survive behind enemy lines. He needed to be a leader. He needed to be thinking. He needed to be creating. And he had to do it without sleep if he wanted to make the assignment deadline.

By day eight he was closing his eyes for not even half an hour, nodding off for five, ten minutes before they all mustered for breakfast.

After a whole night hitting the needle through canvas, he only had half of it done, but he took it to the instructor, wobbly with exhaustion and frustrated. His instructor took out a red marker and circled all the stitches that weren't tight enough, which meant he had to undo the stitches all the way back to the first bad one, and then redo them all.

Another night with no sleep, working even harder and even faster, getting even further behind on the assignment.

The next day was learning how to navigate with a compass and plotting a route between two points on a map, learning in infuriating, pointless detail what every little sign and design meant. It took effort to just to look at the map: he was so tired his eyes kept unfocusing. He kept coming to and realizing he'd nodded off standing up. The instructor became hazy and spectral in his vision; Spencer wobbled, blinked, forced his eyes open, heard his name. Something, words trailing off, then, "Tone . . . Airman *Stone . . . AIRMAN STONE!*"

"Sorry, sir. Can you repeat that?"

"... the next step to plotting your course would be ...?"

"Sorry, what was the—did you ask me a question?" He could barely keep his eyes open. Was everyone looking at him?

"Airman Stone, you're a hazard to yourself and others. Why don't you drop and give me some pushups, maybe that will wake you up." Spencer got down on the ground and obliged, but he figured he was as good as done. He went through the rest of the navigation assignment in a half-waking haze of confusion, and the instructor closed by saying, "Any of you still working on your sewing assignments, we'll give you an extra night. Report before morning chow and present to the instructor in the schoolhouse."

Spencer went back to his bunk, exhausted, demoralized, and sore from all the physical training. He got down on the floor to stretch out his back, just for a minute ... and woke up six hours later. He panicked. It was after midnight, he had to report at 4 A.M., and he had at least eight hours of sewing left that he'd have to do in less than half that time.

In the morning he presented his work, well aware it wasn't near good enough, went to breakfast, and an instructor walked in. "Airman Stone, you're eliminated. Come to the back room, and you'll be served your elimination papers."

SPENCER HAD FAILED AGAIN. This time, he wasn't home in California; he was stranded on base in Texas.

He knew he was still hung over from failing to qualify for pararescue training, but he was proving to himself, with an abundance of evidence, that he was just a failure, period. He lost his motivation, and he started to spiral. Now he was two months into the military, he'd committed to the air force, he'd been ruled out of the only job he really wanted, then the only other one he felt he could really tolerate. Somehow he'd have to find a way to survive four more years in a service whose only two appealing jobs he was now barred from. He was a "student out of training," like a free agent no one wanted. He became a janitor. He had to help the SERE instructors put new mats in the gym, he organized the rooms in the schoolhouse, did whatever glamourless work they needed. Now he had to choose his top six out of a bunch of jobs, none of which were elite, none of which were killing bad guys, none of which were out in the action. He figured the closest he could get was EMT, emergency medical technician, which would at least set him up to be a firefighter back in Sacramento, so he selected that, and after another month he left Lackland, left the world of special forces for good. He gave up on his dreams.

10.

Spencer managed to convince himself that things would work out. On the bus ride east to Fort Sam in San Antonio, he told himself that he still had some direction. He had *some* purpose. But his stomach dropped when he arrived. This base was different. The environment back with all the special forces had been like what he'd always imagined the military would be like. People knew they were elite and didn't have to prove it.

Here people were all marching in unison, singing air force tunes. People cared too much. Worse, people had to conform. Now he had a curfew. It felt like daycare for adults.

Still, he did his best to find some pleasure in it, because what else was there? Be miserable for the rest of his life? So he rolled up his sleeves and dug in. He got on okay. It wasn't thrilling, but he was using his hands. At first, things made sense. If a person stopped breathing, you pumped their chest to make the blood flow. If a person started bleeding, you found a way to stop it.

After EMT training, he moved on to the second phase, five weeks of nurse training. This was more civilized; no more trying to figure out how to handle a wounded soldier in the field. Now you had a hospital around you; you had all the resources and civility of an actual building. He just needed to learn how to use them. He had to learn bedside manner. He had to learn things he'd never have to do in the field: how to use all the things that hummed and buzzed to keep a hurt person alive.

And even though nursing was mostly learning how to work in a hospital, it turned out you had to spend a lot of time in a classroom, too. Whole days studying in a schoolhouse, which activated his reflex against authority, but he tried to keep it in check. He still had no love for books, still wanted to be out in the action, and spending all day in a room with a teacher wasn't his idea of glory but still, he'd found his way into a field he felt fine about. He wouldn't be jumping out of planes like the men on the high-gloss posters, but he'd be useful.

One afternoon as Spencer sat in class, letting his mind wander to the battlefield, a fifty-two-year-old retired army sergeant major approached his wife at the army medical center, just down the street from the classroom. The sergeant major wanted a word about her decision to leave him. The two spoke, the conversation turned into an argument, the argument escalated; she led him outside to a veranda, where he pulled out a .45 caliber handgun and began firing. She fell to the ground and tried to crawl away, but he kept shooting, firing eight rounds before he was done, including one bullet that missed vital organs only because it hit a key fob in her pocket.[1]

Spencer heard the sirens first. Police cars, base security, and state troopers raced by his classroom window.

What the—

An active shooter alert went out over the base PA system and popped up on computer terminals but didn't specify that the shooter was involved in a lovers' quarrel rather than, say, a terrorist attack on a military target, so the thirty thousand civilian and military personal on the base were ordered to follow the "shelter in place" protocol.

Spencer received the order from a nursing teacher who looked up midsentence with panic in her eyes.

"Okay, listen, we have an active shooter on base."

A moment of nervous laughter.

"Guys, listen, you two, get that desk to the door and make sure it can't open. Now! Everybody else, under your desks, this is not an exercise."

It was something in the way she said it, in the cars rushing past—Spencer thought the shooter might be right outside, right there *in the schoolhouse*. A man walking through the halls maybe just a few dozen yards from where he stood, about to kick in a door and start mowing people down. So why were they being made to hide under their desks? They were *military!* Who better to disarm a shooter?

There were protocols for this, since a concentration of military personnel was an attractive target to a man motivated in a particular kind of way, especially if the concentration of military personnel wasn't actually armed and was, instead, sitting in classes, rather like civilians. All the symbolism of attacking the American military, with none of the challenges. So the protocol was rehearsed, and it was very clear. You escape; you do not engage. If you cannot escape, you "shelter in place." You hide. Because if you engage, you create the opportunity for more violence. When first responders come, they might mistake you for the attacker. The idea is that the only people moving are the bad guy and the security forces. So if you can't escape, you find a hiding spot from which you can observe the way in; you "mitigate the room vulnerabilities." You barricade the doors, the windows if you can. You take out radios, turn the volume down, and monitor them closely. You shut off lights so that it looks like the room is unoccupied.

You act, in Spencer's mind, precisely like a coward. He didn't buy it. The notices posted everywhere had clear instructions: how in the case of "immediate danger" you try and "escape/evacuate," and if you can't, you "assess situation/location—what can protect you *(stop bullets)*—look for way in/way out routes—leaders TAKE CHARGE."

This, as far as Spencer was concerned, was what he should do. Take Charge. His own instinct was up against these orders holding him back like a caged animal.

The students barricaded the doors, and the staff sergeant kept yelling for them to get under the desks. He moved slowly, grumbling to himself as he got down on his hands and knees, shimmying under his desk, submitting yet again to the senseless edicts of some undeserved authority. Here was a moment of excitement, and he was being instructed to cower. *Under the fucking desk. We're fish in a barrel.* He felt pathetic. But he was a student, and he couldn't afford to be kicked out of another program, so he did as instructed.

For a while.

He looked across at a classmate under a desk who was reaching for his penknife, they made eye contact, and he nodded at Spencer as if to say, *If this guy comes for us, we're jumping him.* Which made Spencer think that if the shooter really came in while they were all under their desks, he'd be defenseless. He'd probably be killed. Everyone in the room would be killed too. If somebody actually came in shooting, what would he do?

He got up. With the staff sergeant scolding him in an

angry whisper, he got up and stood by the door, readying himself to pounce on anyone who came in. At least if a shooter came in he could engage, wrestle him, maybe slow him down enough to give others in the room the chance to beat the shooter down. The only advantage he had was numbers, and maybe, if he was quick enough, the element of surprise. *Go ahead,* he thought, *write me a little piece of paper.* If he took a bullet trying to confront a shooter, at least he'd have gone down swinging.

After an hour the all-clear sounded, but Spencer had spent most of that time imagining all the different ways this could play out, and one of those scenarios seared itself into his brain. *What if a shooter had come in while I was hiding under a desk?*

What if he was found like that? What if the last image anyone had of Spencer Stone was his body, lying dead, where he'd tried to cower?

If he ever found himself in this situation again, he decided, he wouldn't be found under the furniture. If he died, he'd at least die being useful.

11.

SPENCER HEARS A LOUD PULSING SOUND behind him. Sirens blare, he can hear machine guns exchanging fire and mortars landing. It's total chaos. Before him lies a man squirting blood so powerfully it's almost satirical, a ridiculous movie prop. Three men stand behind him as Spencer tries to decode what's going on. This body is broken, unconscious, and has a brachial bleed; the arm has been blown off and the long artery down the bicep severed right down the middle. So the nub of an arm is pulsing blood out all over Spencer, but more importantly—or less importantly?—the man does not seem to be breathing. Spencer gets behind the body and puts his hands under the neck, cupping it like he's ladling water from a pond, easing the chin back so the mouth and nose are facing up. You do that so if there's something he's choking on or if he has a kinked airway you'll unkink it—but of course it's not kinked; Spencer knows the mechanism of injury, and this guy is obviously not choking. Spencer collects himself. He shimmies back over to the arm and pulls out his tourniquet, sliding the man's arm through the loop, and the man does not resist, of course, so Spencer manhandles the arm. He's not worried about breaks and fractures; he's worried about blood loss, followed by loss of blood pressure, followed by lack of profusion, lack of oxygenated blood to the brain, brain damage, and after that—he doubles the tourniquet over and then pulls it tight enough that he can feel the tissue compressing, like he's trying to permanently reduce the size of the man's arm, but that's good, that's good—now back up to his head, to address the next pressing problem: is he breathing? His chest is not rising. CPR? No, not yet. First he has to establish an airway. The man is unconscious so . . . Spencer remembers—when you're unconscious the muscles in your jaw relax and your tongue can fall back and block your breathing, plus with trauma there could be blood clogging the airway. Spencer rifles through his pack for the long surgical-looking tube with the trumpeted end; he drops it, *damn it,* picks it up, wipes it off, starts fumbling with a pack of lube, tries to tear it open but it slips through his grasp, *fuck,* he picks that up too, tries to tear it open again but loses his grip and the pack goes flying—*fuck, fuck!*—and then decides, *What the hell,* and then he's got his left hand over the man's cheekbones, and he's driving the tube up the man's nose. Gunfire behind him. He guides the tube with one hand and shoves with the other, threading it up the nose and into his windpipe, all the way down until all that's visible sticking out of the man's nose are a few millimeters and the trumpeted end, like a tiny mushroom sprouting from the right nostril. The background noise is no longer there, it's entirely shut off in fact; suddenly it's totally silent, and Spencer feels a tap on his shoulder.

"Airman Stone, congratulations. You just gave this man permanent brain damage."

Spencer takes his hands off and leans back. He wipes sweat off his eyebrow with a forearm. "Don't I need to make sure he has an airway—"

"You do. But did you notice that our friend here has clear fluid in his ears? What might that clear fluid be, Mr. Stone?"

"Aw, crap."

"Not quite, Airman Stone. Guess again."

"Spinal fluid, sir. It could be spinal fluid." The other members of his team stand back.

"Correct! Spinal fluid. And if our friend has spinal fluid in his ears, what does that tell us?"

"He could have damage to his skull."

"That's right! Poor old Rescue Randy here could well have a skull fracture. That tube of yours would have gone right through it. So, to recap: you just walked up to a guy who was already having, if we're being honest, a pretty bad day to begin with, and you shoved a piece of silicone into his brain. Congratulations, Airman Stone, you just lobotomized your patient."

And so it was that an inanimate man, a pretend trauma victim, solidified Spencer's understanding of all emergency medicine's most counterintuitive notions.

A man might need to breathe, but you can't just give him an airway.

A man might need to breathe, but if he's bleeding sometimes you have to deal with that first.

A man might be bleeding out, but you can't always just stick a tourniquet on.

Spencer learned of the human body as an intricate, beautiful, elaborate system of ways to end itself. Cure this, destroy that. You need a tourniquet to stop someone from bleeding out, but if a tourniquet's been on too long, you get necrosis—tissue death. That means that by trying to keep a patient from dying of blood loss you can give them an irreparable limb infection.

Or if the injury is at a juncture, like in the armpit or the groin, you can't very well tourniquet that, because what do you tie it around?

Or, the trickiest of all, what do you do about a wound above the shoulders? A head wound, or a bad cut on the neck. They say "put pressure on the wound to stop the bleeding," but what are you going to do, ball up a towel, or a T-shirt, and shove it into someone's neck? You can't very well put a tourniquet there, because a tourniquet on the neck is the same thing as a noose. So if you've got a patient bleeding out of the neck then . . . then he wasn't really clear on what to do. Surely in combat treating neck wounds must be important, because soldiers wear helmets on their heads and flak jackets across their chests; it's their necks that are unprotected. So what do you do?

He wondered.

You say a prayer and hope something creative occurs to you.

12.

By the time he got to his first overseas assignment, Spencer knew his luck had started to bend in a different direction. He was stationed in the Azores, a string of volcanic islands off Portugal. The airbase felt incidental, an after-thought plopped down on an archipelago of nine verdant, dramatic islands. It felt like being in a Hawaii, or some other island paradise, except that there were a few people in uniform between him and the water. Even the airstrip itself fell off down a dramatic cliff and into the Atlantic.

His shifts were easy, one day on, two days off, and though there wasn't a ton to do on the island, he had freedom, and the time to take advantage of it.

He wanted to go out and explore; no one told him no, but most of the cars were stick shift. No problem, he had time to learn. And because he never used vacation days—he had plenty of leisure time; he never felt the need to—they began adding up.

The base was quiet, and as far as he knew, had been for a while. It had been built to support a little-known weapon in World War II that Spencer remembered learning about back in history class with Alek and Anthony: the blimp. The US Navy dreamed up blimps as a way to fight German U-boats that began terrorizing allied ships in the Mediterranean.[1] But it was a long trip from North America to the Strait of Gibraltar, so when the navy sent its first airships across the Atlantic, they needed a stopover, and this was it. They stopped here, on this strip right in front of Spencer, on their way to the fight. On their way to an air station down in northern Morocco.[2]

But now, not much happened, so Spencer had time for hobbies, and driving stick wasn't the only skill he got to hone on the Portuguese island. It turned out the base had a small jujitsu community. There was an aerobics room with a wall of mirrors on one side and an east-facing window on the other, so you could either watch yourself, or you could look out over the Atlantic while you fought.

Spencer found himself welcomed into a close-knit community of practitioners, both American and Portuguese—people from a different country but with whom Spencer bonded over the form. A lieutenant colonel named John was the highest-ranking belt, so he'd taken on the role of instructor—a fact that filled Spencer with confidence, since John was small and, Spencer was certain, not nearly as strong as him. Spencer looked forward to the first fight. And just as he expected, when the two met on the mat it ended quickly. Except that instead of Spencer submitting John, it was the small instructor who was calm and triumphant while Spencer was left panting and humbled.

But that was the thing about jujitsu, what had drawn him in back when he first started following his brother to classes. A small man could submit you if he knew the form better. When you looked at a stranger across the street, jujitsu reminded you how little you knew about him or her; it worked as a kind of block against making assumptions. That skinny guy with a limp might be a black belt. He could defeat you in hand-to-hand combat if you took him for granted; you just couldn't know. The first roll with John was a reminder. After that, Spencer kept fighting him, kept losing, but kept lasting just a little longer each time.

Then, after two months, he made a series of critical realizations.

The first was that his progress against John was only partially his own improvement. John was letting him last longer and longer: the better Spencer got, the more the smaller man let Spencer exhaust himself while believing he was in the lead. John would stay calm, go with the flow, go where Spencer yanked him, wait until Spencer was winded, and then twist the whole fight in his favor.

Spencer was still trying to use his size and strength, and John was trying to show him that in jujitsu, your body was secondary, incidental to your skill. A large man could be quick, a small man strong.

When Spencer was on the mat with other practitioners, he could sense John watching him closely, nodding along as Spencer improved, learned to stop trying to overpower people, and instead conserve energy, use technique, use leverage, twist physics in his favor.

In the third month, the matches began to even out. "Dude, gross!" John would yell, dodging drops of Spencer's sweat while Spencer tried not to laugh.

"Sorry! What do you want me to do?"

It was then, with the wily little instructor, that Spencer learned the second lesson that had been eluding him. It had to do with one of the fundamental techniques in jujitsu, the way many matches ended. *Hadaka jime*, "the naked strangle" or "rear naked choke": a bicep and forearm around an opponent's neck, the other hand behind the opponent's head, pressing together and clamping the carotid artery. If you've got the carotid pinched, blood to the brain stops and the opponent goes to sleep in seconds, or realizes he will, and submits. You win.

When he first tried to choke opponents out, they responded predictably, wriggling and shifting so that even if he thought he had them under control, he couldn't keep their neck in position. He tried different ways of putting his arms around his opponent, but the thing he was missing was that his arms weren't the only problem. They weren't even the biggest problem.

The counterintuitive notion he'd yet to figure out was that if you were trying to submit someone, just as important as getting your arms in position around their neck was getting your legs in position around their lower body. You had to use your feet as "hooks" to pull your opponent's body back and keep it still, so he couldn't wriggle and loosen the choke. It started with the legs. You could be the stronger of the two, you could be squeezing with all your might, but if you didn't have your feet hooked inside your opponent's thighs, controlling his lower body, he could twist and squirm and keep you from clamping his neck firmly enough to stop the blood flow.

John noticed the flaw in Spencer's technique, pointed it out when Spencer was rolling with others, exploited it when he was rolling with John. Spencer spent hours on the mat, trying and failing to subdue men smaller than him (and sweating all over them in the process). There were times he thought he had it but couldn't get his opponent to submit, and with John, if there was ever space, John found it, exploited it, freed himself from Spencer's hold by twisting his legs and digging his chin down into Spencer's arm, boring a bruise and wriggling room for blood flow.

It kept happening, Spencer getting opponents down to that last step, and the opponent twisting while Spencer's Portuguese and American training partners yelled encouragement.

"Spence, you don't have it, line his chin up with your elbow. And *get your hooks in!*"

"Position before submission!"

"Spencer, Spencer! Go for his legs! It's not just the arms, it's the legs!"

"Get your hooks in, Spence!"

Four months into the tour, Spencer finally submitted John, following John's own guidance. It was a surge of confidence. Just as he'd learned you couldn't take for granted defeating anyone because they could be more skilled than you, so he learned you could beat the highest-ranking fighter around if you trusted your training.

He went back to the fire station—rebuilt just a few years before; another perk of the post here on these islands—connected to the Internet, and typed up a message. "Alek, I'm getting good at this!"

Alek was five and a half hours ahead, at his classified base somewhere in Afghanistan. Spencer wasn't sure if Alek would be asleep or lifting weights in the MWR, the base rec room, but sent the message anyway.

Spencer's screen lit up with a reply. "Good at what, like checking rashes?"

"No, I've been doing jujitsu. I'm finally starting to figure this shit out. I'm not getting my ass beat every match."

"Ah. You're lucky, man. Nothing to do here. I'm like a security guard. I'm a mall cop."

"Well, adventure starts soon."

The idea of a European tour with his best friend still felt more like a fantasy than a plan, but Spencer was beginning to plot out cities. It was only two months until he'd cash in his leave and set out for a three-week trip of a lifetime. Alek was going to have money and time too; his deployment was going to end just before Spencer's leave would begin, so it lined up perfectly. They'd walk through all the sites from their middle school history classes together.

Alek had invited someone else on his deployment, because three seemed like the right number and they'd save money on rooms, but wasn't having much luck. Spencer asked, "Did Strasser decide?"

"Yeah, he can't go. I'm asking Solon, but I don't think he's gonna have enough money."

"Okay. Well let me know. Getting excited, man."

"You have no idea. I'm desperate to get out of here. But I still think we need to park in Germany for a while."

"Yeah, it's just that—there's so much I want to see, you know? This'll probably be my last chance to do something like this. What if I never get to Europe again? I know you have that girl there . . ."

"It's not just that. Don't want to be moving every day, I want to soak it in a little."

"If you just want to stay in Germany that's cool, man, just do that."

"Nah, it's okay. I'll come with you. I want to go to other places in Europe anyway."

Spencer wasn't convinced. By now he knew Alek was only intent on Germany, Switzerland, the places he'd traced his family roots to. And Spencer knew there was a girl in

Germany. But for some reason Alek seemed to be trying to put on a good performance, to convince Spencer he'd changed his mind.

"All right," Spencer said. "Well, we don't have to decide right now, let me know if Solon comes through. What else is going on down there?

"Literally nothing. I just need to get into some action here, I can't just sit on my ass anymore. I'm like praying that we get attacked. I'm going crazy."

"Aw, that sucks. I'm having a frigging blast over here. Drinking beers, hanging on the beach, swimming in the ocean. This is the life!"

"You piece of shit. All right, it's midnight here. I gotta go to bed."

"Hang in, brother. Later."

And Alek was gone.

Spencer had an idea. If part of the reason for the trip was to see in person what their middle school history teacher had taught them about, there was another person who might be interested. He checked the time back in Sacramento and figured it was maybe late enough that Anthony would be awake. Worth a try.

ANTHONY'S FACE CAME ON SCREEN.

"What's up, bro?"

"What are you doing, man?"

"The morning routine, you know."

"All you ever do is watch *SportsCenter*."

"Pshhht. Not just *SportsCenter*. I can't miss *First Take* either. *His & Hers* every day too. That's my religion. Wait, hold up a minute." The image blurred, Spencer saw pixels move, rearrange, Anthony's face resolved again. "So, any action over there?"

"No, but check this out." Spencer unplugged his laptop and panned it around slowly so Anthony could see.

"*Dammmmnn*. It's like paradise. You get to go off base at all?"

"All the time. Actually, I got an idea for you. We're gonna do a big blowout trip."

"In Portugal?"

"No, man, like everywhere. All through Europe. I think I'll have a few weeks saved up by the end of the summer, maybe almost a month, so we're gonna do a big tour."

"Who's 'we'?"

"Me and Alek."

"You should, man. You may get posted anywhere after this, right? You could be back in Texas."

"Yeah, but I'm saying you should come meet me."

"Where do you want to meet?" It was taking Anthony a minute. "Wait—you mean like meet you in *Europe?*"

"Yeah, son! This'll be my last hurrah. You have the summer off, don't you? When else are you gonna go to Europe?"

"I don't have money like *that*. I mean, one day I will."

"I know you will. That's why—look, here's what you should do. Get a credit card. You'll pay it back."

"Man, if your mom could hear you talking like that. I wouldn't even qualify for a high enough limit."

"Just try. Take out a credit card. Do whatever you've got to do."

The more Spencer thought about it, the more certain he was Anthony should come. "This is a once in a lifetime opportunity. When have you not been down for an epic-ass trip? Remember Tahoe?" Right before basic training he and Anthony had gone to a cabin for three days. They were finally twenty-one so they picked up some Coors on the way, rented jet skis, and buzzed along the lakeshore looking at mansions with tanning beds, and four-wheelers out front, pretending to be prospective home buyers. "We haven't had an adventure forever. I have a credit card, and I run it up, but I make my payments on time."

"Yeah, but you have those military paychecks." Anthony wasn't arguing so forcefully. Spencer knew he just needed to push a little more.

"Just get a credit card, man. Go on Credit Karma and see what you qualify for."

Anthony was silent for a moment. "You know—it's funny. Literally just yesterday one of the guys in the store room, out of the blue, started telling me how I needed to be building up credit."

Spencer smiled. They hung up, but as the days went on, he started getting messages from Anthony, whenever he logged on to Wi-Fi at the firehouse.

"Coworker at store room was telling me about frequent flyer miles."

Another one: "Logged on to Credit Karma. They recommended this card based on my credit and it randomly happened to be a card for traveling. Bonus points for airfare and stuff. It's meant to be!"

Then, one day in May, Spencer was checking his email in the firehouse after another shift, when his computer started chiming with an incoming call from Anthony, who had started yelling before his face came up on the screen.

"—it, oh *shit! I got it! I'm approved! It's a ten thousand dollar limit!*"

"Are you serious? *Ten thousand*? My limit's not even that high!"

"So, I guess we're going?"

"We're fucking going!"

13.

A FEW WEEKS LATER, Anthony's messages became less enthusiastic. It was as if some sense had come out of nowhere to change his mind about the whole idea of Europe. He was getting cold feet, starting to worry, and the trip was beginning to wobble, threatening to fall apart.

Once Anthony signed on, Alek had gone back to his original plan. He'd stay in Germany and the Alps where his family had lived. He said he'd still try and meet up, at some point, but Spencer wasn't hopeful. Alek now seemed intent on doing his own thing. So Anthony had replaced Alek, and now Anthony was thinking about dropping.

"What are you worried about, man?"

"I guess homesickness. Remember how I went to Cabo that time for spring break?" It was the only time he'd been out of the country, and he'd been so depressed he didn't even want to see people. "That was five days, and we're going for almost a month." Plus he'd budgeted $4,000 for the trip; the ticket was almost $2,000, and after buying all the luggage and travel gear he needed, he was almost at his limit, before even paying for a single hotel.

"Look, it's just money." Spencer figured maybe he could change Anthony's mood by refocusing on the plan, start thinking about what they were actually going to do instead of what Anthony was going to leave behind. "So look, it's going to be a big loop, right? Italy, Germany, France, and then the big blowout in Spain."

The only thing they couldn't agree on was what extra country to do in the middle. Anthony wanted to go to Amsterdam; Spencer wanted to go to Belgium. They'd sort that out later. The one thing they were perfectly in line for was that it should end on a high. The pretty girls and beautiful beaches of Spain. From everything they'd heard, it was the ultimate party destination. They would end their vacation in Spain.

SPENCER LOOKS UP to see his friend with a weapon point-blank against the man's head, so close Spencer can smell the metal. He pulls and stretches, trying to get his head to the side because he knows how powerful an AK-47 firing is; if the gun goes off, it will rip through the terrorist's head and into Spencer. He is growing tired. He is growing frustrated by the man's wiry strength, and his own inability to knock him out, to submit him, to get him to go to sleep or even just stop struggling, and everything feels delicate because he doesn't know what other weapons or accomplices this man has.

Spencer doesn't have the breath left to say it, but he looks at Alek, tries to make eye contact, and with his mouth clenched and his eyebrows raised, tries to communicate permission to Alek. *Kill this man even though it will kill me too.*

Spencer watches Alek's hands. The gun barrel moves down to the man's head, at an angle that will send the round through it, and into Spencer's neck.

Spencer tightens his grip.

Spencer watches Alek's index finger slide down off the barrel over the trigger guard.

The pad of Alek's finger, moving over the trigger.

Spencer closes his eyes. He has no time and can't assemble his thoughts to say a prayer, but he prepares himself to die with a terrorist in his grasp.

He hears Alek pull the trigger.

Nothing.

Spencer opens his eyes. Everyone is still there; the gunman struggling in his grasp, Alek standing over them, holding the gun, frowning. *What just happened?*

Then metal tearing into flesh, but it doesn't hurt, he feels no pain, he feels it as muted percussion waves coming off the terrorist's body. Thumps. Spencer sees he's not being hit, the terrorist is being hit—Alek is driving the rifle into the gunman, furiously, over and over again. A flurry of motion; more light and metal off his peripheral vision, the shapes arranging themselves so that a realization clinks into place—the terrorist has a pistol—and again Spencer tries to summon extra strength. Spencer's chin is tucked into the gunman's left shoulder, the pistol is in the gunman's right hand, so Spencer can't really see it. The black of the barrel swings across his vision; he tries to bob and weave but he's trapped, nothing to hide behind, and he is wedged into such a tight space between the table and the seat-back that he can't move. There's nowhere to go, not enough time to react; there's nothing more for him to do. *I'm about to get shot in the head.*

Again the eye of the pistol barrel traces across his vision, and by some mercy doesn't go off, but he knows it will soon.

He closes his eyes, turtles his neck to make himself into a smaller target. He moves his head back and forth, trying to dodge the barrel of the gun and use the terrorist's body as a shield, make the angle just a little more difficult. But he can't hide; there's no cover, not enough time; the barrel swings back until it's pointing right at Spencer's head. The gunman pulls the trigger.

14.

"YOU MADE IT!" Spencer was waiting in the lobby of the hostel in Rome when Anthony got out of a taxi looking just about the same as the last time Spencer had seen him, except this time he was dragging a rolling bag, and holding a stick with a camera attached to it. Spencer shook his head. Anthony looked the true city slicker; everything about him screamed "American tourist." If not "fish out of water."

"Holy, shit," Anthony said, "we're in *Europe!*"

"We're in Europe! This is crazy!" Spencer had waited for Anthony to check in at the hostel, saving every bit of their trip for them to experience together, and once they dumped their bags into their rooms they were restless and excited. Now what? Even the hostel itself was new and exciting; they'd never stayed in one before, and this one had *everything*. Its own bar, its own restaurant—somehow that was unexpected and awesome—even just the fact that they had a rack of free brochures seemed like a superfluously generous gift.

"So," Spencer said, "we're here! What should we do tonight?" He turned to the young woman behind the desk. "We just got to Italy. And he just got to Europe for the first time. It's the first day of our trip."

She smiled. "I think I know just the thing," she said in perfect, attractively accented English. "You know we have a bar attached to the hostel? Tonight we have a party bus leaving from there. They call it 'the perversion excursion.'"

Spencer looked at Anthony, who raised his eyebrows. "Would you like me to sign you up?"

The bus had barely pulled out onto the street before a bartender stood up and started passing out unpronounceable Italian beer and colorful shots in little phallic shot glasses. The bus stopped at a bar, then another, then the night became a blur, the bartender passing around more drinks, pouring shots right into passenger's mouths, music loud and pulsing, people sliding up and down a stripper pole set up inside the bus, giggling girls falling off into piles of limbs, Spencer drunk on adventure and liqueur and beer and the perfect weather and the beautiful young bodies all around him, Anthony off talking to some new friend, and at some point Spencer realized he had to take a piss as badly as he ever had in his life. For what felt like hours the bus kept going, until it finally pulled off on an overlook with the Vatican below and the Colosseum lit up in the distance, rheumy and wobbling in Spencer's well-liquored vision; the lights winked at him from miles away, but he hardly had time to consider the history. He was running, hands over his groin, across the grass, past busts of Italian heroes from nineteenth-century wars, past Garibaldi on a horse, racing to a place in the distance where a small tree beckoned to him like a beacon of hope, offering just the small suggestion of privacy he desperately needed. He was so close he could almost feel the relief when he stepped on cobblestones canted by a bulging root; his foot rolled to the right, and he heard three successive *cracks* rocket up his body as his ankle collapsed sidewise.

Then intense, searing pain. *Oh my God. I just broke my ankle.*

The liquor helped dull the full force of the pain, and he relieved himself balancing on one leg, then hobbled over to a stone wall that was probably four hundred or maybe four thousand years old; someone was saying something about it, but all he could do was lean against it and close his eyes, trying to will the pain away. *What did I just do? Holy shit.* In the distance he heard Anthony's voice, laughing at something, then he heard a rustling, opened his eyes, and two girls with exposed midriffs were making their way to him.

"Aw, why dees poor boy stand all alone?"

"You are American, yes?"

"Why you stand by yourself?

The pain receded to make way for his concentration as he tried to turn on his charm, trying to see just how friendly these two girls were. By now Spencer had lost his sense of time, but at some point Anthony snapped a photo with him leaning against the wall, framed by two tanned, lithe bodies on either side, Spencer looking like a man in his element. You wouldn't know his ankle was in the process of swelling to three times its normal size and turning a bruised, livid blue. More time passed without Spencer feeling like time had passed, and then he found himself following a herd of people wobbling back onto the bus, one of the Brazilian girls—was it Luiza, or her friend?—nestled under his arm, Spencer using the illusion of chivalry to disguise the fact that he'd deputized Luiza (or was it the other one?) as a human crutch.

Then they were back at the hostel. Anthony was with a girl he had laughing, and the two of them were stumbling up to the room too, and Spencer realized too late that Anthony had the better angle, the inside lane, stumbling into the room a moment before Spencer could get there, so he turned Luiza or the other one around and started making jokes in the hallway, trying to stall—he wasn't exactly sure what for—but eventually she got tired of standing in the hall of a hostel and went flitting off to some other diversion. Spencer went to peek in the room, cracking the door so as not to disturb whatever assignation might be under way, but found Anthony alone, snoring.

Spencer crawled into bed, thinking, *Hell of a first night in Europe*, and laughing himself to sleep about how the two had ruined two perfectly good chances to kick off the trip with some companionship.

HOLY *shit*. Spencer woke up with his foot throbbing.

The night came tumbling back to him in gauzy flashes, and within a few seconds of opening his eyes he was wide awake, the pain like a bucket of cold water on his face.

He pulled up the sheet and looked; he barely recognized what he saw. The foot didn't fit him; it look like someone else's. It didn't even really look like a foot, but a beat-up overripe vegetable, swollen out in two places and a deep blue color he'd never seen a body produce before. His stomach lurched.

How would he explain this?

How would he spend three weeks on a *walking* tour of Europe?

He nudged Anthony, who stirred, with a groan. "Ugggh. What the hell did we *drink?*"

Spencer wasn't all that worried about Anthony's hangover. He shimmied to the edge of the bed while Anthony groaned more behind him, hung his feet over, and without looking down counted, "One, two ..." and eased himself down, shifting his weight off his butt. The moment the soles of his feet touched the floor, blades shot upward into his shin, a sharp splintering pain that knocked him back onto the bed and forced the breath from him.

"Anthony, man—man, my foot's messed up. It's—it's pretty bad."

"Mmm." Anthony still hadn't opened his eyes.

"I don't think I can walk on it. I can barely stand on it."

Still no reaction, so Spencer shook Anthony awake and made him look down at the foot. Anthony's eyes widened. "Oh, God. That's disgusting."

"I'm not trying to be a wimp, but I don't know if I'm going to be able to do all this walking."

Anthony shook his head. Spencer could see the mix of sympathy and disappointment in his eyes.

The trip is over. The one chance they'd ever have to travel in Europe, in all likelihood, and it was over, after the first day.

Spencer struggled down to the front desk, and a girl rushed to get him a bag of ice.

"I know a doctor who might come look at it," she said. "I'll call him right away."

While Anthony slept off a hangover upstairs, Spencer sat, iced his foot, and internally rehearsed how he was going to tell people that his European trip had ended on the very first day. Before they'd seen any sites at all, or even ridden one of the high-speed trains they had tickets for. Unless the doctor had some miracle cure.

He didn't appear to. When Spencer finally got to see him,

the doctor poked around, took an X-ray, showed Spencer where he'd had a microfracture—but it was hard to tell whether it was new or a childhood injury—then gave him a prescription for ibuprofen and a €120 bill.

Spencer spent the rest of the day hopping back and forth to the front desk for more ice, hoping that by some miracle he would somehow heal, because if he wasn't better by tomorrow—and when had a softball-size bruise ever gotten better in twelve hours?—he'd be on the next flight back to base. He went to bed that night making peace with the fact that his three-week epic blowout European trip had ended before it really began. No Germany, no Belgium, no France.

Most of all, no Spain.

Just one day in Rome on a party bus.

He was asleep before the sun went down.

15.

THE NEXT DAY, Spencer woke up in a wallow of disappointment. Today was the day he'd have to make all the arrangements to go back to base. He figured he might as well give the foot one last shot before making it official. He swung his legs off the bed, put them on the floor, and rose up. He winced; the pain came back. But it was a dull ache, not the knives of pain that shot up through his legs like they were angry at him; more a soreness that enveloped the whole lower half of his leg.

He leaned forward a little—the pain stayed, but didn't worsen. He leaned back, and to the side. He took a few steps. The ankle held. He ripped the laces out of his shoe and squeezed the foot in. It felt like the shoe was four sizes too small, but he got it most of the way in. He took a few more steps.

"Anthony! I think I can walk!"

"For real?"

"I think I can do it. I think—let's keep this thing moving!"

By some small miracle, or else by force of will, the trip was back on.

Next stop, Venice.

THE TRAIN THAT ARRIVED at the station to take them to Venice looked less like a mode of public transit and more like a rocket ship. Or one of those jet cars they built to set speed records over salt flats. It gleamed red; Spencer felt like he was walking into the future.

On board, the train wasn't like trains he'd been on in America. Seats were plush and minimalistic, it was clean, and attendants walked in pressed uniforms, offering drinks. Internet was fast and reliable, the windows were big, and the passengers all seemed to be well-to-do and well put together. No addicts or panhandlers moving through like the subway cars he'd been on, no one asking for money. No criminals.

But most of all, as the train began to pick up speed, it was the *force* of it that struck him. The train was whisper quiet, hitting 150 miles per hour and still accelerating, the countryside blurring past like a movie on fast-forward, and he had a feeling that seemed something like inevitability.

All that power conveying him silently, but with tremendous force, toward a destination.

16.

Spencer could tell Anthony was in a bad mood. That first night put a hurt on him that hadn't totally let up in two days. Making matters worse was the fact that the moment they stepped off the train in Venice the heat hit them, thick and soupy; it enveloped them and felt like an extra layer of clothing. Spencer was too distracted by what lay before him to mind much about the heat—he'd known Venice was a city on the water, but he hadn't thought it would be ... *so* on the water, a whole water world. People used boats like everyone everywhere else used cars. Traffic jams were skiffs stacked stern to bow in a channel, rather than minivans bumper to bumper on a freeway. The directions to the hostel had them getting on a water *bus*.

The water bus was the first of many tests the city of Venice placed before them. Curiously, some people seemed to be just getting on board. Other people were buying tickets. So, um—was it free? Spencer couldn't decide, and Anthony clearly wasn't in the mood for a discussion. All the people Spencer asked for help were either clueless themselves or didn't speak English. So he figured he'd pay the guy selling what might have been tickets for the water bus, and might have been something else entirely, before getting on to try and find their island.

The water bus pushed off and motored out into the Grand Canal. Spencer was loving it, his sense of adventure piqued because he'd been given a new lease on life now that he could walk again. Anthony was having a hard time dragging his rolling bag, which he now realized was a poor choice for backpacking across Europe. Spencer looked back and saw him struggling. "Why do you think they call it 'backpacking'? They don't call it 'roller-bagging.'" Anthony's luggage was designed for buttoned-up businessmen traversing regional airports, not ancient cobblestone streets. Spencer heard a crack, and then Anthony exploded: "Fucking, *fuck* this thing!" Spencer had to turn away to keep from laughing, while the plastic cracked on one of the castors on Anthony's suitcase, splitting off and grabbing at the ground so that the handle lurched out of Anthony's hand and the bag dove forward. *"Damn it!"* Anthony wound up and kicked his suitcase. "Fuck you!"

Spencer laughed into his fist while Anthony started dragging the one-wheeled bag behind him, the plastic claw where the wheel used to be scraping and catching on every single cobblestone.

Spencer had booked the hostel, but they got off the water bus at the wrong stop and didn't realize it at first, so Anthony had to drag his one-wheeled bag around the island in slowly tightening concentric circles as Spencer made wrong turn after wrong turn—"It's gotta be just up there!"—before finally realizing they weren't even on the right island.

Back to the water-bus stop.

More standing in the heat.

Spencer was having a hard time focusing on the directions because he still couldn't get over the fact that he was in a city but that there were no cars. It was like a plane without wings or something; it seemed so strange he couldn't stop looking up and taking it all in, rather than stopping to study the directions and actually figure out where the hell they were.

Another hour and a half circling around streets which— and this was now starting to frustrate Spencer too—seemed to never have signs. How did people find their way here? Did everyone just memorize where they needed to go? It wasn't laid out on any kind of grid, or in any kind of order at all, but seemed designed precisely for the purpose of confusing foreigners. It was just circles upon circles and sets of staircases up and back down that seemed to serve no purpose Spencer could discern other than to raise Anthony's blood pressure.

Up they went, Anthony huffing and sweating and drag- ging his Samsonite over pointless staircases. It wasn't just street signs; there also hardly seemed to be any business signs, or building signs. Spencer figured it was time to ask someone for directions and then realized there weren't any people either. It was actually kind of eerie, now that he noticed it. Where was everyone? It wasn't just a water world, it was a ghost town. It wouldn't be until much later that Spencer learned of *riposo*, the Italian tradition of going home and resting in the middle of the day when the sun was highest and the heat most unbearable. He just thought the city was deserted. Had there been some viral outbreak he hadn't heard about?

Anthony noticed it too. "Why don't we see any people?" Anthony was losing what was left of his patience. "Where are the street signs? Why can't we find this? What the hell are these stairs for?"

Spencer started to see people, but only occasionally, and only poking their heads out of the windows above them, like spectators watching some game, some contest Spencer and Anthony were playing, but whose rules they didn't know.

Finally, a beacon like the tree in the park back in Rome: a small logo in the distance that matched the color pattern Spencer remembered from the hostel brochure.

"I think that's it!"

Anthony said nothing.

"For real this time, I think that's it. Cheer up, man, we're in *Venice!*"

The only sound from Anthony behind him was the rhythmic kuh-*klunk,* kuh-*klunk* of the broken wheel on cobblestones.

Spencer heard raised voices in a foreign language. Italian? He couldn't really tell but it definitely wasn't English, and the closer he got to the hostel the clearer it became that an argument was underway. They walked into the front office and Spencer saw that the noise was coming from a couple yelling at a girl behind the desk. She caught eyes with Spencer, and he could tell she was trying to bite down a smile. It was too late to walk out, so he and Anthony shuffled their luggage to the back and stood awkwardly to the side of the tiny foyer as the girl tried to politely deflect the rage.

Spencer looked at Anthony, who raised his eyebrows. Finally the couple seemed to run out of steam and they barged out. The girl behind the desk looked at the boys and collapsed into giggles.

"What was *that* about?"

"Sorry for you to see that! They yell that they call the police because we don't have the AC. They say it's too hot to sleep so police come to shut us down."

Spencer laughed. "Some people, right? The police?" He

shook his head. "I'm sure we won't be calling the police on you." He smiled. The girl checked them in and pointed them to their room.

When he walked in, the heat nearly knocked him to his knees. "Holy shit." It felt like an oven. Now he understood what the couple was so upset about. Somehow hotter even than outside, like all the heat had risen off the water up the hill and was being pulled in and trapped by this one room. So hot it was hard to breathe. And there were mosquitoes everywhere. Spencer started to count, lost track, and figured maybe three hundred. He tried closing the windows to see if he could stop them from coming in, but a moment after he closed the shutters the temperature kicked up even more.

"Okay, I admit it," Spencer said. "I can't stay in this room. There's no way we're sleeping here. We'll figure something out later."

Anthony just shook his head. He was focused on his phone.

"Wi-Fi working?"

"Yeah. I got a message from John."

"John—wait, John Dickson?" Anthony had a friend playing semipro basketball somewhere in Europe. "He's playing in Italy?"

"Germany. He told me to hit him up when I got to Europe, but he keeps moving." His phone buzzed; Anthony looked down. "He says we should try to meet up when we get to Munich."

For now, Spencer figured they only had one night in Venice, so they might as well make something of it. "All right, come on, we're burning daylight. Let's go see the sights." They showered, changed, and went out to catch the water bus back to the main island. While they stood waiting, Spencer decided he wanted a photo of himself with the water and the buildings in the background, but Anthony was sitting over on a bench, trying to beat the heat by staying perfectly still. Spencer saw a girl who'd materialized out of this ghost town, waiting for the same bus. "Hey, excuse me, do you speak English?"

She laughed. "Yeah, I do."

"Great, great, can you take a picture of me?"

"Of course!" Spencer posed, and asked her if she wanted one.

"That's okay, I have plenty. I've been traveling a while."

"By yourself? I'm Spencer, by the way."

She laughed again. "Hi, I'm Lisa."

"Nice to meet you. And this over here—Ant! Get up. Meet Lisa. Lisa, meet Ant. Or Anthony, I mean."

"Hey, how's it going?"

Spencer had an idea. "Hey, so we're going to the main square, if you want to tag along with us."

So Spencer, Anthony, and Lisa walked through the crowded markets, Anthony pulling out the selfie stick and filming, a signal to Spencer that his friend's mood had improved. They decided to go on a gondola ride, because "when in Rome"—kind of—so they went down to a stand where a group of people waited, started talking to a couple, who turned out to be Malaysian, and soon Anthony convinced the three to split the fare. One by one they stepped on, the woman, her husband, Lisa, then Spencer and Anthony; the gondola driver's eyes bulged at the size of the load piling in, but he managed to steady the boat. He shoved off into the water, manipulating the boat around tight turns and down narrow alleys, sticking out a leg to kick off when they drifted too close to the stone walls. The gondola almost tipped a half dozen times, eliciting woops from the couple, and out in the open water, it started rocking, but the close calls aside, it was just neat little narrow alleyways, passing garage doors leading down to the water, coasting under bridges and passing people eating at waterside restaurants, while Anthony captured every second on his camera.

The evening was beginning to take on that calm, almost magical feel, Spencer feeling careless and free, the Malaysian couple happy to have the company, and there was warmth to the new friends, all huddled together in this small space, bobbing on the water with the city lit up around them.

Lisa told them she was from New York, and that she'd been in Venice for a few days, staying with a local family, which was how she liked to travel, her way of saving money and picking up a bit of the language wherever she went. She'd been on a summer vacation tour of Europe, which she'd decided to do by herself. After the gondola ride she showed them some of the famous churches, her favorite views. She walked with them through the crowded market as Anthony led the way with his selfie stick like a standard bearer, trying to take candid videos of himself exploring Europe, pretending he wasn't the one holding the camera. Since they were doing the tourist thing and in the company of a lady who clearly had some culture, they decided it was time for a classy night. In the main square, they walked past an upscale restaurant; Spencer saw Anthony looking in and said, "Screw it. Let's go here."

They ordered homemade pasta; Anthony ordered a glass of wine, which Spencer had never seen him do, and had a better idea. "Why don't we just get a bottle?" They'd never done that either, ordered a bottle of wine for themselves. They were living it up, in athletic shorts and T-shirts, having a candlelit dinner served by waiters in well-tailored suits.

Over wine, Lisa asked for a full rundown of their plans. "It all sounds good," she said. "Except France."

"What, you don't like it there?"

"Eh, Paris is okay. They're kinda rude there." Spencer looked at Anthony; Anthony shrugged. Lisa lowered her chin and squinted at them. "You know," she said, "you should skip France." Spencer refilled their glasses.

After dinner they strolled through the square like sophisticated Venetians, browsing shops to buy gifts for their families, and marveling at the little toy helicopters that lit up and flew hundreds of feet in the air. They took it all in, the street merchants and performers who seemed to have emerged from the earth just to put a show on for them. They tried gelato with Lisa, walked some more, found a quartet playing classical music, which switched to a string rendition of Coldplay's "Viva la Vida" at just the moment they walked by, as if some celestial MC had seen the three approaching and decided to tee up a more current track just for them.

Back at the hostel, Spencer and Anthony decided to take some of the cool air up on the roof before trying to sleep down in the sauna. Spencer lit up a cigarette, and they looked out over the water.

Behind him, Anthony had an idea. "It feels like all we're doing is traveling. Maybe we should slow it down a little."

"Maybe we should stop trying to do just one day in each place. Stay a little longer." Way off in the distance, Spencer thought he saw a flash. He waited, looking out over the

Adriatic. The sky was almost pitch black, save for the city twinkling behind him, but then he saw it again. Somewhere way out there, a cloud glowed for moment. It was a strange thing: out there, a millisecond of extraordinary power, the earth splitting open and roaring, and here, it didn't even make a sound. Just an instant of quiet light, a hint of something happening somewhere far away. He felt moisture in the air though. He knew it was coming.

"Better go down before this storm hits us."

17.

Munich was all Mercedes-Benzes and BMWs everywhere, even the taxis. Anthony couldn't get over the cars; this time it was Spencer who just wanted to get to the hostel, eager to check email because he was supposed to hear about his next posting.

"A lot of halal shops," Anthony said. He seemed taken with all the Muslims here, Middle Eastern–looking people all over the city. Spencer wasn't paying attention. He was imagining himself at different US air force installations. Some backwater in America? Pápa Air Base in Hungary? Someplace in Europe? Somewhere on their trip? That would be funny. Morón Air Base in Spain, or even Ramstein, right here in Germany?

Which reminded him. "We need to see where Alek is when we get to Internet."

"I got you. Lot of kabob restaurants. So many girls in head coverings."

"I feel like that's all of Europe," Spencer said.

"I need a hamburger. We gotta find a McDonalds."

"Really? A McDonalds? You already need American food? Let's eat local."

"What's local here? Like . . . pretzels?"

"I feel like . . . maybe sausage?" Spencer was still only half listening to Anthony; now he was double-checking the map.

"Maybe schnitzer," Anthony offered.

"Schnitzer? Snitch-er? What are you talking about?"

"Like wiener—snitcher."

"I don't think that's right."

"Pretty sure it's right."

"Dude, what are you talking about?"

"Um . . ."

"Whatever, just, I need a Big Mac. Stat."

"Okay fine, but let's just make it quick. I need to go back and find out what my future holds."

Sated with some greasy American food, they found the hostel with less fanfare than the last time, and connected to Wi-Fi. Anthony pinged his friend, John Dickson. "John's gone again, he's in some town, north of us apparently. He says . . ." but Spencer was still only half paying attention; he was writing to Alek. "We're gonna go to Berlin next."

"All right," Alek wrote back, "I'll try to meet you in Berlin."

Then the message he was waiting for came in from his supervisor. Spencer yelled, "Holy shit!"

"What?" Anthony came over.

"It's Nellis! I'm going to Nellis! They're sending me to Las Vegas, baby!" Spencer was so happy he felt almost guilty. The air force had stationed him at a base in the Azores, which was basically an island paradise, and now, of all the places in the world he could have been posted—it could have been Iraq or Afghanistan; it could have been Greenland or Uzbekistan or Taiwan—he was being posted a short flight from his home, and a place Anthony happened to have family.

"Ah! We gotta celebrate!"

Spencer googled a bar and they set out for the closest one, ready to rage.

But the closest bar turned out to be a red-light bar,

literally, red lights, and bizarre décor: decapitated Barbie dolls, someone's acid-trip idea of a fetish. They each ordered a beer, found no one who seemed all that interesting—or safe—as conversation partners, so they finished their drinks, closed out, and escaped the Bizarro World bar, stumbling out into a gay pride parade that happened to be passing down the street. Spencer remembered a recommendation his mom had made for a place with big beers, so they called a taxi and went there, but that bar was empty.

Next they found a club, but that was mostly empty too.

Then a salsa bar, which was too disorienting—Latin American music in Germany? Anthony still wanted to find a club, but Spencer was getting bored and tired of strange bars so they decided to call it a night. Save their energy. No reason to stay out and, they decided, no reason to stay in Munich for another day. They'd head out tomorrow for Berlin.

Berlin, Spencer felt, was going to be good. He was excited. Excited for Berlin, excited for Vegas after all of it, excited for Spain.

The trip was picking up some momentum.

18.

THE HOSTEL IN Berlin was far from the train station, and in Berlin more cobblestones threatened Anthony's suitcase. And his mood. At least Germany had street signs, and city planning, both improvements over Venice. But the words were so damn long it almost didn't matter. It took another hour to find their way from the train to the hostel.

When they arrived, they knew their luck had fully turned. They had two separate beds, the room was spacious, the air cool and clean. Spencer was still traumatized from trying to sleep in the Venetian oven, so this all came as a relief. They took showers, changed clothes, and though Spencer's foot was still a colorful balloon of inflammation, it seemed to slowly be improving, or at least to not be getting worse, even with all the walking. He took some of his ibuprofen, and they went downstairs to see if the receptionist could recommend a good place to party. As Spencer was talking to the woman at reception, Anthony interrupted. "Does that sign over there say 'Louisiana Soul Food'?"

"Yes, we have American . . . you say 'homestyle' cooking?"

"Wait, really? Soul food in Berlin? Spencer, man, we have to see if it's legit."

So they had soul food in Berlin: fried chicken, mashed potatoes, collard greens, and corn. Spencer stuffed himself and Anthony seemed to approve of everything except for the Fanta. That, Anthony complained about. "It's kind of gross," he said, holding up the bottle, examining the label.

"Probably because it's made with real sugar. I'm not feeling it."

Other than that, Berlin was shaping up well.

At breakfast the next morning, Spencer and Anthony sat silently chowing down, when a girl breezed past the dozen empty tables and slid into the seat next to them. She considered Spencer, then Anthony. Then she said, with enthusiasm that belied the early hour, "Hey! I'm Christy!"

"Uh . . ." Spencer was taken by surprise. "Um, hey," he said. He gave Anthony a look. *She hitting on us?*

"Christy, what's up." Anthony wiped his hand, and offered it for her to shake. "I'm Anthony, this is Spencer."

"So," she said, "what do you guys have planned for today?"

"Well," Spencer said, still not totally adjusted to having a new dining partner, "we were actually going to plan out the day after breakfast."

Anthony chimed in. "You have any recommendations?"

"I'm going on a bike tour later. It runs twice a day. I'm going to do the ten o'clock one, if you want to join."

Not hitting on them, it turned out, just friendly and energetic. What was it with all the Asian girls traveling alone in Europe? Biking seemed like a good idea though; it gave him a little more time without putting weight on his foot. Plus, these girls always seemed to have the inside scoop on where to go and what to see. It was like they kept finding guides, an oracle in every port to help them on their way.

They rode the bikes single file through traffic, stopping occasionally for historical mini-lectures, which Spencer found more digestible than anything he'd learned in school. Perhaps it was for the obvious reason: that it was easier to learn with visuals. Perhaps just easier to learn on his own terms, or perhaps there was something in the air, but whatever it was, everything seemed more meaningful. Perhaps it was the guide, a skinny transplanted Londoner with a hat on backward and glasses Spencer wasn't sure he actually needed—a bit of a hipster, but he seemed to know *everything*. And he seemed to be taking them on a historical tour of war-related sites, as if it were his job to show them only places where the world's great menaces had been confronted.

Out in front of Humboldt University, they saw where the Nazis burned thousands of books, and the guide explained how students were trying to counter that evil by holding a book sale every year. "Their way of getting books *back* to the people," he said, one leg hanging over his bike, looking at Spencer a beat longer than the others, as if this would mean something special to him. "To change what the history is."

They biked some more, then stopped in the Pariser Platz, the square named for the French capital, in front of a series of columns with a statue on top, six stories high. Something about it seemed to draw Anthony in, and Spencer watched him walk a few steps away from the group and begin taking pictures, then put down his camera and just look at it, as if something didn't quite make sense to him. Spencer squinted up toward it.

"This is the Brandenburg Gate," the guide said. "Where your President Reagan told Mr. Gorbachev to tear down the Berlin Wall." The statue at the top had four horses pulling a chariot, like something out of *Gladiator*, except that the chariot carried a woman with wings. "This type of sculpture," he said, "of a goddess with a four-horse chariot is called 'quadriga.' Quad, even you Americans know, is 'four.'" This particular one carried Eirene, the goddess of peace. Sometimes, the guide said, the chariots in the sculptures carried Victoria, the goddess of victory. Often they carried Pheme, the goddess of fame.

This one, he said, had an extra bit of history. It was stolen by Napoleon after the siege of Berlin and taken to France. It was brought back only when the Prussians occupied Paris.

Anthony rejoined, catching the tail end of the guide's speech, and shaking his head. "That's just a big-ass statue to take. How do you steal a whole statue? It's the size of a building."

The guide took them to Checkpoint Charlie. He showed them the *Führerbunker*, where, he reminded them, Hitler killed himself as Russian forces closed in.

"Wait, for real?" Spencer was confused; he looked over at Anthony. Anthony looked confused too. "I thought Hitler killed himself in the Eagle's Nest when American forces closed in on him."

"Your textbooks are wrong. By, oh, about seven hundred kilometers. The *Kehlsteinhaus* is down in the south. Hitler was *here*, with his wife Eva, when he killed himself. And it was the Russians who were closing in, by the way. You Americans can't take credit *every* time evil is defeated."

As he thought about it, it wasn't all that surprising to Spencer. Maybe it wasn't all that uncommon. When you told stories, sometimes you made yourself the hero. Hadn't he and Anthony done that? In their airsoft reenactments out in front of Spencer's house, and in the epilogues they cowrote on Sunday afternoons after *Black Hawk Down* and *Saving Private Ryan*?

The guide shooed them on, the next stop was the Memorial to the Murdered Jews. They parked their bikes and walked through a field of stones. From the outside, it seemed rigid and ordered, like a well-planned and sterile cemetery, but when you walked in, it was disorienting. Some of the stones were only a few inches off the ground; some were two or three times taller than him. It was a maze that swallowed him up when he walked in, so one moment he was totally in shadow, and the next sharp strips of light fell across him.

One moment he was totally alone, and the next he was bumping into a mass of other tourists at a blind intersection.

Anthony followed him, a few paces back, holding his camera up high.

Then the guide pointed to the victory column, another monument Anthony marveled at. "That's a lot of gold to just be out in public. People never go up there to steal it?"

They stopped for lunch, and Spencer learned more about Christy's background. It turned out their newest travel companion had a lot of useful advice about the rest of their trip. She knew France well, because even though she grew up in Florida, she worked in Paris.

"So what do you think," Anthony said. "What should we do there?"

"Well, do you speak French?"

"Ha! No, none. Neither of us."

Spencer laughed. "We barely speak English."

"Oh. I'm fluent in French."

"How long did that take you?"

"I've lived there for four years," she said, and then, she said something surprising. "But I don't think you should spend much time there. Actually, I don't know if you should go at all."

"What, like we should skip Paris altogether?"

"Yeah, maybe just skip it. I'd skip it if I were you. People can be kind of rude to you if you don't speak French. It's also pretty expensive. And they don't really like Americans."

Spencer thought about it; he looked at Anthony.

"No one's really high on Paris, maybe we *should* just skip it."

Anthony shrugged. "I just need my picture with the Eiffel Tower. That's crucial."

"Yeah, but is it worth a whole trip?" Spencer was starting to think that if people kept saying bad things about Paris, it might be time to take it off the itinerary. "Let's at least think about it. Maybe just go straight to Spain." Anthony nodded, and took a bite of his sandwich. "Hey, Christy," he said after a moment. "What do you do there anyway?"

"Do where?"

"In Paris, I mean. What's your job?"

"Oh! I work for a news channel."

19.

AFTER THE BIKE TOUR they headed back to the hostel. Anthony had to take care of some errands and said he was going to stop off and use the Wi-Fi in the room to write his friend John to see if they were any closer to each other.

Spencer went to wait for him in the hostel bar.

He sat down, thinking more about Christy's advice. It nagged at him. When he ordered his beer, he decided to ask the bartender for his thoughts on skipping France.

Two stools down, another patron interrupted. "Where you headed next?"

Spencer looked over. This man was out of place. In his midfifties at a youth hostel, his hair was long and ratty, everything he wore was leather and a little too tight. His voice raspy, with an accent that was hard to understand and harder still to place, but that Spencer assumed was German.

"We're supposed to go to France, then finish in Spain," Spencer said. "The thing is, people keep saying to skip France. We're all most excited for Spain anyway."

"And Amsterdam?" His voice was so raspy Spencer had to lean closer to try and make out what he was saying.

"No, no Amsterdam. We've thought about it, there's not enough time."

The man shook his head. "*Make* time for Amsterdam."

Spencer considered him. He looked like the kind of guy who'd lived hard and aged faster than his years, then tried to

offset the wrinkles by growing long hair and dressing ...
courageously.

"Oh yeah?"

"I just got back from there with my band."

"You—sorry?"

"Band, my band, we were just in Amsterdam."

"Oh! You're in a band? What kind of music?"

"Hard rock mostly."

"Wow. Are the other members all German?"

"Not German," he growled. "I'm from Sweden." He pulled
from his beer. "But I tell you, one of my favorite things to
do when we go up there," Spencer leaned in close to try
and make out what he was saying, "we get some truffles
and head out to the countryside. And you know what I do
then?"

Spencer humored him. "What?"

He smiled, milking the pause. "Nothing. I don't do anything. I just look around."

Spencer laughed. "That doesn't sound too bad."

"You know what else they have? Even if you don't do all
the drugs like I do, they have the nicest people in the world
there. And most of them speak English, by the way." Then he
winked. "Beautiful women too. And history."

Spencer nodded. He could feel himself warming to the
idea. The plan shifted in his mind.

"My friend, forget about France. Go to Amsterdam. You
have to go."

Behind him the door opened. Anthony slipped in and
took the stool next to him. "Making friends?"

"Yeah. And listen, I think we need to change our plans."
He looked down the bar at his new friend.

Anthony waved at the bartender. "Oh yeah?"

"Yeah. I think we need to go to Amsterdam."

WITH THE BARREL FACING Spencer's head, the gunman pulls the trigger. Spencer hears the click. He's still alive—how? How many times has he almost been shot? Will the man pull the trigger again? Alek already has his hands over the gunman's hands, wrenching the pistol away before he can try to shoot Spencer again. Spencer sends strength to his arms to try and squeeze the man into being still, but something yellow flares across his vision—light glinting off a blade. The pistol is gone now, but Spencer is still trapped, and as the blade comes arcing back all he can do is duck into the gunman's neck. He feels cool contact, a dragging across his neck, sees more blood, then their bodies move in opposite directions and Spencer catches a glimpse of his own thumb over the gunman's shoulder. A bolt of fear courses through him. *That's bone—I can see my bone.* His thumb is bent backward and sliced almost completely off, so he doesn't recognize it at first; it's not totally his own, and it feels like he's watching someone else's body in a movie. Spencer hears himself yelling, feels himself struggling, feels the desperate need to create space between their two bodies. He hears himself yell, "He's got a knife!" and flops his body to kick the gunman away, driving the man forward into the middle of the aisle.

Where Alek and Anthony are standing, ready for him.

Spencer scrambles to his feet.

Alek is ready on his left.

Anthony ready on his right.

The gunman crouches in the middle.

The four of them just stand for a moment. Three friends and a terrorist. No one knows what to do now. They stand there in the aisle, and a look of recognition passes between Spencer and the rest, as if all four of them in that moment acknowledge the same thing—*So this just got awkward.*

A beat passes. Spencer is suddenly conscious of an alarm inside the train. When did that start? The noise is awful, aggravating, too much. Has this been going all along?

Another moment passes.

Anthony swings at the gunman first, driving him back toward Alek who jabs twice, and then they're all swinging at him, trying to pummel him into submission, but he won't go down, until Spencer feels a new flood of rage and gets his good hand around the man's back, palms his head, and levers it down, slamming it against the table. Alek jumps on to help pin him down, and the gunman squirms violently, again the wiry strength that surprises Spencer.

"Stop!" Alek yells, putting the pistol right up against the man's head. He doesn't stop; he rotates powerfully, Spencer leans in, using his weight to try and keep his head down against the table. The man torques so hard it seems like he might spin his body right off his own head.

"Stop struggling!" Alek yells again. "Stop! Stop moving! Stop resisting!"

Spencer knows what's about to happen. He can see it as if it already has. Alek is going to shoot him while Spencer holds him down. *His head is going to fly all over me.*

Alek cocks the pistol back.

Spencer thinks, *We are about to execute this man.*

Alek pulls the trigger.

Nothing.

Alek cocks the gun to load a round into the empty chamber. This time he offers the gunman no chance. He holds it up to the man's head, and pulls the trigger again.

Again the gun does not go off. The man's struggling kicks into an even higher gear. Now Spencer grabs him around the shoulders, spins him around and jumps backward again, again flying across the seat, again trying to work his forearm under the man's chin, wedge it in against his neck, compress the arteries, choke his brain of blood.

Spencer can't see.

He has a second wind now, but it won't last much longer. Blood is running down his face from the wound on his forehead that has swollen his eye almost totally closed, down his neck from a wound he can't yet see, his hand is soaked in blood from his nearly severed thumb. None of the weapons seem to work, so there's no way to subdue the terrorist, and now the box-cutter blade is nowhere to be seen.

The gunman is punching him again, arcing his fists back and up into Spencer's face.

"You don't have it," he hears Alek yell, his best friend trying to guide him to a better chokehold. "Get it deeper." Spencer adjusts, still can't choke him, then, a memory: the jujitsu group in Portugal, the lieutenant colonel yelling at him, "Put your hooks in, put your hooks in! It's not just the arms, it's the legs!" Spencer shimmies his heels up over and in between the gunman's legs, and he pulls, begins to slow the gunman's torquing, and feels his forearm set satisfyingly under the gunman's neck, right where it fits, a puzzle piece finally settling into place.

He leans back and squeezes hard, using his weight to tighten the chokehold, which now feels snug.

Fists keep coming back so Spencer leans into them, taking the punches, keeping his hold tight, trusting his training, trusting Alek, until he thinks he can feel the punches begin to weaken, and soon the gunman's hand is just dragging, open palmed, over Spencer's face.

Then he's asleep. The alarm wails.

AYOUB

Ayoub followed his father to Europe in 2007.

Ayoub's father was trying to make a go of it in the capital, so that's where Ayoub went to join him, but he began getting in trouble.

In 2009, he was arrested on suspicion of selling hashish.[1] He wasn't a user, there just wasn't much else to do for money.

And anyway, he was not extreme in his faith; he never minded sitting with the people who got high. Mostly, he considered himself an athlete, five-a-side soccer his favorite pastime.

In 2013, the family moved down to Spain to the mouth of the River of Honey, Rio de la Miel, a city called Algeciras on the bay of Gibraltar.

It was a place of uncomfortable contrasts, a weigh station for oil traveling across the Atlantic, where small fishing skiffs bobbed next to giant cargo vessels. A rich fishery but also one of the busiest transshipment points in the world, a place where millions of dollars' worth of commerce occurred in the space of every second, and yet Ayoub lived among poor immigrants, and almost half the city was unemployed.[2] Ships passed with thousands of tons of cargo, but in Ayoub's neighborhood there was little to do for money besides sell scrap, sell hashish. All around was natural beauty, but Ayoub lived in decades-old dilapidated public housing with peeling white paint.[3]

Legend held that there was once a giant 150-foot statue of the prophet Muhammad, one theory being that it was built to warn the Muslims of an impending Christian invasion.[4] Another was that the statue protected the land with magic, with winds and currents, and only when the giant prophet was toppled could ships pass and international trade begin.

Modern Algeciras was a place in whose alleys and side streets you could become lost and anonymous, yet was situated in a province known for the proliferation of watchtowers. The place Ayoub moved to had once been a merchant paradise; the towers were places from which merchants could watch people and cargo arriving. In Ayoub's family there were merchants too. His father sold trash. Ayoub sold hashish. Each dealt only in the things he himself didn't use. They had no watchtowers. From the housing project in which they lived, they could not see the people and cargo arriving, mostly from America.

Ayoub was a normal young man; he took advantage of the beaches with other friends[5] and played soccer often, but like most others his age, he was constantly looking for work. In 2012 he went back to Morocco, and was arrested again on suspicion of selling drugs.[6] When he came back to Spain, he was done. He wanted out of the drug world.[7] He'd had enough, and wanted something better.

This city though, Algeciras, was a major transit point between two continents with a huge unemployed underclass—in that way, a city tailor-made for drug trafficking. Staying out of it was hard; it was hard to find other sources of income when an obvious one was always there, but Ayoub was trying.[8] He sought discipline in prayer, found some structure there, and began worshipping with a half dozen different congregations.[9] Near his home, in the space between a market[10] and an immigration detention center,[11] his father helped convert an auto repair shop into another mosque.[12] It followed the concept of Taqwa,[13] which means "God fearing," the *idea being that followers must always have the Almighty in mind. Always be on guard, lest they do anything that would displease God.*

It was a good fit for a young man trying to avoid a world of crime around him. It was a mosque in which men and women prayed together.

But Spanish police believed it to be a threat. They had it under surveillance the moment it opened, and the moment Ayoub stepped inside it he brought upon himself a new problem, though it was one he was not yet aware of: He was placed under surveillance, and marked as a possible threat.[14]

He could not know how this mark would stick with him. He did not know how it would affect his future. He kept working hard; he stayed out of trouble. When he wasn't praying, he worked in a teahouse.

He lost that job too.

He couldn't find another.

Ayoub was seeking refuge in religion just as, twenty-five hundred miles[15] due east, in the direction he prayed, there were rumblings that would affect his own life and millions of others. Two groups of Islamic extremists had merged. One a division of the Syrian resistance called the Nusra Front, the other calling itself the Islamic State of Iraq; together, they rebranded as the Islamic State in Iraq and Greater Syria, or ISIS. Their mission was so bold that for a long time they were dismissed as dreamers. Other radical groups rejected them as fantastical, and even Al Qaeda cut ties with them. What ISIS wanted was no less than to bring about an actual Islamic state. They wanted to restore the caliphate from over a millennium ago. And just as Ayoub was looking for a way out of the drug game, ISIS was becoming a movement that demanded to be taken seriously.

In January, it actually took over a city, Fallujah, frighteningly close to the capital of Iraq.

A few weeks later, it took an even bigger city, one on the north bank of the Euphrates, called Raqqa. This was important not just because Raqqa was a major metropolis, and not just because ISIS had effectively erased the border between Syria and Iraq. The city had been the capital of the Abbasid caliphate, twelve hundred years before, when the Muslim world was the center of science, discovery, fairness, and order.

ISIS was holding the old capital of the state they sought to restore.

The idea of an Islamic state was beginning to seem not just possible, but imminent.

As it made a stronger and stronger case that it could conceivably achieve its goals, it offered disenchanted youth everywhere a chance to be part of a world-changing cause. The places it fought were rich with people easy to demonize. In Syria, freedom-loving rebels were underequipped and poorly organized, trying to stave off a brutal dictator who sent a professional military to push barrel bombs out of helicopters and onto children.

The ISIS leader, Abu Bakr al-Baghdadi, issued a recruiting call.

His message was calibrated precisely for young men struggling to find meaning. He wanted to inspire "volcanoes of jihad"[16] all over the world, which would drive away the infidels whose meddling in Muslim lands had poisoned them, and turned them into places where honest young men couldn't find dignity. If the meddlers could be driven out, the world of justice and peace and discovery—the caliphate—would emerge again.

Many ISIS fighters were as interested in booze and women as stereotypical American infantrymen, so while becoming a holy warrior may have been for some a way to serve their faith, for many it was just their only path to glamour. Baghdadi offered the sign-and-drive equivalent of purpose: no money down, bad credit, no credit, just initial here and welcome aboard. He provided rules, a project, a way to be part of something bigger than oneself, a thing to tell girls about.

The imams loyal to ISIS were skilled at taking in the complaints of each young man and fitting them into a narrative of persecution against all Muslims. This was a narrative that would resonate immediately with young men like Ayoub, who had to either accept he was not very successful at anything because he was not very good at anything, or choose to believe the world was rigged against him.

Or at least, in Ayoub's case, that Europe was rigged against him. And Europe was taking on a new significance for ISIS.

ISIS wanted to fight its enemy not just in Iraq and Syria and other hot zones in the Middle East, but "even outside of it if possible, so as to disperse the efforts of the alliance of the enemy and thus drain it to the greatest extent possible." The reasoning was simple. "If a tourist resort that the Crusaders patronize ... is hit, all of the tourist resorts in all of the states of the world will have to be secured by the work of additional forces, which are double the ordinary amount, and a huge increase in spendings."[17]

Drain their blood, drain their wallets. That's why it emphasized that "to be effective, attacks should be launched against soft targets that cannot possibly be defended to any appreciable degree."[18]

Targets, in other words, like passenger trains.

Some countries stood as obvious choices. Places where the message would resonate, and where foot soldiers might be found. France, for example, had the largest Muslim minority on the continent, but the Muslim community there was mostly an under-class. They made up almost 70 percent of the prison population. There were nearly 11,500 known radical Islamists in the country, according to French surveillance data,[19] and regard for ISIS was high. If ISIS wanted a place away from the Middle East, with a potential supply of both young recruits and soft, symbolic targets, they could hardly do better.

France presented itself as an obvious new theater of war.

In 2014, Ayoub's new job took him to France.

A subsidiary of the telecommunications company Lycamobile was recruiting from Ayoub's neighborhood, and they offered him work.

It was his first break. Finally, gainful employment and a chance to leave his parents' home.[20] The company gave him a polo shirt with a logo, a cart of cheap gifts, pamphlets to hand out on the street, and dispatched him to a part of Paris called Saint-Denis.[21]

There was excitement to be had there, especially for a soccer fan like Ayoub. The national stadium was in Saint-Denis; the French national soccer team held their home matches not far from where he worked.

It was also ghettoized and postindustrial.[22] Ayoub had been plucked out of Spain and plopped down in a largely Muslim area many outsiders considered too dangerous to enter at night, and which the French ministry of the interior designated a "priority security zone."[23] He was living in a part of Paris with half a million Muslims, 40 percent unemployment, and the highest violent crime rate in the country.[24] It was a place where police did little to protect the local population, or even to punish them, sometimes pulling out entirely for fear of sparking riots.

In Saint-Denis, the symbols of authority were pulled from the people and positioned as enemies.

Ayoub tried to get by, living among others who were in various ways like him; other Muslims, other North Africans, other émigrés from former French colonies.

It was a seasonal gig; he had a six-month contract. But he felt good about it; he thought it was a good job,[25] and his father thought it was a healthy chance for a new beginning after the boy's youth spent more or less adrift.[26] It wasn't a glamorous job. It was going out on the street to give away cheap trinkets and sign up other Moroccans for SIM cards. But he was a good employee.

And because he was there to appeal to the Moroccan expatriates, it was a chance to take pride in his own culture.

In France, Ayoub was quiet. He arrived at work via public transport,[27] spent the day dutifully putting up posters, handing out flyers, trying to sign people up,[28] and going home. His employers found him diligent; he was finding his way.[29]

A month[30] into his new life, Spanish authorities[31] who'd been surveilling Ayoub's mosque back in Spain learned that he'd gone to France. They alerted the French authorities.[32] Ayoub was placed under a state security "S form," which gave authorities legal clearance to spy on him.[33] A month after French authorities got this intel, Ayoub was dismissed from his job.[34]

The company's explanation was that they'd found his working papers[35] were out of order,[36] and didn't believe the address he had on file was correct.[37] But back home, when they heard the news, Ayoub's parents were livid. His father thought the company was criminal for treating people like that.[38] Still, Ayoub had no recourse. He was now stuck in a foreign country. He was under surveillance, *without family, without an income, desperate for a way to make a living.[39] He was a young man without a job or legal status in a country where Muslims were an underclass, where they filled most of the space in most of the prisons, and where there were thousands of known radical Islamists.[40]*

With apparently nowhere else to go, he stayed in Saint-Denis[41] for a few more months. Soon he stopped calling his father.

Then authorities lost track of Ayoub El-Khazzani.

PART II

SPECIALIST ALEK SKARLATOS

TUE AUGUST 11, 2:27 PM

Solon Skarlatos:
Dad almost blew through a red light.

Alek Skarlatos:
Hahaha dont wreck my car

Solon Skarlatos:
Lol I had to tell him it was a red light
lol. Saved our lives and your car

Alek Skarlatos:
Wow . .-. U should drive

20.

Thirteen kilometers north of base.

ALEK CLOSED AN EYE and looked down the barrel of the gun.

He was somewhere in the middle of Afghanistan, hiding in a dried-out ravine, aiming at an enemy tank.

He kept quiet, kept his breathing shallow behind the rifle, and prepared to fire a four-inch armor-piercing incendiary round at three thousand feet per second, right into a tank driver.

This was no airsoft gun. Alek had grown up since the days fighting in the yard with Spencer, and so had his toys. This could kill a person. This could kill a *vehicle*. His head was canted to the right, cheek against the cheek piece, left eye closed, right eye against the scope. The spotter threw a veil over him for camouflage and then ranged the tank. "I've got five hundred fifty—I've got six hundred meters out."

Alek thumbed the dial, adjusting the minute of angle and nudging the barrel up to account for the inches of drop across that distance as gravity pulled on the bullet.

"I've got twenty-seven," he whispered to the other shooter. "You got it?"

Six hundred meters was easily within range, but every second he waited the chances of staying hidden got worse. Time to get on with it.

He adjusted the rifle barrel. The tank was off center and

he had a better angle at the front, so he was aiming for the driver's cabin, trying to put the round right through the driver's slit from a third of a mile out. If he missed it by a millimeter he'd still kill the driver, but if he hit his mark he'd take chance out of it entirely, make the armor piercing redundant; the round would go right through the slit, through the driver, across the cabin, into the other flank, and probably out the other side. The driver wouldn't stand a chance. If an insurgent happened to be standing on the other side of the tank, he wouldn't stand a chance either. A .50 caliber armor-piercing incendiary round would cut him in half.

The other shooter was aiming for the rear. The engine block. He would shoot the round through the tank's engine while Alek killed the driver—you take out the legs and the brain at the same time. But if one fired before the other was ready, they'd give up their position without disabling the tank, and then hell would be unleashed on them.

It only worked if the boys were in sync.

Alek flicked the safety off just as on the other side of the tank and out of his line of sight, three children ran up to the tank and began playing next to it.

"Scorpion to Base," Alek radioed, "ready to fire, requesting permission."

"Base to Scorpion, permission granted, fire when ready."

Alek dropped his finger off the trigger guard and put his finger on the trigger.

BASE WAS THREE HUMVEES parked at an elevated position a half mile back—a half mile over which Alek had to drag the thirty-pound antitank sniper rifle, five feet long with the barrel, so damn cumbersome he almost didn't notice an unexploded mortar right in his path. Who knew how long it had been there, waiting to take him out, end things right then and there. Thank God, or chance, or whatever, for putting that little rock right in the one place it had to be to send him stumbling off his path so that his foot planted next to the mortar, instead of right on top of it.

Now he lay, finger on the trigger, waiting only for the other shooter to get his range dialed in so they could both shoot at the same time. But time was of the essence. They had to shoot fast, before they got spotted.

Behind the tank and out of sight, the children continued playing quietly.

Alek was impatient. "You got it?" They needed to fire soon. Even if they hadn't already been seen, a tank stayed in one position only so long. He brushed his finger over the trigger.

The other shooter got locked in, and the spotter took over. "I have control, countdown from five, four . . ."

On "one" both shooters would fire, but Alek's round wouldn't have an engine block to stop it. It would go right through the tank and kill a child, maybe three children.

"Three, two . . ."

"Base to Scorpion! Base to Scorpion! That's a negative, *negative*, Scorpion! Hold fire, we're seeing kids back there!"

Alek caught his breath and dropped his finger off the trigger. He'd come within a hair of shooting.

"They're playing behind the tank, hold fire. I repeat, both teams hold fire!" The radio clicked off, then clicked back on. "Guys, we've got trouble. Team Alpha, Team Bravo, we're starting to get some attention."

Another pause. This was becoming a shit show.

"Base to both teams, we're surrounded up here." Alek looked up at his spotter, who was frowning. "Both teams, both teams, stand by for E and E."

Alek radioed back. "Scorpion to Base, what's up back there?"

"Base to Scorpion! Base to both teams! Throw smoke and *go!*"

Normal "escape and evade" was to back up slowly and discreetly to avoid being seen, but whatever the hell was happening back there was serious enough that they were being told to give up their positions, to get up and run. Alek pulled the pin and heaved a grenade out of the ravine, a puff of smoke shot up and hung for a moment giving at least a semblance of cover, and he humped the rifle up to his shoulder and started running as fast as he could back to the Humvees.

Up on the knoll, villagers had surrounded the vehicle; they just kept coming, circling, the crowd growing and surrounding them and the NCOs didn't know who was friendly and who might not be, but they just kept coming, like children of the corn, so the NCOs started yelling, "Let's go, guys, time to go!"

The first truck pulled out, then the second. Alek was pulling security on the third truck, so once the other two had gone he threw the sniper rifle in the back, jumped in, and then the last vehicle pulled out, throwing up a cloud of dust so the villagers disappeared in the rearview.

Then it was quiet. "Strange," the soldier riding shotgun said, "no beggars on our tail. Guess they're not following today."

Yeah, Alek thought, *that is strange.*

Another voice on the radio, the team leader. "All right, gentlemen, let's pull off here and do a sensitive items check." They'd egressed so quickly they didn't have a chance to make sure they hadn't left any gear behind, so they pulled to the side of the road and opened the back gates on the Humvees to count it all up. Alek began looking through his truck.

A chill ran through him.

"Shit, where's my ruck? *Where's my fucking ruck?"*

Suddenly it was obvious why the villagers who'd seemed so intent on confronting them had simply let them go: they had what they wanted. They'd dropped the gate and grabbed Alek's rucksack as the Humvee pulled out.

This was bad. This was very bad. Alek did a quick recounting: the ruck had high-caliber ammunition; it had—shit, it had a GPS with classified military technology. His officer in charge would get demoted for this. This was military technology being compromised and potentially falling into enemy hands, and suddenly what had been a live-fire sniper training drill, shooting at the abandoned burnt-out carcass of a Soviet-era tank, was becoming a very real crisis.

"Okay, no one bugged-out faster than we did," the section leader said, "so let's focus on the vehicles first." Vehicles move the fastest, so if they could make sure no one was driving out of the village with the stolen bag, they had at least a chance of tracking it down before the bag and its classified contents made it to some Taliban outpost.

They piled back into the Humvees and drove back toward the village, cutting off vehicles along the way, dragging drivers out, searching bodies, searching trunks. Alek was mortified that he was the reason people's jobs were at risk, and angry at the locals for stealing his rucksack, but at the same time, he was having fun. *We never get to do this, go out and search vehicles.* He was grateful for the action, the excitement, which came as a relief.

The reality was, his mission in Afghanistan had been until this day, extremely quiet. It was boring. His unit provided security for a base special forces used, so other guys went out and saw action while Alek and his friends were just glorified babysitters. He followed local staff around to make sure they didn't steal toilet paper when they cleaned the bathroom, he sat in the watchtower on his best days, wishing something exciting would happen to him. Alek woke up every day and he didn't go to war; he went to work. He clocked in, did nothing, clocked out. His life at war was as mundane as it had been back in the States. More so, and with fewer menu options. His only diversion, before the ten-day sniper training, was going down to the MWR to do laundry or lift weights, and mostly, to chat with Spencer online about the trip he was going to take when he got done with his tour.

"Tour," that was a funny word. Here he was stationary. He would only start a real "tour" when he left.

NONE OF THE VEHICLES had Alek's rucksack. Could one have snuck by, or gone a different route?

Now he was nervous, but still excited. He was part of solving a real crisis; he just wished he hadn't caused it. They zigzagged back down the road until they were pulling into the village they'd left, and they knew, by process of elimination, that the bag was either long gone, carried miles away on some road they didn't know about, or it was here, in this village. The team initiated a KLE, a key leader engagement, which translated to basically "talk with the important guy," but they were antsy. The villagers had been acting strange, not outright hostile, but suspicious, and Alek's team wasn't sure whom they might be harboring, whom they might be loyal to, behind those blank, appraising stares.

"Skarlatos, you take the turret. I'm going to take the terp so we can talk to these folks and see what we can find out." Alek had left his normal rifle at base because this was a sniper drill, so he hung the M107 over the turret, feeling a little ridiculous with so much firepower against apparently unarmed people, at such close range. He was a mall cop with a bazooka. He was still a little embarrassed for having put his team in this position, but he'd been desperate for a release, desperate for all that pent-up adrenaline. He looked through his scope and when he saw a man coming toward his NCO with the rucksack, Alek readied himself for the man to pull out a weapon.

The villagers bartered to give the ruck back, asking that the soldiers leave the villagers a field knife and some spent shell casings. They were asking for the team's trash. Alek's NCO agreed, and as he carried Alek's bag back to the Humvees, Alek said a little prayer, asking that nothing would be missing.

He opened it and looked in.

"All there?" The section leader watched him closely. The bag had been dumped out and repacked; he knew that because nothing was in the same place, so he was at first uncertain whether anything had been taken. As he rifled through it to the bottom, he saw that, in fact, something had been. It wasn't all there. The villagers had repacked the bag, but they'd clearly lightened its load. Another pang of anxiety shot through him. What would he say happened? He'd have to admit he lost a GPS, classified technology, let it fall into someone else's possession; maybe he'd be discharged, or even worse, his seniors would be discharged ... But sitting at the bottom of the pack, the GPS was still there.

They gave it *back?*

Who knows how much they could have sold that for. He was relieved. Then almost puzzled. A villager could earn a year's wages selling that; why'd they give it back?

They'd returned his ammo too. Couldn't they use that?

All they'd taken, now that he could see all the contents clearly, was a scope-tightening wrench, the water from his CamelBak—but they'd returned the CamelBak itself—and a hat with his name on it.

Someone in that village was running around the desert with SKARLATOS written on their head.

Someone had a sense of humor.

ALEK RETURNED TO BASE feeling good. He hadn't had the chance to shoot at even a pretend enemy in a tank, or a real enemy in the village, but by chance he'd had a few bonus hours of action, of freedom, and his worst fears had been averted. He was a little embarrassed, but everyone in the team agreed to keep quiet about his lost rucksack.

By the end of the next day, everyone on base knew. The special forces guys who got to go out and see real action ribbed him for it: Alek's first contact with the enemy was getting fleeced by unarmed villagers. Alek laughed along with them; it was all in good fun, but it felt like being the little brother. Forced to stay home while the real men went out to play ball.

Not that there was much action anyway. Afghanistan wasn't where the world's attention was anymore. Now the real bad guys were ISIS, and there weren't very many of them in Afghanistan. Jihadists going to fight in Syria, or to be trained there; the passage of extremists through Turkey.

Which was funny when he thought about it. His grandfather was Greek, but he was born in a part of Greece that was, back then, under Ottoman rule. Turkish rule, in other words. So his grandfather was born in Turkey, and now Turkey was the gateway to jihad. Not that his grandfather was an extremist; his name had been *Sokratis,* after all. "Socrates," just like the philosopher.

Although he *was* a resistance fighter. A guerilla. He was an insurgent, and here Alek was, trying to fight an insurgency.

But that was just it. He wasn't really fighting at all. He wanted to be a soldier, but instead he was a housekeeper. Before he'd left for his deployment, his mom came up to Oregon to say goodbye, and she'd made a big thing out of how she'd felt a sense of fear about him going to war. She'd been ill with it, she said, but then God spoke to her. "He told me that something very exciting's going to happen to you, Alek, and I can't wait to see it. I can't wait to see what he has in store for you."

God was wrong. Or Heidi misheard him, because there was no excitement. Nothing happened. Nothing besides one drill that went awry. The war in Afghanistan was winding down, and the only real missions available were gobbled up by the special forces guys. They were the ones who got to fight what was left of the war. They were the ones who got to kill bad guys. Alek followed janitors around.

21.

EVER SINCE THEIR history class at the small Christian
school, Alek had been pretty sure he wanted to be in the
military. That class had been the one respite from the whole
long trauma he suffered there, and he still felt moved by
history, by wars; he wanted to be part of them.

Perhaps it came from family too. The stories he heard
about two grandfathers who each led heroic, interesting
lives—he felt it was maybe in his blood. Wars were the
culmination of history; wars were where you left your mark
on it.

And he loved guns. The military would be fun; it would be
cool. He knew early on it was what he wanted to do. It just
took a few twists and turns to learn exactly how.

One important step came just after the small Christian
school. When he left with Spencer, he found himself caught
between two worlds. He and Spencer were wading into the
new one together, but the rest of Alek's friends, his entire
community, had all been at the school, which was also his
church. Most of his life revolved around an institution he
now felt alienated from.

Spencer seemed driven to go out and find new friends,
but Alek didn't think he could be authentic, and be super-
ficial enough to socialize, at the same time. He knew none of
these people. How could he pretend to have anything in
common with them? Spencer could at least connect with
people about things like basketball. Alek preferred to paint.

He started doing landscapes with his dad, then one day someone knocked a vase off a table and Alek looked at it, lying there on the floor, shattered, and thought it had a strange kind of appeal. He set up an easel and used oil paint to re-create the broken vase on canvas. It turned out well; it was still strange, but it was pretty, and interesting, and he liked it, so Alek began painting abstract art in most of his spare time. Which was a nice diversion, but a solitary one; not exactly a path to camaraderie.

And he couldn't quite reconcile himself to the fact that he *needed* a new community. He'd had one, and it was just a few miles away. It felt strange to pretend his old friends didn't exist. Spencer got up one day and walked out to try and find a clique, but Alek didn't feel motivated to. And he felt if he tried, he'd only hold Spencer back.

"It's okay," Alek said that day, sitting on the school bench, "you go ahead." And he let Spencer go.

His dad started talking around then about moving up to Oregon, because he had real estate investments up there, and it's where Alek's stepmom came from. Alek's dad asked him whether eventually, maybe after graduation, he'd think about moving up with him, and though Alek couldn't quite put his finger on why, the idea appealed to him.

Except, why wait until graduation? Why not go now? Spencer was off making friends; Alek didn't have any here.

He loved Oregon the moment he landed. It was a slower pace of life; it was more solitary, more space. He didn't miss Northern California. He missed his mom and his family; he missed Spencer and Spencer's family; he missed the compound on Woodknoll Way, but he didn't really miss California.

Besides, Spencer seemed to be doing okay without him. When they spoke, and when Alek went home to visit after they'd both graduated, he got a taste for how Spencer was getting on with his life. Spencer had a job he said he liked at Jamba Juice, and new friends. Friends who struck Alek as a little directionless, hippies really, but they seemed to care about Spencer. Spencer appeared to be unbothered by the fact that he was going to spend the rest of his life gaining weight and making smoothies. The only adventures Spencer would ever have were going to be getting drunk with friends who had exotic piercings.

To Alek, that seemed boring. Alek wanted more.

Back in Oregon, he was enrolled at Umpqua Community College, with a part-time job at Costco, but he decided it was time to begin thinking seriously about the thing he'd always planned for. Time to think about which branch of the military he wanted to join.

For a civilian, he knew the military inside and out. He knew every branch, what they did, how they spoke, what their lives were like.

But he wanted to be careful, smart, and not everyone had great things to say about their branches.

Some people returned from deployments talking about how big of a mistake it had been. Something in the back of his mind said, *Try it out before you sign your whole life away.* So he needed a way to dip his toe in the water before diving in, and he decided on a branch full of people with other careers. People who worked when they weren't deployed, as analysts and consultants, middle management at big Oregon-based companies like Nike. The Oregon National Guard would be his carefully plotted entrée to the military.

Just when he'd made his decision, he got a text from Spencer. "Hey, man, big news. I'm signing up for special forces! Air force pararescue, baby!"

Alek thought before replying. Was that a joke? Spencer? In the special forces? Alek had studied every service inside and out and considered pararescue. Did Spencer actually know how hard it was? Did he think he was just going to waltz in and qualify for one of most elite branches of the military? Spencer was, what, fifty pounds overweight the last time Alek saw him? He'd never make it. Alek thought about checking his friend, sparing him the heartbreak. What if Spencer hurt himself? Clearly Spencer needed advice from someone who knew what he was talking about, before he got hurt, or embarrassed. *How do I say this without being an asshole?*

He deliberated, trying to figure out how best to be a good friend, and finally decided it wasn't his place to be critical. Maybe Spencer would come out of it on his own. But Alek didn't want to encourage him too much; he needed to be careful, not build up an inflated sense of hope that might devastate Spencer when it popped. So after a long pause, he finally just settled on something neutral. "That's great, good luck."

And he thought about how even though Spencer would never make it, it still must mean something that they both, independently, decided to join the military at the same time. Maybe that's what happened when you were best friends.

Even when you didn't have a plan, friends did things together.

22.

THE TWO FRIENDS HAD A PLAN.

It was the spring of 1941; the Nazi occupation of Greece was just a month old. The fascist Italians had tried and failed to take the country, so their Axis brethren came to bail them out with the full force of the German Twelfth Army. The Germans sent panzer divisions and the Luftwaffe, laying waste to the country on their way, and the advance took only weeks. When they reached Athens, they went straight to the Acropolis to raise the Nazi flag, so that the swastika could be seen from all over the city, and all over the cradle of Western civilization there would be no doubt about who was in control.

During the occupation that followed, thousands of Greeks died, many of starvation, many from harsh punishment as the Nazis tried to prevent a resistance.

What the Nazis did not count on was an almost absurdly brave plan carried out by a couple of young men.

Their plan should not have worked. The odds were against them. Two teenagers against the Twelfth Army. The Acropolis was heavily guarded and had only one authorized entrance, so they'd have to run a gauntlet of Nazis to get there. The boys decided they needed to sneak in from the side, but that presented another problem: the Acropolis was guarded by nature as well, with steep cliffs all around. They had to find a different way in, so they took the natural next step: they went to the library. They rifled through encyclopedias looking for ideas, and within the pages on historical sites around the city, the places in which the beasts and gods fought and formed alliances in ancient Greek mythology, they found a hint. A brief mention of a cave with a fissure leading all the way up to the top of the Acropolis. They scouted it out and decided it had as good a chance of success as anything else they'd come up with.

They went out and secretly scouted the perimeter of the Acropolis looking for evidence, found an old archeological site at the northwest cliff face with a wooden door and a rusty old lock. They skirted the barbed wire, broke the lock, forced the door, and went into the cave.

They found the fissure from the myth, and while it was impossible to tell for sure, it seemed at least possible that it went deep and high enough.

The boys barely made it home before curfew, and even when they did, they received chilling news. Two hundred miles to the south, German airborne troops had begun an invasion of Crete. Crete wasn't only a symbol of Greece's continuing collapse to the Nazis, it was the country's biggest island, and a base from which to project power over the Mediterranean and Middle East Theater, so it wasn't just meaningful for Greece—whoever held Crete held a powerful advantage in the whole war.

The boys decided they needed to move faster.

A few nights later, just after news broke that Crete had fallen to the Nazis, the boys went back to the cave.

They were armed only with flashlights and a penknife, but they were able to use old planks from the archaeological dig to climb up through the shaft, and they found themselves at the base of the Parthenon, partially lit by a quarter moon.

They waited until guards had wandered away from the belvedere, which served as a lookout post at the east end. When the coast was clear, they crept over to the pole, pulled out the penknife, and sawed at the rope until the giant Nazi flag came tumbling down.

When Athens awoke the next morning, a giant symbol of evil was gone. It was like a huge black cloud had lifted, and a vision of what could be took over. Spirits rose all over the city, and a palpable sense of opportunity grew throughout the country. The day the flag came down changed the course of history, because it showed what a few normal people could do. It inspired thousands upon thousands of people all over Greece, proving they could have a real, *visible* effect on their own lives, on their world. On the evil in their midst. That bare flagpole inspired a resistance movement against the Nazis and drove tens of thousands of people all over the country to join it, among them a thirty-two-year-old shoemaker named Sokratis Skarlatos.

SKARLATOS JOINED THE RESISTANCE. He lived in the city of Alexander—*Alexandroupoli*—so he became a guerilla fighter there. He trekked through the Evros Mountains with an old rifle and waited for opportunities to sabotage his oppressors. Eventually he was captured and held in a camp near the Evros River, but he was wily and bold. He escaped, dodging bullets as the guards fired at their fleeing prisoner, and dove into the Evros. He fled into the Rhodope Mountains, traversed north, then came back across the river and hid in the foothills, waiting for the right time to go home.

As soon as he did, Skarlatos was recaptured.

This time, he wasn't given a chance to escape. The Nazis had a more creative idea for him. He was a shoemaker, after all, so he might as well put his skills to use. They conscripted him into the Nazi war effort, sent him to Germany, and assigned him to a plant in the east where he would help make boots for soldiers.

He was good at it; he was made a supervisor. He'd gone from being a freedom fighter to being just about the opposite, manufacturing one of the most recognizable symbols of oppression, the Nazi jackboot. But still, he'd found a way to survive. And he found a girl: a teenage leather cutter in his charge who caught his fancy.

Skarlatos rode out the war at the boot factory, and when it ended he took his young bride to a small town on a lake at the foot of the Bavarian Alps. Übersee, it was called, "over the water." They had a son, Emmanuel, and when the Iron Curtain fell, the old freedom fighter took his family to the land of opportunity.

Colorado, then Oakland, where Emmanuel grew up, met his first wife, a customer service rep for Greyhound named Heidi Neuberger, and in October of 1992, a boy with heroism in his blood was born. He was given the name of the greatest Greek of them all, Alexander, with a slight tweak suggested by a speech therapist at a Lamaze class, to make the full name easier to say: Alek.

He came from a people who'd fought one of the world's greatest evils, and done so with hardly any weapons. It was this history with which he'd always felt the need to commune. It was why he took to history class, even when little else in school held his interest. It was why he loved guns, maybe even part of what drove him to join the military. He grew up wishing he could go see where his grandfather was born, to see where he'd fought, and loved, and found a way to survive among the Nazis. He wanted to see where his father was born. And after his tour in Afghanistan, he would finally, finally have the money to do it.

23.

"GERMANY FIRST. We gotta go to Germany." Alek was in the MWR after shift, messaging Spencer. After another boring day. He hadn't realized quite how boring life on a base in Afghanistan was going to be, but he knew he wouldn't have many chances to spend money. He knew that his best friend was going to be stationed in Portugal, and he knew both of them would finish their tours with some savings. He wanted Spencer to see this part of him, a part he himself was only beginning to understand.

"Alek, I'm getting good at this!" Spencer's messages were so enthusiastic Alek was almost jealous. He'd seen pictures of Spencer's base—it was like a beach resort or something. Spencer didn't know what it was like to be at a *real* posting.

"Good at what, like checking rashes?"

"No, asshole, I've been doing jujitsu. I'm starting to give my class instructor a run for his money." Spencer and his jujitsu. "Anyway," Spencer wrote, "adventure starts soon. I'm getting excited, man."

Spencer had no idea. Alek was desperate for it to begin. Spencer asked, "What ended up being the deal with your friends?"

"Strasser can't come," Alek wrote. "Honestly I don't think Solon will either. I know he wants to but I don't think he has the money."

"Sucks."

The planning was getting complicated, partially because

Alek was spending too much time doing it. In reality he didn't really need to be doing this now; he'd have plenty of time to plan later, after his tour, because he had to go back to the US for demobilization before he could fly to Europe. He planned anyway though, because for him it was a diversion, one of the only ones he had, the one fun thing he could do while stuck here on a gloryless tour. So he over-planned.

"So," Alek wrote, "then when do you want to come back through Germany?"

"It's just that there's so much I want to see, you know? This will probably be my last chance to do something like this, there's a lot to do. I know you have that girl there . . ."

Lea. He *knew* Spencer was going to bring that up eventually. She'd been a German exchange student in Oregon, and he'd met her over a friend's Snapchat he photobombed. Then they began talking, and once he started planning his German tour, he decided he wanted to see her. But the plan to see her when he was passing through Germany evolved into something more; she'd invited him to stay with her at her family's house, and now he figured he might spend a few days with her.

"It's not just that," he wrote Spencer. "Just don't want to be moving every day, I want to, you know, soak it in a little."

"All right, well, we don't have to decide right now. Let me know if Solon comes through. In the meantime, whatever happened with the sniper training?"

"I'll tell you about it later." The last thing Alek wanted to talk about was being here. "But basically, I'm still really bored."

"Don't worry. I'll have a couple of beers for you. "

"You piece of shit. All right, it's midnight here. I gotta go to bed."

"Hang in, brother, later."

Two days later, after his shift, Alek went down to the MWR to lift weights, and decided to check his messages first. He had a Facebook message from Spencer. "Good news, I think Anthony's coming."

Alek had to think for a minute. *Anthony?* "Anthony from middle school you mean?"

"Yeah, he thinks he can get the time off. He's just trying to get a credit card now." That was random. Of all the people to invite. Alek hadn't seen Anthony in what, five years, seven years? What was Anthony like now; would they all still get along?

It was good though; Spencer would have someone to travel with on his speed-of-light tour of Europe, and Alek felt okay letting them do their own thing while he went to trace his roots. He'd catch up with them for a city or two, then go back to his own spirit quest.

By the time his deployment was over, he had it pretty much figured it out: Germany, then Paris with Spencer and Anthony. Maybe Barcelona. He wasn't quite as high on Spain as they were; mostly he wanted to get back to Germany where he could continue tracking down his own history. When he'd see the eastern side. Austria to see where his father was born. Cross the border, see Switzerland. Then Prague, where he had a cousin, and finally he'd fly out of Frankfurt. He wanted Spencer to go with him; he felt it was something important about him he wanted Spencer to see, but didn't want to pressure Spencer to do something he didn't want to do, but might end up doing out of duty.

So Alek decided to tell a little lie, "I actually want to do some of that EuroRail stuff too," he wrote. That way he'd get to see Spencer, without taking Spencer off his path. Alek would go back to Germany afterward, to finish his journey on his own.

So the plan was set. He closed his computer and went to the gym. Just another month of his boring deployment, idly hoping, wishing, for some action before his adventure could begin.

FINALLY, AFTER WHAT FELT like a decade, he was done. Sitting in the belly of a C-17 Globemaster rumbling down the runway at Bagram Airfield and lifting up into the cloud cover. Someone said something about a sandstorm in Kuwait, which explained why the plane was diverted to Qatar to wait it out. Before the long flight from the Middle East to Texas for demobilization, they had to stop in Germany to refuel. *Such a roundabout way*, he thought. He was on his way to see his roots, and there they were, right out the window, almost close enough to touch, but the path took him all the way back to the US first before he was free.

24.

HE PUT THE RECEIVER on the vise block, then threaded the magazine catch into its hole. Then he flipped it around and slid a spring over the magazine catch, and tested the movement. It had to be smooth, because this was the mechanism that would drop the magazine out of the rifle so you could reload. He tested it. He stuck an empty magazine into the receiver and it locked in place. Good. He pressed the button and the magazine slid right out. *Good.*

Next he attached the bolt catch into the receiver, so that after firing the last round the bolt would stay back. That way if you sprayed a whole magazine at a bunch of targets, you could stick in another magazine and the bolt would already be back, poised to fire another round.

He lubed up the roll pin and tapped it into the hole for the bolt catch. He threaded on the safety selector, slid the grip onto the receiver and screwed it down, watching closely to make sure he didn't kink the spring. The safety had to move smoothly too, so that when he was ready to shoot it would snap easily and definitively to "fire." So far so good.

He wiped the sweat from his forehead and stretched his neck.

Next the trigger spring over the trigger, the hammer spring over the hammer. He flicked the safety to "fire" and stuck the trigger into the opening in the bottom of the receiver, the disconnector on top, put the hammer down, and tapped a pin in place to secure the whole assembly.

Now the weapon had a trigger. He attached a trigger guard, the barrel, gas bolt, and a flash suppressor. Then a scope.

After four hours of careful work, he was done.

He lifted it up and inspected it. He flicked the safety on and off, pulled the trigger back a few times, ejected and reloaded empty magazines. Everything worked. He carried it over to the table in the rec room and set it with the others; he'd assembled an arsenal. He had assembled weapons for long-range, AR-10s equipped with scopes, and AR-15s with red dots for closer range, the red dots being lighter and quicker at acquiring targets in close quarters. Urban environments; vehicles.

He was doing this mostly from boredom. Also he wanted to earn a few extra dollars while waiting for his journey to begin. He'd asked friends in Afghanistan if they wanted weapons, and if they did, he offered to build the weapons for them, customizing the guns for whatever their needs were. All they had to do was the background check for the lower receiver, the part the government considered a firearm, and the rest Alek could handle. He liked working on weapons anyway; it was quiet meditative work, time by himself with his thoughts, and it was positive, constructive work, bringing something into being. It was like painting, which he used to love, and anyway he had a month after his deployment before he was due to meet Lea in Germany. By the time he left, he'd made a dozen semiautomatic weapons for his friends.

25.

ALEK LANDED IN FRANKFURT, flush with money from his deployment and the little extra from the guns he'd made. Lea picked him up at the airport, and together they drove the hour to her home in Heidelberg. Alek was struck by how pretty it was, green and scenic, and everything seemed organized. He met Lea's family; he met other people in their town.

Lea's family had an extra room set up for him, so he put his bags down, and his dip into history began immediately. Lea took him to the castle in Heidelberg, rich with competing legacies, having changed hands over the course of almost a millennium, and which was somehow almost miraculously preserved despite all the destruction to so many other German cities during World War II. It had been the headquarters of the American forces in Europe when America was helping to fight Nazism. It was a place where much of the destruction was done by the Germans themselves. During *Kristallnacht*, the "Night of Broken Glass," two synagogues were burned down, Jews were killed, and afterward they were deported en masse, but the Americans did no damage. The city, somehow, never fell victim to the strategic bombing the Allies visited upon so many others.

Alek found his own way to make his mark. He had Lea take a picture of him holding a miniature American flag, just in the right place, so that it looked like it was one of the heralds flying from the high turret of the castle. Claiming Heidelberg castle for America. A perfect way to start.

Lea took him to Rothenberg, to see buildings older than Alek's country, another perfectly preserved medieval town that escaped the bombings in World War II. It was a city along the Romantic Road, and nearly unchanged since the Middle Ages. He bought a stupid-looking German hat, but he thought it was funny. That night when Spencer wrote to check in:

In Munich, So much history

Alek thought, *you have no idea.*

It was a funny thought, now that he stood there: his mom's father coming from America to Germany, just as his dad's dad was doing the opposite. The next day he took Lea to help him find the café where Heidi's dad had gone after getting his stripes, halfway through 1953, and Alek bought Lea a beer there, at the very place Nicholas Neuberger, Grandpa Nick, had celebrated becoming a sergeant, sixty-two years before.

It was a café next to the old Heidelberg bridge over the Neckar, and being there put Alek in a pensive mood, think-ing about the other things Grandpa Nick had told him. He told Lea how Grandpa Nick was raised in poverty in upstate New York during World War II, and the military was his chance to satisfy his wanderlust. He'd come to Germany, as a mechanic based in the Rhineland during the Korean War, but his furloughs took him farther; he'd told Alek about his favorite trip while stationed in Germany, down to Spanish Morocco.

It was the summer of 1953. Nicholas Neuburger had time off and money to burn. He wanted to see Africa, so he went down to Gibraltar with some other GIs and caught a ferry to Morocco. It was there that he'd had one of the most bizarre, inexplicable experiences in his life, a thing so out of context that he'd written it down and placed it in a scrapbook, because he didn't think anyone would believe him otherwise. He didn't even tell the story until two generations later, when his grandchildren went up to his ranch and asked about his time in the service.

Sitting where his grandfather got his stripes, Alek remembered that weird old story. The summer of '53, Grandpa Nick riding on a train across French Morocco with other GIs on the way to Casablanca. Most of the passengers were sleeping, but Grandpa Nick was awake. He couldn't sleep because there was a group of Frenchmen—or at least he figured they were French because they were wearing suits and had pale skin—laughing and carrying on, so every time he dozed off a shriek of laughter and rapid-fire French woke him up. He sat looking out the window, watching the passing countryside. At 2 A.M.—and he knew it was 2 A.M.; on this matter he was certain—he saw a band of men on galloping horses, wearing robes and swords with blades as big as butchers' knives, ride up beside the train. The horses kept picking up speed, galloped ahead of his car, then the train slowed, stopped, the horsemen boarded, and they moved into Nick's car, waving their blades like they might just tomahawk anyone in their way. It all happened in what felt like an instant. Before Nick knew what was happening they were in his car, right next to him, grabbing a man in a suit who, now that Nick looked at him closely, seemed by his complexion to be Middle Eastern. The bandits, or whatever they were, grabbed the man by the hair, and as they yanked his head his eyes met Nick's with a look of pleading, of terror.

A look not just of surprise; it was as if some terrible but not wholly unexpected thing was happening to him, something he might have been worried about, might have been running from.

The horsemen dragged him off the train, and the French revelers who'd kept Nick awake now looked directly at him, and spoke to him in English that was so crystal clear it alarmed him, like their bodies had suddenly been possessed. "Do not move. Do not say a thing."

They stared right at him.

Out the window, he saw the Middle Eastern man in Western clothes slumped crosswise over a saddle. His body was limp. Nick couldn't tell if he was dead, or bound, or unconscious. And then the horses galloped off. The train started again. He never learned what happened. So it stuck with him; he wrote down the story with the date and time and put it in that scrapbook. He never forgot about it, even in his old age, because it was a story that didn't yet have an end.

"wow, THAT IS A CRAZY STORY." Lea seemed impressed by Alek's lineage, and Alek began to feel proud of it. He felt his own journey echoed Grandpa Nick's, the military providing the means to finally find his own history, and he was falling into a comfortable rhythm here. Each night he slept at Lea's house; each day she drove him to another site in southern Germany.

She took him to Phantasialand, a theme park in Cologne for a familiar kind of fun, riding roller coasters and wandering through the huge parts of the park designed as world neighborhoods: Chinatown, Mexico, and the one Alek found the most interesting, Deep in Africa. There they rode the one everyone seemed to be talking about, the Black Mamba, an inverted coaster that passed through towers meant to mimic the mud-brick walls and jutting crossbeams of North African mosques. They banked through near misses, the whole ride designed to make you think you were going to run into some great danger, but then at the last minute, you'd bank hard off your course and be diverted to safety.

He was most taken with how everything in that section of the park all the way down to the bathrooms had the pointed arches he recognized from photographs of mosques. Everything was adjusted for history, for place and time. Walking through that part of the park was like walking through the souks of North Africa. The attention to detail amazed him. Stalls with thatched wood roofs, red dirt paths—he felt like he could be walking through a city in Tunisia, or in Morocco.

Each night he slept at Lea's house, and each day she showed him something new.

He wanted to get soccer jerseys, so she took him to a huge sporting goods store in Mannheim, where he bought two for his brother Solon, the biggest fan in the family. Solon had been desperate to come on the trip, so Alek figured he'd take a few jerseys back for him. For himself, Alek bought a blue-and-red-striped Bayern Munich jersey, and had Lea ask the store to screen-print his favorite player's name on the back. He liked it so much he decided to try and wear it every day. He would be wearing it four days later when the entire European press corps descended on him.

He was supposed to be with Lea for just a week, but it felt so good with her family, and they were so kind, and he was saving so much money, he couldn't think of a good reason to leave. On his eighth day he heard from Spencer that he and Anthony were in Germany too, but up in Munich, and Alek was having too good of a time down south to leave.

On his tenth day, after coming back from a hike with Lea, he had a Facebook message from Spencer:

Headed to Berlin!

Alek still didn't feel like leaving.
After his eleventh day:

Just met this weird rocker dude at a bar. We've changed plans. We're going to Amsterdam! Will keep you posted.

By then Alek figured he'd put Lea's family out long enough; might as well start the reunion now. So on his twelfth day in Heidelberg, Lea drove him back to Mannheim. He caught a bus to Amsterdam but got off at the wrong stop and had to catch a cab the last twenty-five miles.

On board the 15:17, Alek looks out the window from his first-class seat as the last of the Netherlands passes by. He's bored, and a little antsy. He's eager to squeeze the last bit of fun out of this trip because now that his tour in Afghanistan is over, the most interesting part of his life is over too, and that turned out to not even be very interesting. All he's had is a few weeks in Europe, and then in a week or two he'll be back in Oregon, working at Costco, taking night classes at community college, sleepwalking toward some degree he doesn't care all that much about.

Spencer sleeps to his right, sealed into his own world by noise-canceling headphones. Across the aisle, Anthony sleeps too. Why hasn't he been closer to Anthony? In hindsight, Anthony is the kind of person Alek likes being around. Laid back, unaffected. Genuine. And yet he hadn't talked to Anthony in seven years. Not since junior high. They'd been a handful, the three of them, in seventh, eighth grade, tearing through the neighborhood with paintball masks, BBs welting each other's skin and plinking off doors and windows. Leaping over downed trees in the forest behind the old elementary school, imaginary infantry charges, piling into the basketball coach's living room to play Call of Duty until their eyes watered and their thumbs ached. Acting up in class, the three of them, their own civil disobedience against the family who ran their school. It was Spencer who had pulled Anthony into their friendship when Anthony arrived at the school, wide-eyed and friendless. Alek remembers being fine with it, liking Anthony even then—Anthony, who seemed dumbstruck by every aspect of suburbia. It was almost like having a little brother, a plebe to indoctrinate into their way of life, except that Anthony was actually a grade ahead.

Alek gazes out the window at rolling fields, burnt straw-brown by late summer heat. He looks down at his phone, just in time to see the pulsing blue dot cross the line. *We're in Belgium!* he thinks. FN Herstal is here. Fabrique Nationale d'Herstal, one of his favorite gun makers. All those rifles for the US military are made somewhere out there. Is Steyr from here? No, Steyr's Austrian. It was in Oregon that he got his first real gun. He had time on his own, and he began to find solace in weapons. Not just the paintball and airsoft guns he and Spencer and Anthony had battled each other with in junior high; when he got to Oregon, his dad bought him a real 12 gauge, and Alek found purpose. He had something to share with his younger brother. How to fire it, how to clean it, how to take it apart and put it back together. Each weapon was a sophisticated machine, but also simple, and elegant, and sexy, and just fucking cool. They had histories. Firearms manufacturers changed ownership, armed the Allies, armed the Nazis—what kind of weapons did the Vietcong use, the Sandinistas? It was a hobby that folded into the one subject he'd always felt most at home with, since he and the two friends next to him had bonded back in their middle school history class.

26.

THEY STUMBLED OUT onto the street in Amsterdam, drunk and giddy. They'd found a club, drunk too much, danced too much. Alek woke up in a heap on the floor of the hostel room, head throbbing, but content. He'd get his own room tomorrow night; he was desperate for a bed. On Friday they were supposed to catch the 15:17 for Paris, but already he was thinking they'd skip it, catch a later one. Amsterdam had exceeded his expectations, and they all wanted more time here.

"Oh, man, how crazy is this?" he'd said when he first caught up with them at the hostel. "The first time we're all together after, what, *seven years?* And it's in Europe!"

Of course, he'd thought it strange at first, random, that Spencer invited Anthony on their European trip. His bonding with his best friend, this last hurrah before a boring pedestrian life, it felt altered at first. Now that they were all together again, though, it felt right. Old friends, a new place. A city none had explored, opening itself up before them. The place itself was old meeting new, gleaming space-age structures rising out of cobblestone streets with centuries of history.

They went out at night, went to a soccer game during the day. They drank beer while the sun was still up, they made friends easily here. There was a chemistry to this place where the three had finally come together after so many years. Was it just him, or did the place buzz with its own energy? Alek didn't want to leave.

That was his style; he was beginning to understand that about himself, and he wasn't ashamed of it. To stay in a place, get to know it, get to know the people, maybe find a girl. Spencer and Anthony, they still seemed to want to see as many places as possible, burning through Europe like the whole continent was on a limited-time offer. Alek wanted to take it slow, soak it in. In Amsterdam, for the first time, Spencer and Anthony agreed.

"Spencer, man," Alek overheard Anthony saying, "we might need to stay here for the weekend!"

Anthony said Amsterdam reminded him of home; the weather was like home, sunny but breezy, the topography favored Sacramento. Plus the only reason they were supposed to leave was to go to Paris, and Spencer said people they'd run into along the way kept trying to divert them from it. "We met this girl at our hostel in Berlin," Spencer said. "She told us Paris is just really expensive. She said it's actually pretty boring, and people are like—they're actually kind of *rude*."

"And Lisa in Venice was the same," Anthony said. There'd been a girl on their train to Amsterdam too, an Australian who'd already done all of Europe, and tried to convince them not to do France. So why not just skip their train and catch a later one? There were at least a dozen trains a day.

They went on a bike tour out to a farm, Rembrandt Hoeve on the Amstel River, owned by an eccentric Dutchman who made clogs and smoked gouda. They biked past houses along the canal that Alek could've sworn were cockeyed, and then the guide explained that they were, that they leaned over the water so that things hoisted up from the canal wouldn't swing into the façade; it had the effect of making it look like the world was about to fall on top of them as they rode past.

They rode by the Amsterdam Bos, a giant park, bigger than Central Park in New York City, where the wealthy held fox chases and protesters had chanted against the Vietnam War.

Everything was easy, the weather was perfect, the people were perfect; Alek had so many things left to do.

So why leave? Why leave Amsterdam? No one had a good reason. Why not just stay here longer? He wanted to get a haircut here. Anthony and Spencer had gone without him while he was on the bus up from Mannheim. They'd stumbled across a Jamaican barber while biking to the laundromat, and Anthony was so excited to find someone in the Netherlands who could cut a black man's hair that he made Spencer get the same haircut. The two looked sharp; Alek wanted in.

Then there was the club they kept hearing about that Anthony wanted to go to. But it was only open on weekends, so if they kept their train reservations they'd miss it.

Plus the girls were kind here, and the boys all agreed that Dutch people were attractive. "I think it's cause everyone bikes," Spencer said, "so they have nice legs."

Alek laughed. "Is that your medical opinion?"

And they hadn't been able to see Anne Frank's house yet; they could do that if they stayed. It was history, after all, that had brought the three of them together, in middle school, and was part of what brought them to Europe in the first place. They couldn't leave without seeing it; it wouldn't be right, like making a pilgrimage and skipping the temple at the end.

"So I guess it's decided," Alek said. They sat outside a bar after walking through the red-light district, logged on to Wi-Fi so they could look at maps and pick a new train time. "We'll just skip Paris."

"Yeah, or at least delay the trip," Anthony said. Paris would still be there next week. Anthony wanted to stay, Alek definitely wanted to stay, and Spencer wasn't about to stand in their way. So the plan was they were going to skip the 15:17 to Paris.

They would leave tomorrow, or even Sunday, or maybe just wait until Monday. Alek would get his hair cut, they'd go to the club, they'd have plenty of time to see Anne Frank's house. It was decided.

AND THEN ALEK FELT SOMETHING nudge up against his thinking, like a small voice in a distant room, urging him to leave this place.

He didn't know how to explain it to the others and didn't quite understand it himself, but he realized he'd changed his mind.

He asked Anthony. Anthony had changed his mind too. Anthony also didn't really have a good reason. "Maybe we should just stick with the first plan," was all he could muster by way of explanation for his own reconsideration.

There were a dozen good reasons to stay. There was no good reason any of them could think of to leave. And yet, they all agreed to leave. None of them knew exactly why, but they all felt it.

27.

AT THE TRAIN STATION in Amsterdam, Anthony asked Alek to take candid pictures of him looking off into the distance. "They're not candid if you ask me to take them."

"Just get me from the side." Anthony was in a pensive mood, or at least trying to look like he was in a pensive mood. He put his arms across the bench and gazed off into the distance. When he lifted his arms, his fleece hiked up and Alek could see the purple of the T-shirt he was wearing underneath.

"Anthony, you're not wearing a Lakers shirt are you? We're in Europe, wear a soccer jersey! Borrow one of mine. Or borrow one of Solon's, I have extras."

"I'm good, no shame in it! I'm proud to support Kobe." Anthony looked off across the platform and said, as if to himself, "The Black Mamba."

"The what?"

"The Black Mamba." Alek was still confused. "It's Kobe's nickname. You didn't know?"

"That's weird, I went on this roller coaster in Cologne called Black Mamba. All Africa themed."

"No shit?"

The train finally dinged into the station, and Alek picked up his bag, but as he moved toward the train, a woman approached. "Excuse me," she said with a British accent, and an arm out toward him, "would you boys help my father board the train?"

Behind her, a frail old man with wisps of white hair offered an embarrassed smile.

"Sure, ma'am." Alek held the man by his elbow while Spencer got the other, and Anthony grabbed their suitcase with his free hand. When the train doors whisked open, Alek helped him up the high stairs, then helped them get settled in their seats while Anthony loaded their luggage.

"Bless you, boys," the man said. "Thank you for your help."

"No problem," Alek said. He turned to Spencer. "You know where our seats are?"

"We have first class. I think it's up there, but this seems fine to me."

"Yeah, fine by me."

They sat down and settled in.

Fifteen minutes passed.

Half an hour passed.

SPENCER GOT UP.

"All right, tired of this," he said. "I'm bored. I'm gonna go check Wi-Fi on the other cars."

Spencer disappeared into the forward cars. More time passed. Spencer burst through the door with his fists in the air.

"Found it! First class is that way. And the Wi-Fi works there."

They waved to the elderly man and the woman who'd diverted them from their reserved seats up front, and moved forward through carriage fifteen, through carriage fourteen, up to carriage twelve.

Up in first class, a train attendant brought them snacks and tiny Coke cans. "Oh my God! So adorable!" Alek was in a bored, giddy mood and found the smaller than average soda endlessly funny. "They're so cute! Spencer, look at this baby soda!"

Spencer groaned. "Alek, shut the fuck up."

"Well, Spencer's in a grumpy mood."

"All right, I'm putting my headphones on." Spencer, the noise canceling headphones firmly affixed to his head, slumped back in his seat and closed his eyes.

THE TRAIN SLOWS. People rise, people reach for their bags, a sea swell of arms and leather and canvas. Spencer and Anthony don't stir.

Alek watches absently as passengers get off, passengers get on. Brussels. He takes a picture of the station. He decides it's boring.

Then, out of corner of his eye, a person on the platform catches his attention.

A curl of blond hair, a confident walk: the attractive train attendant he flirted with earlier, leaving the train. No!

Alek looks around and sees more people in uniforms leaving. *Crew change,* he thinks. *Damn, she's gone. She probably thinks we're a bunch of idiots.* Then, *We are a bunch of idiots.*

He watches her leave with a hint of disappointment. He does not see that as she walks away, a North African man passes going in the opposite direction, approaching the train.

The man crosses the platform, angling just out of Alek's field of vision, and boards behind Alek.

He has enough firepower to kill nearly everyone on board.

Alek takes pictures as the train pulls out of the station. He thinks about waking up Spencer. He wishes something would happen. He tracks on his phone how far they are from Paris; he follows on Google Maps to see what route they're taking, and if he recognizes the names of places they pass. He looks out the window, watches more countryside pass by. He messages the girl in Germany. He messages a friend from his deployment. He messages a girl in Oregon. He looks out the window some more. He looks down at his phone again, playing a little game with himself, trying to predict exactly what time it will be when the train crosses the next border. He texts the two girls. He tells them where he is; he watches the route he is taking on his cell phone.

At approximately 5:55 P.M., just after the little blue dot moves across the screen into France, everyone stops receiving messages from him.

Alek hears luggage dropping off a shelf behind him. Something with a weighted base, because the sound is extremely loud and he hears a tremendous cascade of broken glass. Before he can turn around, a man in uniform blows past his vision at a full sprint, and without thinking, Alek falls to a crouch and turns in the foot space, looking back through the gap between the seats where he can see, swaying in and out of his narrow alley of vision, like some kind of specter moving through a nightmare, a shirtless man with a machine gun, walking slowly toward them.

Adrenaline hits. His vision narrows. The train evaporates around him and all that exists in the whole world is one man with a weapon thirty feet in front of him. Alek's vision is a single sphere, like looking through binoculars; he is watching a video game through a gun sight. He thinks, *Go—let's go*, but means it only partly, feebly; a message to his friends next to him whom he can sense are now awake, he only knows he's said it aloud because he feels it vibrating from his lungs, hears the words returning as an echo. Then Spencer blurs across his vision and Alek realizes he's sent his best friend to charge the gunman.

Another clear thought: that Spencer is defenseless, exposed, and alone.

28.

MEANWHILE, 150 MILES to the south, Alex Daniels, the press attaché for the US embassy in Paris, was finishing dinner. One of the perks of the job was you could host friends on long layovers, and these were a few Palestinian citizens of Israel on a fourteen-hour stay with their kids. Daniels was only five weeks on the job at the embassy, and had tried, and then given up on, meeting press contacts. No one was around. The press, like just about everyone else in France, was on vacation for the month of August. After a week of trying, he'd decided he would wait for *la rentrée,* the grand French tradition of coming back to work in the fall.

It turned out, he wouldn't need to wait that long.

First, his work phone rang.

It was a Friday night, so he let it ring, and said goodbye to his guests, whose taxi had just pulled up.

His work phone rang again.

When it rang a third time, he figured it might be something important, so he picked it up. "This is Agence France-Presse, we just learned three marines stopped a terrorist attack on a train from Amsterdam to Paris. Would you care to comment?"

Daniels cleared his throat. "I don't have any more information at this time, I'll have to get back to you."

He took down the name and number. And then he did what all good press attachés do when blindsided by a story: he turned on the TV.

The phone rang again. Another reporter. Then another, and the blizzard began. Daniels tried to get in touch with his deputy, who was already buried because he was the duty officer that weekend, which meant he was getting not only press calls, but calls from every worried American in France.

"I'm sending all the press to you," he told Daniels, "and I'm going to take all the duty calls." But by that point Daniels was already hopelessly behind. He was already forgetting who had called from which outlet. He needed triage, and he no longer had a deputy to help, so he started making a list of everyone who'd called and in what order, but it was fighting a hydra, the list growing longer than he could keep up with. He'd never seen anything like it. While up in Arras, Alek and Anthony sat together in a hotel room well into the night trying to figure out what the hell had just happened. Alex Daniels was doing the same down in Paris.

Across the city, not far from the embassy, Rebecca Robinson woke up Saturday morning to an urgent call from her colleague Rick Holtzapple. Robinson was the ambassador's assistant, and Holtzapple was a political affairs officer, but since August was the slow season, the embassy had fewer people on hand than usual. The deputy chief of mission—the second in command to the ambassador—was back in America on annual leave, so Holtzapple was filling in for her. But the ambassador was gone too, taking a weekend away with her husband, which left Holtzapple effectively in charge of the whole embassy. Robinson was getting a call from the most senior person on staff. On a weekend.

"Something's happened," Holtzapple said. "We need to call the interior minister."

Robinson took a shower, put on a sundress and sandals—it was a Saturday in August after all—and went down to the embassy. The calls started before she could sit down. She learned that, coincidentally, an embassy employee had been on the same train everyone was talking about, and had called the embassy's security officer. Embassy personnel had known almost the moment it happened, but no one, not even the employee on the train, knew *what* had happened. All he'd been able to report was that the train stopped, rerouted, and a bloody man was carted off; the news outlets were all repeating the same thing: three marines stopped a terrorist.

Daniels arrived several hours after her, having tried to triage from home for most of the morning. Before he got to his desk, Robinson stopped him. "Alex," she said, "this is your *Charlie Hebdo* moment. Welcome to Paris."

Robinson went about setting up calls with French government officials, per Holtzapple's request, starting with the minister of the interior, who was in charge of the national police and the other law enforcement bodies. Then she, the executive staff, and the consular team all switched their attention to what had become the most pressing task: securing the safety of Americans who had been in harm's way, and for all Robinson knew, still were. Here the consular staff was critical, since they were the ones specially trained in providing emergency services to American citizens abroad. If an American was seriously injured, they needed to know what hospital he was taken to and whether he was receiving good enough care. America needed to take care of its own.

But there was a problem. Robinson and the rest of the

staff felt responsible for the well-being of three young Americans, but didn't know where any of them were. All they knew was that the one named Spencer Stone was in the hospital, not even *which* hospital, and the other two were completely in the wind. By now Robinson had learned their names, Anthony and Alek, but those two could have gone anywhere. Were they okay? Were they targets? Would they get back on a train and leave before the FBI could debrief them?

And there was a second problem. Robinson and the consular team needed to make sure the one named Spencer was getting adequate care, but even if she could find him, she had no authority, and the consular team didn't either. The boys were marines; the embassy's consular services didn't extend to active-duty military. It had to be military to military.

Robinson called the defense attaché, Lieutenant Jim Shaw, who'd already set out for Arras with what amounted to a satellite embassy—two vehicles, two assistants, and a team from the FBI's legal attaché office. Here a key piece of mis-information proved fortuitous. The fact that everyone still thought the boys were all marines compelled Shaw to bring enough personnel, and enough vehicles, to accommodate all of them. For now, his focus was finding out how badly Spencer was hurt, what hospital he was at, what kind of care he was receiving, *and* trying to find out where the hell the other two were.

First, Shaw found out that Spencer was transferred to a hospital in Lille. He'd nearly severed a thumb, but he was doing okay. And that was another extraordinary stroke of luck, an act of God, or just an uncanny coincidence: when the terrorist attacked, the nearest station happened to be thirty miles from a leading medical center with a renowned orthopedic program. At the moment Spencer's thumb was cut, the nearest train station was Arras, so when the train was diverted, it delivered him right to one of the best places in the world to repair precisely the injury he'd sustained.

Spencer was conscious and stable but he didn't immediately know where Alek and Anthony were; he'd been surrounded by French-speaking people and wasn't sure what was going on, but through the French officials buzzing around him, Shaw was able to reverse engineer the last several hours and track the other two boys down to a hotel in Arras.

Then, yet another problem: someone had leaked their location, or else a wily reporter had trailed one of the military attaché vehicles, but either way, there were hundreds of reporters set up outside both the hotel and the hospital. The boys had become rock stars, literally overnight.

Back in Paris, Rebecca Robinson had spent much of the morning into the afternoon frantically trying to help Shaw find the boys and fielding phone calls from an already immensely grateful nation. The president of the railroad association called, the president of the train company, ministers and other government officials called, all this on a Saturday in August when they shouldn't even be in the city—all calling to thank America, to thank the embassy. She'd never experienced anything like it. Not only had those boys performed just about the greatest act of heroism, as far as she was concerned, that had ever been performed, but now *she* was receiving appreciation from every corner of the country. It was like an immense gift the boys had allowed her, without even needing to show their faces and claim credit for themselves.

UP IN ARRAS, Alek sat watching the flurry of activity. He'd had about enough of this, dozens of different officials in all sorts of uniforms all showing their authority. No one spoke English except for Chris—thank God for Chris—translating for him and Anthony, even letting them use his phone to call their families.

At least now some other Americans were in the picture. A defense attaché from the embassy in Paris had arrived, having tracked them down by finding Spencer at the hospital and asking the pool of police gathered there where the other two Americans had been taken.

But that was the other thing. Spencer. Why wouldn't they let him see Spencer?

One of the FBI agents came into the office he and Anthony were sitting in. "Boys, you're going to be receiving a call."

"OK—"

"It's going to be from the president."

They went into an office with a conference table, sat down next to a couple of empty bottles of Coke and a giant stack of bottled water, one of the agents put an iPhone on speaker at the center of the table, and Alek tried to contain a grin. *Is this a joke?* He looked at Anthony, who was more nervous; he kept pressing the button on a pen. They whispered jokes to each other, waited, whispered more jokes, and then Alek had a frightening thought. *What if the president's actually been listening the whole time? He's probably thinking, what the fuck are they*—and then a voice came over the speaker. "Introducing, President Obama."

"Hey, guys!"

Holy shit! How do you respond to the president? Should Anthony speak first? Should I? After a pause Alek said, "Hello, sir," but he said it at the exact time Anthony said, "Hello, Mr. President," so what came out was an inaudible jumble.

Shit. Bungled that one.

Obama waited a minute. "Uh, listen, I was just talking to Spencer and I told him, like, when I have a class reunion kind of thing, we just have a beer, we don't like, tackle terrorists or anything."

Anthony laughed. Alek let Anthony take the floor this time, but now Anthony and the president were talking over each other, thrown off by the slight delay on the telephone line. They both waited, then both started speaking at the same time. Then they both waited, and both started speaking at the same time again.

"Yeah, it was an interesting reunion," Anthony said, at the exact moment Obama said, "You guys have more exciting get-togethers—" and then Anthony tried to respond anyway.

"I can say that."

Bungled that one too. It was getting embarrassing. This time Anthony and the president both stopped, each out of respect for the other, neither wanting to talk over the other a third time, so now Alek felt the need to break the silence. But what do you say to the president of the United States?

"Well, yeah, we didn't plan it. But, uh, maybe next time, we'll work something out." *What the hell did I just say? What does that even mean?* Another awkward silence. This time Anthony tried.

"It's gonna be hard to top—" but the president was trying to talk again, then stopped.

"It's gonna be hard to top this one."

"I think so. But listen. I just want to let you guys know how proud we are of you. I know you're gonna have a chance to meet President Hollande. I just talked to him and he, on behalf of the French people, was just expressing such gratitude for what you guys did and I just wanted you guys to know . . . Aleksander, you're representing the army like . . . " Obama didn't seem to know exactly how he wanted to phrase it. "Like nobody's business."

And Alek laughed. He laughed at the president's loss for words, he laughed from a place of pride, he laughed at the fact that they'd just stopped a terrorist attack and perhaps mostly he laughed at the absurdity of the whole thing, of having a stilted conversation with the president of the United States of America over an iPhone speaker.

29.

Down in Paris, at about four thirty in the afternoon, Robinson and the executive team heard from the defense attaché again.

"You've got to get up here. The press is everywhere." The situation was quickly becoming untenable.

Robinson, Daniels, and the rest of the team got together with other embassy staff to figure out what to do. No one in Arras was equipped to handle the press, let alone what was quickly becoming the story of the summer, if not the year. The boys had suddenly become the most sought-after news items on the continent. It was a perfect storm, a story happening in a month with nothing else in the news to compete, less than a year after the attack on *Charlie Hebdo,* and it was on a train that had just passed through two other countries. It seemed like just about every reporter from all three nations was trying to get a piece of the boys.

Then the photo started making the rounds: Spencer coming out of the hospital, squinting into the sun with his arm in a sling, giving a wave. Robinson was an adult watching young people wander into a situation they could not possibly be prepared for.

She wanted to get them in front of her and under her own care. She wanted to get them behind Daniels, who could filter the onslaught of media attention and help keep things sane.

Daniels said, "Let's get them to Paris."

Robinson nodded. "Let's get them to the residence."

The residence wasn't just the ambassador's home; it was a huge, luxurious mansion. Robinson wouldn't have been making a much more extreme offer if she'd suggested the president's bedroom at the White House. But the residence offered two tactical advantages. Already reporters were beginning to anticipate that the boys would end up in Paris, and news vans were beginning to set up outside the embassy. There was still no press at the residence, because even though it was just a few minutes away, why would press be at the residence? To see an ambassador who wasn't even in town?

And critically, the alternative was a hotel. Paris was a city obsessed with celebrity; hotels in Paris were notorious for leaks. At the residence, the boys would be safe and away from reporters. Daniels would be able to control press access.

"I'll deal with notifying the ambassador," Robinson said, "and getting the residence staffed up."

Holtzapple nodded. "Okay. Let's do it."

There was just one more thing Robinson was worried about. When she saw the picture of Spencer Stone after his operation, the image that flashed across her mind was the crumbled wreckage of a Mercedes-Benz in the Pont de l'Alma, where Princess Diana died with paparazzi in chase.

"They need a police escort."

FROM THE THIRD STORY of the police station in Arras, Alek looked down and saw at least thirty reporters gathered outside. "Anthony, come look at this."

"Oh, shit. This is major!"

Shaw came in to the room. "Okay, guys, it's time to get going. We've got a car waiting for you, and Spencer's here."

Out of the corner of his eye, Alek saw a familiar figure walk into the room, and sure enough, there was Spencer, eye still swollen and dark, arm in a cast, but cleaned up and beaming. Alek threw up his hands, next to him Anthony whooped and threw his up too. Spencer raised his good hand, and they all laughed, celebrating like they were back on a basketball court in middle school after hitting a buzzer beater, an emotional reunion after being separated for a day that had felt like a month. "Spence," Anthony blurted out, without even waiting to say hello, "how'd you get up so fast? How'd you know?" But before Spencer could answer, Shaw came in and took them down to the car, which turned out not to be a car but a whole motorcade, which pulled out of the driveway, filed onto a four-lane highway where—it took Alek a moment to notice—only one of the lanes was open. Only the lane for them. They stopped on the highway to pick up a police escort and then took off again, the highway almost totally deserted. And whenever there was a civilian vehicle up ahead that wasn't moving, one of the motorcycles peeled off from their flank, caught up to the car, matched speeds, and at over eighty miles an hour reached out, tapped on the driver's window, gestured for them to roll it down, put a hand into the driver's cabin right up against the driver's face, and showed in no uncertain terms that the driver needed to get off the road.

Alek had never seen anything like it. It was a high-speed high-wire act.

"Jesus," Anthony said to the men in the front of the car. "Where do they learn how to do that?"

"They get sent to America for training."

Behind them an SUV trailed, overflowing with men carrying automatic weapons. When an old navy-blue sedan started gaining on them and ignored the outrigger's hand signals to fall back, the SUV swung out so it was right next to the sedan, the glass came down and one of the men hung halfway out the window with a machine gun pointing right in the driver's face.

"Holy shit," Alek said, "that's an MP-5!" That gun could fire eight hundred rounds a minute and the man was aiming it at a civilian vehicle, yelling at the driver with words Alek didn't have to speak French to know were R-rated. All that just to clear a safe passage for him. This was the coolest ride Alek had ever been on; better than shooting at tanks in Afghanistan, better than a roller coaster in Germany. This was like the two combined. Anthony yelped and then laughed when they almost hit a charter bus, but it reminded Alek of one of the near misses on the Black Mamba, everything on rails, everything controlled, even when it didn't seem to be.

They raced through the French countryside, watching France's finest performing all manner of high-speed theatrics, zooming south down the A1 autoroute, which ran right through Saint-Denis—the poor suburb Ayoub lived in (and which would, in several months, be the target of a series of coordinated terror attacks around Paris). Then they veered off into the capital through the other northern suburbs of Paris, toward the residence of the US ambassador.

ALEK SPRINTED through the hall in a robe, holding a magnum of champagne like a microphone.

"We get robes!" It was like *Home Alone*. A huge palace, with a fine dining room, ten hot Pizza Hut boxes stacked and waiting. Who eats ten pizzas? Fridges full of champagne, closets full of luxuriant robes; it was time to go crazy. Alek felt an overwhelming impulse to jump on every single bed.

"This is the Ben Franklin Room?"

"That's where the president sleeps!"

"Well, shit, gotta jump on it!"

"They said Charles Lindbergh slept on this."

"Fuck it, gotta jump on that one too!"

Spencer was lying on one, while Alek and Anthony jumped on all the beds like four-year-olds. "Spence!" Alek yelled. "Come on, man, you're missing out—who you talking to?"

"I'm FaceTiming. With my sister."

"Kelly!" Alek felt a little manic, a little drunk on all the energy and excitement, on talking to the president, on beating up a terrorist, on racing down through France in a motorcade surrounded by machine guns; mostly, on being in a mansion wearing a robe with all the free booze he could drink. He dove onto Spencer's bed with the champagne in his hand. "Kelly! What's up!"

"Hmm," she said. "So it looks like *you're* doing okay."

ALEK IS STANDING over Spencer, who's in the aisle fighting the terrorist. Alek can't remember getting there; he doesn't remember running down the aisle. He has the feeling he lost connection with his own body and only just now tumbled back into it, jolted awake in time to see his best friend fighting a terrorist. Alek has become a vector, heart rate sky high and blood vessels constricted, jetting chemicals around his body, sugar and oxygen, so that he's twitchy and wired, hyperalert to some things and oblivious of others. He's kicking the gunman, trying to soften him for Spencer. He senses Anthony nearby, but he's concerned only with finding someplace soft on this man to hit. Spencer is moving wildly, trying to get around the man's back with a forehand over his neck, and then Spencer's left his feet, the two bodies flying across Alek's vision toward the window. Alek can hear the pain of it, his best friend's head slamming the glass and blood staining the train window; his senses are crossed and confused, sounds and sights shading into one another, but through the daze he is acutely aware that Spencer does not have the chokehold he thinks he has.

Then that the man is pulling a pistol from somewhere, a Luger, raising it behind him so that the barrel is up under Spencer's chin. A spasm of energy—Alek grabs the man's hands, wrenches the weapon out and reverses it, holding it against the man's forehead. A clear signal in Spencer's eyes—do it.

Alek slides his finger over the trigger guard and prepares to do the unthinkable, *but if this man isn't stopped he will kill my best friend.* Alek holds the pistol to the man's head and pulls the trigger.

The gun clicks. It is not loud.

The man is still alive.

"Shit." Alek cocks it again, but when he pulls the slide back his eyes laser into the ejection port, and in the moment the slide moves back on the barrel he can see into the chamber—there is no round there, no magazine even. The gun is empty. He chucks it and lunges for the AK-47, feels its reassuring weight in his hands. This weapon he knows is loaded.

When he points it at the gunman, the gunman has pulled out a blade and is starting to jab it backward at Spencer, but Spencer doesn't seem to see it, doesn't seem to know, or has just lost his senses, because Alek is watching his friend bleed and his friend is not letting go. Then Spencer sees what's happening.

"Shoot him," Spencer says.

"I'm trying!"

Alek puts the barrel of the machine gun right on the terrorist's head, right against his skin. And he knows he has no choice. He must kill this man so that this man does not kill Spencer, and maybe dozens of others. Alek pulls the trigger.

Nothing happens.

Alek is now angry, he starts jamming the slant break of the machine gun barrel into the man's head, jabbing as hard as he can and aiming for the temple, thinking maybe it will break through, channeling his anger, trying to drive it right through the man's skin and into his brain. But he is frustrated, the man is not still, and Alek isn't hitting his target, he wants nothing more than to drive the weapon right through the man's skin and make him stop, every fiber in Alek's body wants to extinguish this man right now, but the muzzle slips off, misses the temple, and Alek drives it right into Spencer's eye before he can pull back, but he cannot stop, he is driving the weapon, putting all his weight into it, it is exploding out of his arms into the gunman's head, and then Alek notices that the man's eyes are wide open and locked on him. Like he recognizes Alek.

Alek is trying to destroy him.

They are staring into each other's eyes.

30.

ALEK SAT IN AN expensive room on the second floor of the ambassador's mansion: a big room with all mahogany everything, even the walls, a big desk in the middle flurried over with printer paper. People rushed in and out of the room with so much urgency it felt like the terrorist attack was underway rather than having just been averted. Everything was moving a million miles an hour. Alek had just stepped into this world of convoys and police escorts and even spies. They'd met with the CIA at the embassy; Alek could have sworn they favored appearance in their recruiting because it seemed like every other member of the division was some young attractive woman.

"This is some spy shit! We gotta get a picture," Anthony said.

"You can post that, but you better not call us CIA." Alek watched Anthony's face turn to puzzled, like he wasn't sure if they were joking or not.

And now Alek sat in the mahogany office, across from Chief Randy Griffith, watching the American government maneuvered to do things he hadn't known were possible. Or legal.

It was Sunday afternoon. Whatever the hell it was that happened on the train—Alek still wasn't totally sure—had happened just two days ago. They were going to get the Legion of Honor, the highest honor France gave, tomorrow.

They work fast in France.

By the way people were whispering around the embassy about the award, Alek could tell how meaningful they thought it was. "You guys deserve it," people said, in serious, subdued tones that added a sense of solemnity to the occasion.

But while Alek and the boys would receive a nation's highest honor from its most powerful man tomorrow, their families were about six thousand miles and nine time zones away.

Anthony's dad was home in Sacramento, about to fly across the country to New York to do an interview.

Alek's mom was in Sacramento too.

Spencer's mom was next door to Alek's mom.

Not only were they an ocean plus a continent away, but none of their families could possibly understand what was happening yet. Alek had yet to see an accurate news report himself, so he could only imagine what they were saying outside of this room, outside of this embassy, outside of this *country*.

Here, the news was still reporting that three marines had stopped a terrorist in France. Alek had been able to talk to his brother briefly, and the others had talked to at least someone in their families too, and everyone was beginning to get a sense of what had just happened, but things were happening so fast it was hard to keep track.

What was the time difference again?

What day is it back home?

What day is it here, for that matter? They'd been moving so much and had been at it so many hours it felt like they hadn't been in any one place long enough for its time to apply.

Across from him, Chief Griffith was working himself into

a lather. This was the beginning of what would be nearly a year of surreal experiences, maybe a lifetime of them. He was working with Anthony now. "Anthony," the chief said, "focus. We don't have much time. Where is your dad?"

"Sorry, he's home."

"Home—so Sacramento?"

"Yeah. Or no! No, sorry, New York. He's going to New York for an interview."

"So he's in New York now?"

"Wait, today's Saturday? Or Sunday. No, he was *leaving* today for New York."

"Not anymore he's not. Get him on the phone."

Anthony called his father, who picked up after four rings, groggy, barely awake.

"Dad, go to the airport, you're on the next flight to Paris."

"Son? What time is it?" Anthony checked the clock. "It's one P.M. Or, where you are? Where you are, I don't know, early. But you gotta get to the airport."

"I'm supposed to go to New York today."

"Not anymore. You gotta cancel that, you're coming to Paris."

"Paris . . ." He trailed off. Alek could hear Anthony's dad on the other end of the line trying to work things out in his mind. "I don't have a ticket to Paris."

Chief Griffith chimed in. "Tell him to let me worry about that."

"Dad, just go to the airport," he said "We've got it covered."

Alek smiled. That must have felt cool to say.

"And, Dad," Anthony said into the phone, "the flight leaves at 8:09. Don't be late. If you don't get on that flight, you won't get here in time."

"Okay, I'll be there." Pastor Sadler was coming to his senses. "I'll call the commissioner, see if he can get me a police escort so we can cut through traffic."

While Pastor Sadler took off through the early morning in Sacramento, Chief Griffith and the embassy staff in Paris got to work clearing the way for him to get on board, which meant dealing with two immediate problems.

First, the flight was due to take off in less than an hour. If Pastor Sadler kept a steady pace of eighty miles an hour from his house all the way to the airport, he'd get to the airport just outside of thirty minutes before take-off. The airline might not let him check in, and TSA probably wouldn't let him through. Griffith yelled for Robinson. Robinson had an idea: they had a TSA staffer *at* the embassy. Robinson called the TSA rep and told him to simply get to work, connect with the agent on the ground in Sacramento if need be. Calls began going from Paris to the TSA office in Sacramento.

The other problem was that even if he managed to deal with the TSA issue, the flight was oversold, so Anthony's dad likely wouldn't have a seat by the time he got to the gate.

Sure enough, Anthony got a call around a quarter after four—seven fifteen in the morning Sacramento time.

"They're not letting me through, it's too close to the flight."

One of the embassy staffers had Pastor Sadler put the TSA agent on the phone. "These boys just got off the phone with President Obama. You do *not* want to be the person who screws this up."

Sadler got through.

Next, Griffith got on a call with an executive at the airline, while Anthony's jaw just about hit the floor. The embassy seemed capable of getting anyone they wanted on the phone.

Pastor Sadler was now at the gate. Alek could hear all this happening in real time, like listening to a radio show of a high-speed chase. Next step, the gate attendant. "Okay, listen, Mr. Sadler, here's what you have to tell her." Griffith laid out the script.

"You want me to say *what?*"

"And tell them if they don't make that announcement— and this is very important—if they don't make the announce- ment, you tell them that plane is not leaving. We will not let it take off."

They could hear Anthony's dad over the speakerphone talking to the gate attendant, and then the gate attendant speaking into the PA. Alek couldn't believe it was working, but Griffith was getting frustrated, because the gate atten- dant wasn't delivering the whole message.

"Pastor Sadler," Griffith interrupted. "Tell her she has to tell them *who you are.*"

"I am, she won't tell them."

"This isn't going to work," Griffith said. "No one is just going to get off a flight if they don't know *why.*"

The gate attendant radioed the message again; again she didn't deliver the critical part; so the attendant was making an announcement that two people needed to get off, but not telling them why.

"Okay, this isn't working. Hang up. I'm going to try some- thing else."

"Call you back, Dad!"

Griffith snapped his fingers at someone passing outside the office. "Get me someone from United."

"You're calling the airline? How are you just going to . . ."

But Griffith was already talking to the official on the phone.

"Listen, we got your SAC to CDG through Dallas on the tarmac and I need to get two people onto that flight, the parents of one of the train heroes. We're trying to patch into the cockpit but we're getting some resistance—okay—okay, great. Thanks."

Griffith addressed Anthony again. "He's going to make sure. That plane is not taking off without your parents."

He's getting a message to the fucking plane!

Finally the whole message made it to the plane, was relayed over the PA, and a married couple—two air force veterans—volunteered their seats. It was almost 8 A.M. when Anthony's dad got on the plane, just minutes before the scheduled take-off. They'd delayed a transatlantic flight, with hundreds of people on board, just for Anthony's parents.

HAVING WITNESSED THE levers of power operating to get Anthony's family in the air, Alek tried to picture his own mom and Joyce. What would Joyce do? Shriek? Laugh? Would she know that Spencer was okay?

Would his mom be fretting, worried that some terrible detail had been left out of the news?

Both women were, it turned out, in respective states of mania trying to figure out (a) what exactly had happened, (b) whether this award was really going to be given to *their* boys, and if so, (c) how the hell they were going to get to *Paris* in twenty-four hours.

Both mothers, when first confronted with only the sparsest information—"terrorist attack," "your son," "France"—had sat staring at the television, as if simply by looking hard enough they might force it to cough up some piece of information it was holding back. It didn't.

Joyce was half excited, half terrified. It *seemed* Spencer had done something good, and it *seemed* he was okay, but she didn't know either for sure and she had no other details. She felt the need to do something; she couldn't just sit there and let her imagination drive her crazy, so she did what she always did in times of crisis. She went out to buy milk.

"I don't even need milk," she said out loud, when she was already halfway to the market. And then, "I'll drink it eventually." It was reversion to a habit she'd developed when the kids were small, Spencer still right there under her care, when she'd buy half a dozen cartons of milk and stick them in the freezer, then bring one out when it was needed and let it thaw overnight. It was one of the ways she saved trips to the market and therefore just a little extra time looking after her three wild children; one of the small tricks she'd developed as a single mother, but that had become muscle memory. Spencer was off somewhere far from her reach, shirtless and bloody, and she did the one thing that made her feel the way she felt back when she was able to protect him with her own arms: spend a little more time with him by pillaging the dairy aisle.

Heidi did almost the same. She still had a young daughter she had to pick up from school; she couldn't just sit in front of the TV all day. Plus she had an appointment to get her nails done. Should she cancel it? But she wasn't getting any information, and sitting at home was driving her crazy. *Well, I guess our day must go on.* In the midst of her idle banter with the stylist she said, "You won't believe this, but my boy I think took down this terrorist in Paris."

"Wow, that's interesting."

"Interesting?" Did she not hear me?

Then she went to pick up her daughter. It became a day of trying to deal with huge, grave events by focusing on the most mundane things, the small things she could control. At the picnic tables where parents gathered waiting for their kids, she couldn't contain it; she needed to tell someone. "Hey," she grabbed the closest woman by the elbow and said, "I can't even believe this, but I think my Alek took down that terrorist they're talking about in France."

"Oh really? Are you going to the fund-raiser this week-end?"

What is going on with these people! While she was trying to figure out why the city was so maddeningly indifferent to her momentous news, the media clearly wasn't. Joyce called and said, "Channel 10 wants to interview us."

"I don't really want to interview," Heidi said, but then she couldn't articulate exactly why.

"I don't either," Joyce said. "I haven't washed my hair."

"Maybe we should do it anyway. It feels important."

So Joyce and Heidi sat down next to each other, with the living room lit up by camera lights, and answered the reporter's questions. "I spoke to Spencer," Joyce said, her voice beginning to crack, "and he said, 'I would have been killed if it wasn't for Alek.'"

"And I spoke to Alek, and he said the same thing: 'Mom, if it wasn't for Spencer, I'd be dead.'"

"I really feel like they had a divine intervention and they were saved, because the gun was at his head and . . . he tried to shoot twice . . ."

*   *   *

WHEN JOYCE FOUND OUT the boys were going to receive the Legion of Honor, she knew she wasn't going to miss it. She didn't need to be told twice that the medal was a big frigging deal; everyone in all three families needed to be there. Heidi, unsurprisingly, was on the same page.

But figuring out how to get to Paris in time for the presentation was a puzzle. Last-minute tickets to Paris at the height of tourist season cost thousands of dollars. She didn't have that cash on hand. *Think, Joyce!* She was a problem solver; she always had been, plus her job as a workers' comp adjustor for the state had primed her to deal with people in times when they were at their most desperate, or most manipulative. Now she tried to channel both mindsets. She needed someone who had the means to get them there, someone who could use a vanity project, maybe someone with a private jet to loan, and for whom money was no object and a little good publicity was worth any price—and then it struck her. Donald Trump!

"Oh, please," Heidi said, "come back to earth. We need to figure out a real solution."

But Joyce felt she was on to something. She adjusted her glasses on her nose, fired up the computer, went online, and started pelting requests at every Donald Trump–related website, Facebook page, and real estate company she could find. "Could you please tell Donald Trump that we, the parents of the boys who stopped the terrorist attack, would like to borrow his jet."

Alek's mom decided to try her own approach. Divide and conquer. "Okay, you work on that. Alek's commander, Colonel Prendergast, said if I need anything I could call. I'm going to go see if he can help."

"Okay," Joyce said. "I'm going to stay here and wait for Donald Trump to return my call."

Heidi had the first sign of success. She got through to Prendergast and asked him if he could help them get to Paris in less than twenty-four hours. A silence on the other end of the line.

"Actually, I have an idea. Sit tight, I'll call you back."

Thirty minutes later, he called back. "I might have something. It's a friend who flies a private jet for a big CEO. I don't think he ever loans out his plane, but we're going to ask." The pilot had received the request in an email while on the golf course, and decided to forward it to his boss.

The next update from Alek's commander came just before midnight.

"Okay, be ready. We have the plane for you, but you're going to have to leave at six A.M. to get there on time, so get yourselves to the airport.

"The Sacramento airport?

"The Oregon airport. Get yourself to Oregon, the private jet will fly you over from there." Heidi shrieked. "Thank you so much, you are a saint!" Then she collected herself. "Ahem. I have my neighbor, Joyce? She's Spencer's mom. Can you take her, too?" She waited a moment, then added, "Also, if it's not too much trouble, the boys' siblings?"

There was a pause. "Um, I'll—I'll check the plane's capacity, I guess."

"Great! And one more thing."

"Yeah?"

"How are we supposed to get to Oregon?"

Prendergast had another idea. Since he was in the National Guard he had a day job too, as an analyst for Nike, so he had frequent flyer miles piled up, and he decided to donate them so Joyce and Heidi could get last-minute tickets from Sacramento to Portland.

When they arrived just before dawn in Portland, Joyce still couldn't quite accept that someone's personal plane, unless it was Donald Trump's, would be able to accommodate all of them, much less carry them thousands of miles across the Atlantic. But when they landed in Portland, a van picked them up, took them to the airfield where the private planes were kept, and they couldn't believe their eyes. It wasn't just any little private plane, it was an eleven-passenger Falcon 2000 built by, appropriately enough, a French avionics firm. The owner's crew was standing by, waiting to give them the grand tour of the most luxurious plane they'd ever seen. Everywhere they looked was some glimmering wood panel that with the push of a button revealed a tray of snacks or some other fancy swag. The pilot welcomed them aboard, Joyce found her way to one of the La-Z-Boy–sized, fully reclineable bucket seats, shimmied around in it, and then all of a sudden her feet flew up and the seat-back went down so that she went from upright to horizontal in about a nanosecond.

She lay there, stunned, for a moment.

"Okay yeah," she said, "I admit it. This is plush."

Heidi rolled her eyes and smiled as the pilot fired up the engines.

31.

ALEK MARVELED; somehow it had worked out.

Not somehow; he saw exactly how. It was the US embassy defeating obstacles left and right. The lesson was that nothing was impossible if you had the willpower and a long enough list of contacts. He watched Chief Griffith and Robinson and dozens of other people snapping fingers to get CEOs on the phone, like placing an order at a deli. He saw them get messages *into the cockpit* of a commercial jetliner sitting on the tarmac in Sacramento. A few hundred passengers heard a message directed from a cluttered second-floor office six thousand miles away. Was that even allowed? Could you just . . . keep a plane from taking off?

Now Anthony's dad and stepmom were in the air, Alek's mom had persuaded his National Guard commander to donate his frequent flyer miles to get them up to Oregon, and convinced the Columbia Sportswear CEO to loan them his private jet. Everyone was airborne. All the families were on their way.

Spencer's sister, Kelly, had been in Los Angeles when the boys boarded the 15:17 to Paris. She'd taken a job as a high-profile nanny and by sheer coincidence, she was getting ready for her own very first trip to Europe; she'd been invited to help take care of her boss's children. Kelly had just gotten her passport and had all her tickets in order, though at the moment calls started coming in about events on the train in Paris, she was at work in Los Angeles, chasing kids around the house, trying to corral them and get them packed and ready for their overseas flight.

Joyce was the first to call, at 12:26 P.M.

Kelly missed it; she'd left her phone on the counter and replaced it with a tiny Velcro shoe—she was chasing after a child wearing the other.

Her phone rang again; she stopped and caught her breath long enough to see she'd already missed two calls from her mother. Then the phone dinged with a message. It was a picture message, and when she loaded the picture, she went cold: her brother in a wheelchair, shirtless, covered in blood, his face bruised, eye swollen shut.

Some kind of joke?

"Just call Solon," her mom said, when she called back. "He's the one who knows." At that point, Solon was the only one who'd talked to any of the boys directly.

"Okay." She called Solon.

"Hey, what's up, Kelly?"

"Solon! Thank God. Is Spencer okay? Are the boys okay?"

"Yes, Kelly, your brother still has both of his balls."

"Solon, *what?* You're not helping!" Maybe his way of dealing with the gravity of the situation? Or did he really even know everything was okay? Was he trying to obscure the fact that things actually weren't okay? Kelly wasn't sure, but before she could begin to really panic, her boss called. He was in Europe; he had more information even than the families. "This is the craziest thing I've ever heard. I can't believe it's your brother."

"I can't believe it either. What's it like over there? What's happening?"

"You have to go see your brother. Come over with the family and we'll get you to Paris."

"What about the kids?"

"Don't worry about the kids, I'll figure something out. You have to go be with your brother."

"Right, right." She still didn't know what had happened, only that Spencer had been hurt, and that it looked bad.

She somehow managed to get the kids corralled and into the car, to the airport, through security, onto the plane, got the kids' hand luggage in the bins and their bodies buckled in, made sure they were okay, and then threw back an entire glass of white wine.

SHE LANDED IN COPENHAGEN and called Spencer on Face-Time, hoping to find some kind of conclusive information about her brother's condition, and also to find out what the hell had happened. The screen fizzled and crackled to life, and she saw what looked like terry cloth. The image backed away and resolved, and she saw Spencer, and then Alek, and then Anthony, all three of them wearing luxurious-looking bathrobes, each holding bottles of champagne.

"What up, Kelly!" Alek had launched himself onto the bed so that his face came crashing onscreen, and that was it: Kelly couldn't control herself. She started laughing, and laughing, and couldn't stop; finally knowing they were okay was like the first real breath she'd taken since hearing something had happened on a train. "Okay, boys," she said, when she finally got herself under control. "Behave yourselves. I'll be there soon." As Kelly made her way from Denmark to Paris, and the three boys partied in the ambassador's residence, a few thousand miles to the west, the Columbia Sportswear CEO's private jet had reached its cruising altitude, and the pilot came out. "Okay, ladies, why don't you give me your passports now and I'll take them to . . ."

Joyce's eyes widened. *Passports!* It hadn't even occurred to her. She was at forty thousand feet, cruising toward France at six hundred miles an hour, and she did not have a passport.

DANIELS HAD YET ANOTHER problem to deal with. The press interest hadn't let up; it had grown only more intense. He'd tried to keep them at bay as best he could, but he didn't want to lie to reporters. He batted some requests away by invoking security concerns, which were legitimate, but they weren't much of a bulwark against the tidal wave of media requests coming in. It became increasingly clear he was going to have to call a press conference.

Robinson and Daniels got the boys dual American- and French-flag pins, and made sure they were ready: no stains on their shirts or smudges on their faces. And then Robinson had an idea.

"Do you guys want a few minutes before you go downstairs? Maybe we can take a few minutes to pray."

They got in a circle, and Robinson led; as she spoke, they each in turn began to cry. By the time they finished, there wasn't a dry eye in the room.

After the press conference, Alek was starting to feel stir crazy. He'd been cooped up for so long with so many people handling him, and the Legion of Honor ceremony was tomorrow; he needed to get out and be alone, or at least be just with the people he cared about. Spencer, Kelly, now Anthony, Rebecca Robinson who'd become like a close, protective aunt. "Hey, Rebecca," he said, "can we get out of here?"

"You know," she said, "I have an idea. Why don't you boys walk me home?" She cleared it with the security folks, and they walked out into Paris.

"And you know what? Let's take the long way to my house. Let's visit a few of the things you came to Paris to see in the first place."

They walked up to the Arc de Triomphe; they all sat there and waited for the Eiffel Tower to light up. And then they just walked. They walked down the avenues, past the cafés; it was getting darker, getting on to that anonymous time of night when you can see only shapes of other people, not expressions, not faces. For those moments, they were just a group of friends on vacation in Paris. They walked down Avenue George V to the Crazy Horse Saloon, and Robinson elbowed Alek playfully. "Guess what that is." She had a mischievous look. "That place is famous for its burlesque shows."

Anthony laughed. "It's so great that someone's telling us these things, because we never would have figured this out on our own. It's funny, we've kind of stumbled into having our own tour guides the whole trip."

Robinson looked at Anthony, standing there in front of the Crazy Horse, like she knew what he was thinking.

"Okay, Anthony, get over there. We gotta get some pictures." While they were posing, a couple hurried over to them. "Are you guys . . . are you *the* guys? Can you take a picture with us—do you mind?"

Alek looked at Spencer, who was just as surprised as he was.

"Well, sure," Alek said.

The couple sidled in.

"Damn, that's bright," Anthony said, squinting at the flash. The couple scurried away, giggling to each other, and a silence fell over the group. Alek breathed deeply, and for a moment tried to just enjoy being there, with these people. Sitting there, with their families in the air, they all just enjoyed the silence.

"You know," Robinson finally said, watching the couple leave, "I think this is it. From now on, I mean—from now on you're out in the world."

AFTER ALEK STRIKES HIM five, six, seven times, the man's arms begin to slacken, his struggling is dialing down, the blade has fallen from his hand. Alek's best friend is covered in blood, but the man is beginning to lose consciousness, so Alek just watches his eyes begin to close. Alek speaks to Spencer: "You don't have it, you don't have the choke in, you don't have it." Spencer adjusts; Alek's strikes have weakened the gunman enough that Spencer can shift around until he has a good chokehold, and Alek wills Spencer not to let go of the man's neck. Just to be sure. Spencer holds it. A train employee comes running into the frame, steps in front of Alek, and begins slapping the gunman in the face.

"Okay, he's unconscious, you can stop choking him."

Alek feels rage. *Where was this guy before? Back the fuck up. Where were you when this guy was trying to shoot us?*

A new gust of motion; a British businessman is there, in his sixties, Oxford shirt, glasses, buzz-cut, he will introduce himself as Chris and prove to be a steady, calming presence, but for now is important because he speaks both the languages.

As Spencer drags the terrorist to the floor, Alek sees the long-haired man on the ground gushing blood. *How did I not see him before?* Alek thinks the man might die if he doesn't get help, but there are other tasks that need to be performed. Alek quickly establishes a division of labor. "Spencer," he hears himself saying, "go get that guy." He points to the bleeding man. Maybe he just looks at the man. Spencer puts his hands in the man's neck as if Alek could direct them there just by looking.

The bleeding stops.

The British man has a necktie in his hands and is binding the terrorist's legs and hands behind him. The British man has gotten hold of some kind of cable too, and has the loose ends in his teeth, pulling them tighter.

Alek can focus on his next task.

He picks up the machine gun again, cocks it, puts a new bullet in the chamber, extends the butt stock so he will have better control of the weapon, and goes back to make sure no one else is hit, and that there are no other terrorists on the train. He walks toward the next train car, but something catches his eye. In the one fluid motion with which he manipulated the weapon he ejected the old round, which popped out of the barrel and bounced onto a seat, where it now lies, as if waiting for him to find it.

Alek looks closely, and suddenly he understands why his friend is not dead. The terrorist had aimed at Spencer, pulled the trigger, and the weapon did exactly what it was supposed to do. A spring pushed a bullet into the chamber, the trigger moved the firing pin, the firing pin struck the bullet. Then the unlikeliest of malfunctions occurred, just about the only malfunction possible in an AK-47. The bullet, which Alek now holds between two fingers and examines closely, has a perfect, deep dent in the back. Just like it's supposed to. Just like you'd see on a spent shell casing after a bullet had fired.

Only this time the bullet didn't fire. It had a bad primer. The firing pin struck the bullet, but the chemical reaction that was supposed to initiate simply did not happen. The bullet simply did not ignite. The little piece of brass refused to do its one job. And it saved Spencer's life. Which meant it probably saved everyone else's too.

ALEK STARTS MOVING back through the train. The only notions occupying his thoughts now are tasks that need completing; advancing to the next level. He feels logical, as clear as he's ever been, a computer operating without noise, silently running a single program. He is not thinking—it does not feel like thinking—it is ratcheting down a checklist. He moves into the next train car, following the terrorist's path in reverse, moving past the bathroom where the attack began. He walks through carriage thirteen: empty. The café car: empty. He registers the detritus of fleeing commuters: open laptops, cell phones, iPads, books. It looks like a place from which people have dematerialized in the middle of whatever they were doing. A marooned plastic cup, lolling on a table after falling from a hand that has disappeared.

Another empty car, then another.

Then, in the last two cars, a sight that nearly bowls him over. Every single person huddled together, hundreds of them.

For the first time, the gravity of it strikes him. All these people. *If that man hadn't been stopped in the front—if we hadn't stopped him—and he'd made it back here with all that ammo, to all these people, confined in one small place with no way to escape* . . . the immensity of it pulls him from his state.

"Is anyone hurt?"

He goes back to the second train car from the front. He begins clearing the AK-47 when a train employee comes to him with damp paper towels to help clean up blood. The train employee is trying to be useful. It enrages Alek. Alek has shifted into a military kind of perception, dividing labor, triaging tasks; his level of adrenaline is still high, only now it's mixed with the emotional tidal wave that started to swell when he saw the huddled passengers at the back of the train. He is not prepared for a distraction from the tasks that need to be done. This man is disordering a To Do list and Alek is too amped up to accommodate disorganization. Things in their order. It's not time to clean up—that's a step whose turn has not yet come—the employee is throwing it all out of order.

Alek tries to ignore him. He asks Chris to ask the man for some space. Chris has an innate ability to speak sense into people. Chris whispers to the man and the man retreats. Alek finishes emptying the weapon, places it on a seat, moves to Spencer's side. He asks Spencer if he can help. Spencer is trying not to move, trying to keep the bleeding man from moving, but Mark is groaning, and his wife is insists Mark got shot in the chest. Alek knows Mark did not get shot in the chest, but he does not know how he knows. Spencer seems to agree, but he says, "Check anyway."

Alek takes the box cutter from the terrorist and slices open Mark's shirt. He does a blood sweep, running his hands all over Mark's torso to see if blood comes up, which would mean there was another wound. He doesn't find any. He stands up.

He looks at Anthony, who has a look on his face like he's just witnessed some ridiculous slapstick accident, a man and a banana peel. Alek doesn't know what's funny. Did he do something? Say something? Is there a smudge on his face?

And then he understands. All of it. There is a terrorist tied up on the ground, Spencer is bleeding in a million places, and meanwhile the train is whirring along quietly, a big smooth machine oblivious to the menagerie inside it. Alek is on the same page now. He stands next to Anthony, this friend he had not seen since middle school, a person he was surprised was coming at all, a person he didn't totally get, and the two of them, without even really needing to say anything, know they are thinking exactly the same thing. It is all absurd and ridiculous, and together they stand there and laugh.

THE TRAIN PULLS INTO THE STATION, Alek still thinking about the absurdity of it all. He needs space. He wants to be next to Anthony, but Anthony has gone off with a policeman and is trying to recount what happened. Alek wants to go be with Spencer, but Spencer has a swarm of EMTs around him. Alek doesn't want to be with anyone else. There are too many people around. He's tired of being confined in such a tight space with so many people trying to take charge.

He sits by himself on a bench, alone, a little like an old man at a park whose friends have all left him, and he begins to think.

It is a process that will last months, years, but he is beginning to see a series of uncanny coincidences.

That they left Amsterdam when they did, even though none of them really wanted to. What was it that pulled them to Paris? Why did they decide to ignore all the people who told them to skip France? Two separate girls traveling alone whispering into Anthony's and Spencer's ears as if the devil preferred to send his messages through spunky young Asians.

What made them come to France anyway? A sense. He thinks of all the coincidences:

That they were on this train. So close to staying in Amsterdam and taking a different one.

That they were even in Amsterdam at all, when none of them planned to be.

That they kept failing to meet up in Germany like they were supposed to.

That they were in the right train car, after the old man and his daughter took them three cars back. That the Wi-Fi was bad. If it had worked, they would have stayed back there, been back there when the man started shooting.

Or was that some force trying to keep them out of harm's way?

That Spencer had been too cheap to join any kind of gym for exercise except jujitsu, so he knew a form of fighting that worked on anyone.

That Spencer's roundabout path, failing pararescue, failing SERE, had taken him to EMT and given him just enough skills to save that man?

Alek's own obsession with firearms, so that he knew exactly what to do, how to handle the weapons the terrorist brought on the train. What if it had been anyone else?

That Anthony had become obsessed with capturing everything on camera so he had footage, pictures of everything, everything an investigator could hope for.

Or back even further, that his mom moved into the next house down, not twenty feet from Spencer's. That their moms were so similar. Both had been flight attendants, both had just been divorced, both had kids almost the same age, so similar their families had congealed into one. That their names came right after one another alphabetically, and that when Anthony came to the school, his had too. That Anthony kept getting signs that he should come on a trip he couldn't afford. His coworkers telling him he needed to travel young, just as Alek's other friends were dropping out; that the first credit card he qualified for was a travel credit card.

That when the man started shooting, the closest train station was here, not even thirty minutes from a hospital in Lille that happened to have a renowned orthopedics program. As if the train was being diverted exactly to where Spencer needed to be for any hope for recovering the use of his thumb.

The one million things that had to happen for them to be here, to stop the attack. Then to keep them safe.

The coincidences piled up in his mind to something immense, almost too much to bear. It was as if they'd found themselves in the center of a cosmic tug-of-war, one invisible force pulling them away from the attack, the other pulling them toward it.

As if Joyce's prayers and Heidi's prayers, in living rooms

back in Sacramento within earshot of one another, were competing. One pulling them to safety, the other pulling them to mission. Somehow they'd each pulled just enough, just the perfect amount, so that they'd gotten both.

AYOUB

In January 2015, two heavily armed brothers stormed the offices of a weekly satire magazine called Charlie Hebdo and opened fire. With military discipline, they killed eleven people, injured eleven more, then shot and killed a national police officer outside the building. France deployed the army, and the brothers took hostages, but they were shot and killed before the end of the day.

The shootings shocked people in the country and beyond. Nearly four million people demonstrated in France, the phrase Je suis Charlie, "I am Charlie," in solidarity with the magazine, ricocheted across the Internet, and though the magazine typically sold fewer than a hundred thousand copies, the next issue sold almost eight million, and in half a dozen languages. The world mourned for Charlie Hebdo.

Ayoub El-Khazzani did not.

Ayoub resented this reaction.

On social media he posted old photos of the violence colonial France inflicted upon Africa. He said France was a terrorist state for what it had done. He posted videos explaining theories that these attacks by Muslims were faked, just hoaxes meant to marginalize Muslims yet again. Ayoub proclaimed, "I am not Charlie Hebdo." He had no sympathy for a magazine that mercilessly insulted his religion. That was just picking on the weak. He began posting videos of Saudi sheikhs of the strict Salafi tradition preaching, on sites devoted to religion.

And, still mostly lonely, he spent the rest of his time reading up on love, how to fashion his hair, how to lose weight.

More than a year after going off the radar in France, on May 10, 2015, Ayoub El-Khazzani popped back up. He was in Berlin.

He was boarding a Germanwings flight to Istanbul,[1] the gateway to jihad in Syria.

Because he was under an S-Card, his movement was caught and the intel was passed to Spanish intelligence the next day.

Security services lost the trail after he landed in Turkey,[2] but there was little doubt where he was headed. Syria was a place where fighters were trained to join the jihad there or, ever more frequently, trained and then sent home to carry out attacks on European soil.

On June 4, he returned to Europe on a flight from Antakya, a Turkish city on the Syrian border.[3]

He went to Belgium.[4] Belgium was a country with the highest concentration of jihadi volunteers in Europe.[5]

He stayed with a sister above a Carousel minimart in Molenbeek, a district of Brussels,[6] where he was surrounded by people like him; its population was largely Muslim, and also largely of Moroccan extraction.

It also had a thriving illegal arms trade. It had the highest unemployment in the city. It was crowded and graffitied.[7] It provided ample disaffection for those on the path to violence, or who had traveled far and wide in search of opportunity but had found none.

And it provided weapons. It was weapons from this slum that were used in Paris in the attack on a kosher market, and at the shootings at the Jewish Museum in Belgium.[8]

That summer, while Spencer, Anthony, and Alek prepared excitedly for their EuroRail adventure, Ayoub went on a backpacking trip of his own,[9] traveling between Belgium and Germany, as well as Austria, France, and Andorra. He traveled, each time, by train.[10]

Then, just as Spencer was leaving Portugal, and Anthony and Alek were saying goodbye to their parents, Ayoub finally called his. He had not spoken with his father for a year and a half.[11]

It's August 21. It is hot and humid, with little relief. A nearly windless day.[12] Ayoub purchases a burner phone[13] and activates it.

Ayoub leaves his sister's home. He walks up to the roundabout with a small park in the middle but no grass, just pigeons. Up Rue Piers, where he enters the Ossenheim metro stop, going underground just before the street meets a field with young men playing soccer. He rides past the new car washes, a thinning, littered woodland, abandoned and hollowed-out automotive parts warehouses slowly filling up with bottles and old dolls and car tires.

Past the giant slaughterhouse recently converted into a covered playground. A whole tour of urban decay in less than five minutes.

He comes back up at the Clemenceau station by the school with the faux graffiti wall. Vivre ensemble, *it says. "Live together." And* Paix, *for "Peace." As he moves through a park with public exercise equipment bolted to the ground all around him, the South Tower rises nearly forty stories high right in front of him, a giant gleaming beacon emerging from the train station. As he makes his way toward it, he moves through another area full of firearms; the region around the station is a widely known hub for the black-market weapons trade.[14] The whole country of Belgium is, really. A storied history of firearms manufacturers, like FN Herstal,[15] combined with lax restrictions and the country's status as a transit hub for people fleeing other wars allowed Belgium to become a country saturated with firearms. Then after a wave of violent crimes hit, new gun control laws were enacted, but the weapons were already there; their sale continued by simply moving underground, where they combined with a wash of black-market weapons flowing in since the Balkan Wars. As people fled to Belgium from the collapsing Soviet Union, a community of Balkan expatriates grew, many of whom knew how to access old Soviet munitions reserves back home. Which turned out to be veritable gold mines.[16] So by the time the government finally tried to crack down, it was far too late. There were millions of unregistered weapons already in circulation; they'd simply moved to the black market.[17] There could be no better place to assemble an arsenal without authorities knowing.*

He enters the station, angled glass with white lettering, French station name in one direction, Dutch in another.[18] He is six stops and less than two miles from the Maelbeek metro station, where twenty people will die from an explosion during a coordinated ISIS attack eight months later.

Big yellow posters list times and destinations. He asks for a ticket to Paris. The clerk offers him a seat on the next train, originating in Amsterdam at 11:17, and the one after that, the 13:17[19] to Paris.

Ayoub decides he will wait for a later train, #9364. He does not say why. He does not appear to have a reason, though Thalys employees know the Friday #9364 is one of the busiest trains on the route. It's the end of the week, it's right at closing time, and August is high tourist season. That train is usually packed. And because in the summer Thalys attracts young people on short-term contracts looking for spending money or a foot in the door, the train's staff that day was both younger and less experienced than usual.

Ayoub pays €149 in cash and the clerk hands him a ticket for first class on Thalys #9364. The 15:17 to Paris, originating in Amsterdam.

He proceeds to the platform, a nexus of old and new. Gleaming red trains whine into the station looking like long rocket ships, passing antique-style roman-numeral clocks, a gesture to the old days of rail transport. Backlit billboards show smiling white vacationers enjoying their holidays all around the continent. Above Ayoub the roofs are the same old corrugated metal that covered the slums in cities he lived in, holding back rain when it came but making it sound angry, pounding down like the sky itself wanted in. Sheets of metal just like the ones his father collected and dealt for scrap. Gauzy, filtered sunlight falls through transparent seams in the roof, as train #9364 pulls into the station.

Ayoub approaches.

He walks past an elegant young woman, tall and thin and blond and draped in burgundy fabric that matches the train, matches her heels. A train attendant, on a crew change.

Ayoub is not focused on her. Ayoub is about to win glory, and he carries power in his backpack. He has a 9mm Luger semiautomatic pistol. He also has a blade from a box cutter, a bottle of gasoline, a hammer, a backpack with eight fully loaded magazine cartridges, nearly three hundred rounds of ammunition, and a side-folding Draco AK-47 semiautomatic assault rifle with a slant-cut muzzle and a collapsible butt.

He boards in first class.

The stairs under the train doors retract; the train managers radio to each other, and the train begins to move. It happens without sound. Like the world has tipped just a little and the train has begun to roll downhill. The hum of the engine kicks in, but it is faint and feels far away. It is astoundingly quiet. Even the people speak in hushed tones, as if discussing something grave or private. The loudest sound is the pneumatic hiss of the doors between the cars opening and closing, as confused passengers finally find their assigned seats.

The train rolls out onto the tributary of tracks multiplying in front of the station. It picks up speed, passes the junkyards, moves onto a smoother track, picks up more speed. Within minutes of leaving the station, it is traveling at over 150 miles per hour.

Ayoub leaves his seat and enters the carriage-twelve lavatories.

He plays a YouTube video on the phone he has just activated; on the screen in his hand, a speaker incites the faithful to take up arms in the name of the prophet.

Ayoub removes his shirt.

He straps the backpack and Draco machine gun across his bare torso.

When he is finally ready, he opens the door and walks out.

He sees something he has not anticipated: a curly-haired man seems to be waiting in line to use the toilet.

Ayoub feels a shift in weight on his shoulders—a second man has grabbed him from behind, and now the curly-haired man is grabbing, twisting, torquing the machine gun;[20] Ayoub feels it slip out of his grasp and now the curly-haired man has the gun and Ayoub reaches for his pistol and gets his finger over the trigger guard.

A crack echoes through the carriage. Glass shatters. The men leap backward. The machine gun clatters to the carpet and the curly-haired one crumples; in an instant a bullet has passed through his shoulder blade, pierced his lung, and struck his collarbone.

"I'm hit," he says. He has locked eyes with his wife, and is staring at her through the seats.[21] "I'm hit."[22]

He is no longer holding the machine gun.

Ayoub picks up the weapon and realizes he has space around him. "It's over," the fallen man says. Legs and arms are in motion, bodies sprinting in different directions, the pistol like a starting gun, Ayoub is under way. One man has taken off toward the back of the train, the train attendant is sprinting toward the front, past the letters on the door panel, THALYS—WELCOME TO OUR WORLD, *and Ayoub swings the Draco forward and decides to follow the attendant. Ayoub is in control. It is working again. He has a bag full of weapons and a train car full of unarmed targets, enough ammo for all or at least many of them. He is in power, he is winning justice for the weak and oppressed, he will make this country bleed. There are more voices now, and a flash of sky blue[23] growing bigger in his vision. A ridiculous sight, a body running toward him. This is surprising, but the man is an easy target and he's running down a perfect shooting gallery: the train car boxes him in, the man has no cover, seems to have no weapon, is not threatening. Ayoub barely has to aim. He lowers the weapon at the man and pulls the trigger.*

The gun doesn't go off.

He pulls the trigger again.

The man is close, the gun's not going off, the one thing everyone knows about this kind of gun is that they never jam, he tries to cycle it but he's flustered now because the unjammable gun seems to be jammed so he grabs the wrong lever and accidentally activates the safety, now the trigger won't move, and he's out of time. The man is almost on top of him so he swings the weapon up into the man's face just as the man arrives but the man has so much momentum that Ayoub is driven back and just as he's coming back off his feet there's a gap so he can see two more bodies, a shorter man in the red-and-blue stripes of the Bayern Munich soccer club and a tall man with skin like his, and then Ayoub is on the ground and the gun is gone from his hands, and he begins to fight.

PART III

ANTHONY SADLER, KNIGHT OF THE LEGION OF HONOR

WED, AUG 19, 11:35 PM

Anthony Sadler:
Still alive dad, loving Amsterdam
like deeply in love lol

Pastor Sadler:
Lol That's great Son. People are nice?

Anthony Sadler:
The Nicest! The language is Dutch
but mostly everyone speaks English
and they are just genuinely nice people.
The most black people I've seen yet
also I was surprised. We went to the
black neighborhood in south East
Amsterdam and it was cool

Pastor Sadler:
Wow!

Anthony Sadler:
We've literally just biked the whole
city, takes about an hour but it's not
ridiculously big so that's nice and
beautiful! I love show you tons of pics

32.

IN THE MONTHS AFTER it was over, there was this feeling. That they had disrupted something large, used up all their good luck in those few moments, and had none left to spare.

A feeling that their parents' prayers had tugged them to just the right place at the right time and then protected them once they were there, so that an alert man would see the terrorist first and take the only bullet; prayers that had poisoned the primer on that next round so that the gun didn't go off and charging the weapon wouldn't help. So that none of the boys were killed, but also so that none of them had to kill.

The odds of all that happening were so astoundingly low, so overwhelmingly against them that it must have taken the full force of prayer, of God, of whatever it was that allowed you to confront a universe canted against you and prevail. The feeling Anthony had was that their luck, their parents' prayers, might, therefore, be exhausted.

And on a more tangible level, a troubling idea lingered. A question that a reporter had asked his father at a press conference, just after he returned to the US. Was he worried that by stopping a terrorist attack, the boys had invited reprisals on themselves?

All of it mixed together and simmered, and produced in him an unsettling sense, humming along in his mind, always in the background but still always there, that the other shoe would drop. It was only a matter of time. The universe would eventually correct itself.

On October 1, it began to.

It was another lost twenty-six-year-old. Although this time instead of a terrorist on a train to Paris it was a community college student in Oregon, and this time there was no one there to stop it. Nine people died, and then the gunman shot himself.

Anthony turned off the TV before the reporter could poison his mind with any more of the details, which he knew by now were not likely to be accurate anyway; he understood the press better after they made him a marine. Anyway, Anthony was getting tired of news that had to do with death and violence. He had no more stomach for it.

He saw Spencer the next day on their way to New York, and Spencer told him Umpqua Community College was where Alek had gone before deploying to Afghanistan.

Where Alek would be right now, in fact, if he hadn't accepted the invitation to be on *Dancing with the Stars*.

When Anthony next saw mention of the shooting on the news, it was all about Alek. Alek leaving the show, Alek going home to be with his people. This part didn't feel fair. There was a subtext to even showing Alek at all, and Anthony wondered: Will there always be a question, held in people's minds, about the three of them? *Could you have stopped it? Where were you* this *time?*

Was he now expected to be a hero wherever he was?

It was an immense amount of pressure, and every time he turned on the news something else dark and violent had happened. Each event fit into a story in his mind, a growing narrative of violence, and each one was pressure on him and his friends.

Alek had helped save a bunch of people once. Alek would have been on campus if he wasn't dancing on TV. Were they trying to say Alek was partially responsible for people dying? Would that be with them forever?

33.

ANTHONY THOUGHT HE'D come down, found some level of normalcy. But the energy still coursed through him, this weird pressure, a thing he'd accomplished; they'd diverted the course of world events. They'd nudged history aside in a small but perhaps significant way, maybe changed what textbooks would say in the future.

It was pressure, it was the most powerful high, it was many things at once. It was neurotransmitters firing in a hundred different directions for a hundred different reasons.

No one could really understand what they were going through, because *they* didn't really understand what they were going through, and they'd already been pulled in so many different directions, so many competing media requests, that they hadn't had the chance to sit in a quiet room together, just the three of them, and figure it out.

Not since the police station in Arras. And even then, Spencer hadn't been there.

The embassy in Paris, but there they were either cracking champagne bottles in the ambassador's residence, or they were surrounded by crowds nearly euphoric with gratitude.

They hadn't really reflected, and the pressure of it was still there. Latent, but bubbling, bubbling.

Anthony was still wired, still jacked, still had flashbacks to when it happened; not so much sounds and images playing across his memory but the feeling of it, the adrenaline, the power, the moisture in his palms and the sense he could run through walls. Little things he didn't even register, he wasn't even conscious of, could make him feel the way he felt on the train. He didn't even need to be thinking of the train. Something would happen, a sound, a sight, a color, something that evoked a moment on board, and then it was automatic. A part of his brain would shift just a little, and the adrenaline would come coursing through again. His body prepared itself for war but war wasn't there.

It happened first at a club in Manhattan. Spencer was holding a drink, an aloof partier bumped into him, the drink spilled, and the guy just stared at Spencer, didn't apologize, offered no indication of emotion at all. Anthony shifted to put himself between Spencer and the stranger, since Spencer still had one arm in a splint. Anthony said, "Stay back" to Spencer and that's when the guy swung.

Anthony lit up with rage. Sparks fired across his retinas. Security guards were there in an instant but Anthony was electric with anger and energy now; the guy had flipped a switch and turned Anthony to "go." The guards perp-walked the guy out the front and ushered Anthony out the back, but the moment they pushed him out the back door Anthony ran the block over and found him in front of the club next to a line of cabs.

"What's up now, huh? Security's not gonna help you now!" Anthony ran at him, their bodies collapsed together, the guy was on the ground, Anthony started swinging, his body going back and forth, wrestling with a stranger just as he and Spencer and Alek had wrestled a stranger once before; the guy's friends circled and Anthony turned to face them. "What's up? You guys want some too?" Then back to the man on the ground, his fists finding flesh, letting it all out, until he felt his whole body pulled back through air as if out of a dark dream where he'd lost control, Spencer's good hand around the back of his belt drawing him back to real life.

The next clear thought he had, they were in a cab pulling away. *Did that happen?*

THE NEXT DAY, Belgium's prime minister awarded them the country's highest commendation.

It was an upscale reception. Anthony's stomach swam and his head throbbed. But it was a catered affair; the UN General Assembly was in session so senior diplomats from all over the world had descended on New York City, and it felt like all of them were here in their finest attire, mingling and congratulating Spencer and Anthony. Which was wonderful, but Spencer and Anthony were operating with two hours of sleep between them and respective force-12 hangovers. Butlers carried champagne and bottles of Belgian beer, which felt like a slow form of torture. Anthony burped. He looked at Spencer, who was hurting worse than Anthony, but then Spencer gave an *oh well* half nod, plucked a beer off a passing tray, and put it to his lips. He recoiled.

Uh-oh, Anthony thought. He's gonna hurl right here.

Spencer put a fist to his mouth and burped again. He looked at Anthony. Spencer tried another sip; Spencer was brave. Anthony, inspired, smiled at a waiter and picked up a glass of champagne. The thought of alcohol was nauseating, but so was the thought of passing up free champagne. This was a matter of principle. When the champagne was free, you drank it.

34.

THE VIDEO SPENCER SENT was dark and jerky, like a grainy image from a security camera at a crime scene, the bodies too close. Like Anthony's own videos from the train, or one of those found-footage horror movies. Was Spencer drunk? Or was it just too many bodies moving and dancing? Anthony tried to make out where Spencer was; by now Anthony could tell most of Sacramento's bars by the inside décor, since he could get into any of them for free and often did. But too much was going on for him to see clearly.

"Spencer, where you at?"

Spencer didn't reply. Anthony hoped he was okay. He put his phone on the nightstand and fell asleep.

He woke in the morning to his phone leaping off the table with messages and missed calls. His father had tried to call him six times, so Anthony returned that one first.

"Son, Spencer got stabbed last night."

"What?"

"I'm trying to get details now. But he's at the hospital. I'll let you know when I know. I've got Joyce on the other line now."

"Is he okay, though?"

A pause. "He's in the hospital."

That's not an answer.

It took most of the day for Anthony to learn what had happened, to be satisfied that it was not a terrorist tracking the boys to Northern California. It was a fight that had taken place outside a bar.

But it was bad, worse than Anthony understood right away. Spencer was in critical condition, so Anthony couldn't even see him. Not for two days, while Spencer went in and out of surgery.

And still, Anthony didn't grasp how serious it was until he went to the hospital, into Spencer's room, and Spencer pulled down the gown so Anthony could see the stitches crawling up his chest.

"What happened?"

"Open-heart surgery. They got everything. They nicked my heart."

Spencer seemed to be appraising Anthony, seeing how fully he was grasping this. "Anthony, they called the homicide unit out."

It took a moment for that to register. *Homicide*. You don't call homicide when someone's hurt. You call homicide when someone's been killed.

"They thought I was dead." Spencer was quiet for a moment. "But the other thing is . . ." he paused again. "I did too. I thought I was dying. I sat down on the sidewalk after they stabbed me and closed my eyes, and I thought I was closing my eyes for the last time."

Anthony couldn't think of what to say. "So what happened?"

"I woke up on the sidewalk, a paramedic was giving me a sternum rub, telling me, 'Wake up, wake up!' I was like, 'I guess I'm still alive.' Then I just remember being on a gurney here at the hospital, everybody standing over me working, you know, but this homicide detective keeps trying to squeeze in and ask me questions, just trying to get information like he didn't think I'd ever be able to." Spencer paused. "To give him information again."

Anthony was overwhelmed. His best friend, with whom he'd already been through one life-threatening situation, who'd really, as far as Anthony was concerned, saved Anthony's life, and who was now lying there, having only barely survived, cut and torn up and stitched back together.

Anthony wasn't so worried about him physically, since by now it was clear that as bad as it was and as close as Spencer had been to dying—again—he was going to make it. Anthony was more worried about what Spencer was feeling. He worried about his friend's mind. Was Spencer feeling the same pressure Anthony did? People called Spencer "Captain America," and they meant it to celebrate him, but it was also pressure. It meant that if you got hurt, you failed. If other people around you did, you were a failure. Anthony felt for him. He just couldn't think of what to say, which was a brand new problem he'd been having since the train. Finally he just sighed and said, "You motherfucker. You just won't die, will you? You just won't fucking die."

Spencer closed his eyes. Anthony felt emotion welling up inside him, but still couldn't think of anything to say, not even to his closest friend, that would fit the gravity of the situation. "I'll see you when you get out, man. You'll be all right, okay? You'll be all right." And he left.

35.

THAT WASN'T THE END. The shooter at Alek's college, the terrorist reprisal attack on Spencer that turned out to not be a terrorist attack, but just a street fight, but then turned out to be almost fatal ... it was happening; the boys were paying back for the luck they'd had.

Anthony was in biomechanics class early on a Friday afternoon when his phone started buzzing with messages coming from numbers he didn't recognize. THEY COULD'VE REALLY USED YOU IN PARIS.

On the drive back to his apartment, more came in: Y AREN'T U SAVING PARIS RIGHT NOW?

Then another, and another; he parked in the driveway and pulled up the news on his phone, and his heart sank. He went inside, sat on the couch and turned on the TV. The same images scrolled again and again; nighttime in Paris, with a local time stamp, excited anchors talking over each other, but the banner across the bottom of the screen said it all: 18 KILLED IN PARIS SHOOTINGS.

This has to do with us.

The banner changed. AT LEAST 30 DEAD IN PARIS ATTACKS.

Then it changed again. FRENCH PRESIDENT DECLARES EMERGENCY, CLOSES BORDERS. And again: AT LEAST 60 DEAD IN PARIS TERROR ATTACKS.

He felt weary. He was, in an instant, exhausted with violence, and he couldn't watch anymore. He still had a hard time trusting the news, so he turned off the TV and hoped they'd screwed up again, somehow got the details confused and drastically overestimated the death toll, or maybe even got the whole thing totally wrong, maybe a hoax, but already something heavy had fallen in his stomach and he thought, *We did this to Paris.*

Anthony looked back at his phone; the headline on the CNN website still saying sixty had been killed IN SHOOTINGS AND BLASTS; HOSTAGES HELD. He willed it not to be true, to be a mistake, at least for the count to start going in the opposite direction.

The headline changed to a big black banner, with big white letters: MORE THAN 100 KILLED.[1]

He couldn't shake the notion that he was at fault. That *this is because of us. We stopped an attack, and they had to come back ten times worse to let the people of France know we didn't stop anything.*

He did not feel what all the people sending him messages felt. He didn't wish he'd been there. Instead he felt he'd been so stupidly lucky when he was there, and he felt guilt. He and Spencer and Alek had stepped in the way of fate, and fate had come roaring back with a vengeance. Terrorists were responding to the three of them, and using hundreds of innocent people in France to make the point that you couldn't stop history from happening; you just could maybe change when and how bad it was.

We've done this to them.

It would be months before he could fully accept that his reaction was wrong, that he hadn't somehow inspired a reprisal attack, and that instead the mastermind planned at least four other attacks that had stalled out before, and as many as six. His name was Abdelhamid Abaoud, and though he was involved in Ayoub El-Khazzani's plot against the train[2] and might have felt pressure because of past failures, he had many wells to draw from beyond what happened aboard the 15:17 to Paris. If Anthony and Alek and Spencer, and the others there that day—"Damian A" who slowed El-Khazzani down, and Mark Moogalian who tried to grab the machine gun and got shot, all before Anthony even woke up, and Chris Norman who helped bind El-Khazzani and then spent about two straight days translating—if any of them had happened to be somewhere else, had not been there to stop the attack, there was no reason to believe it would have stopped the mastermind from planning more. It would have meant that instead of a hundred thirty people dying in one attack, four or five hundred would have died in two.

But at that moment, it didn't matter. No amount of reasoning would have helped him shed the awful thought that he was responsible.

And there was another reason he felt so personally connected to the killings in Paris. It wasn't just that he'd convinced himself he'd somehow inspired them. It was because he now felt a closeness with the city. It was funny, in a way, that this city they'd kept hearing lukewarm things about on their trip, and which they were just about to skip altogether, instead gave him his fondest memories.

Partially, of course, because the appreciation was amazing, breathtaking, and so obviously genuine. It was not about celebrity; it was about humanity. It hadn't felt like people in Paris wanted to be around them because they were famous— he didn't even feel famous yet. The people there made Anthony feel like he and his friends had given a tremendous gift. People didn't want a part of them, people wanted to make sure the boys were properly thanked. So after Anthony turned off the TV, that's what he started thinking about.

Paris, just after the train. The city's people; the beginning of his fame. He sat in front of the blank TV screen, thinking about those four days they had in Paris, and everything that came after.

36.

THE DAY BACK IN AUGUST when Anthony and his two friends received France's highest honor, their biggest problem was what to wear. Another funny contrast: they were surrounded by the luxuriant splendor of the ambassador's mansion in Paris, but their clothes were mostly dirty, and anyway none of them had thought to bring formal attire on a backpacking trip across Europe. The best they had were sports jerseys covered in blood. There'd been no time to go shopping, certainly not to get anything tailored, so they were about to receive the Legion of Honor from the president of France while wearing gym clothes.

Chief Griffith had an idea. He disappeared, then came bursting back into the residence with a bag full of clothing. "Okay," he said, "try these on." A pair of khakis for each of them, borrowed shoes, belts. "But make sure I get all this back."

"Damn, Chief," Anthony said, holding up a pair of slacks to eyeball the size. "Where'd you get this stuff from?"

"I borrowed it. From the marines. From *actual* marines. So unless you want America's finest coming after you, you better get it all back in good condition." He'd run down to the embassy's marine detachment and raided their closets, but no one had suits or blazers. Apparently marines didn't have any more reason for three-piece suits than backpackers did. The best they had was polo shirts. So the boys headed down to get the nation's highest award looking like frat brothers on their way to a barbeque. Later, when the news broadcast images from the award ceremony, anchors would try to explain away the visuals that rolled with the reports, saying things like "The three of them, dressed . . . *casually*, received France's highest award . . ."

Anthony didn't much care what he was wearing. When he walked into the embassy lobby with the others, the whole crowd assembled there erupted in cheers. And it didn't die down; it just kept going. Someone leaned over and said in his ear, "You stopped our 9/11." They kept roaring, the excitement feeding on itself, the fact that they'd cheered for so long becoming itself something to laugh and cheer for, and finally Anthony decided it might go a few more seconds, so he took out his camera and began filming. Still, the crowd didn't quiet. It was the most thunderous applause he'd ever heard, and he started to get a sense of what this meant to people.

They got in a black SUV for the short ride to the palace. A line of reporters, a royal guard; Joyce, Heidi, and Everett arriving with them after flying through the night, landing at Charles de Gaulle Airport less than an hour before the ceremony, stepping off a plane to a waiting motorcade, and racing through the city. Anthony was happy to see more familiar faces, happy to see Heidi go up to Alek, hold his face in her hands and say, "Remember what I said to you before you deployed? This is *it!*" Which seemed nice, whatever it was about, and Alek smiled, but Anthony's parents weren't there yet.

"Okay, sir?" A skinny Frenchman had taken him by the elbow and led them to a stage, pointing out an X where Anthony was to stand. "He's going to come up to you," the man said, as if "he" was a waiter or something, rather than the president of France. "He's going to pin the medal on you, shake your hand. That's it."

"That's all?"

Anthony's X placed him next to Chris, while Alek and Spencer stood on the other side of the podium. The skinny man attached a radio to Anthony's ear so he could hear a translation, but when the president addressed the crowd he spoke faster than the translator could keep up, so Anthony didn't know whether to smile, look serious—the one thing he had never, ever doubted was his ability to act appropriately in any situation, and now he had no idea. He forced his face to neutral.

Where's Dad?

The president started talking.

"One need only know that Ayoub El-Khazzani was in possession of three hundred rounds of ammunition and firearms," the woman in his ear said, "to understand what we narrowly avoided, a tragedy, a massacre. Your heroism must be an example for many and a source of inspiration. Faced with the evil of terrorism, there is a good, that of humanity. You are the incarnation of that."

Anthony scanned the crowd. Many important-looking people. His father still wasn't there. Was there a problem with the plane? Had he not been allowed on board in Sacramento at all?

"We're not weak as a society faced with terrorism, we are strong when we stand together." Anthony tried to keep his gaze forward, but noticed the president glance in his direction. More important-sounding oratory in French. "If something happens," the voice in his ear said, "you have to respond. You have to do something." That didn't sound very official. It sounded like something Anthony himself would say.

In fact it sounded like something he *did* say, at the press conference yesterday—a shiver ran through him. The president of France had just quoted *him!* Now, he could let a little smile crack on his face. And as he scanned the crowd again, out of the corner of his eye he saw a door to the left of the stage open, and his father and stepmother slip in. Anthony locked eyes with each of them, gave a nod, and they smiled back. What he saw on his father's face was raw, unfiltered pride that his father was trying hard to contain. Anthony wanted to laugh, to let his whole face light up in a smile, *Can you believe this, Dad!* but he tried to put his serious face back on, lest the president of France say something sad or tragic while Anthony was grinning like an idiot. A moment later, the president of France was standing in front of him, pinning the country's highest medal just under his collar, and kissing him on both cheeks.

IT BEGINS SIMPLY. Anthony was asleep, now he's not. Spencer is looking at him with strange eyes because a body has just blurred past them.

Then Spencer is gone.

The adrenaline hits Anthony and he thinks, We have to do something, and Alek is already out of his seat following Spencer. Anthony gets up and moves through the train car like he's on a gas-powered dolly blasted forward and he's next to Spencer in something like a second. Alek is leaning down, he is picking the machine gun up, light hits the metal and triggers something in Anthony. The barrel in Alek's arms moving toward the seat where Spencer and the gunman are twisting. Sound leaves him and knowledge comes and slams into Anthony like a heavy, open hand smacking the round of his head: Alek is going to kill Spencer.

Anthony has been injected with a drug that affects not him so much as everything around him, so limbs move like they're moving through thick liquid, slowing them all down except his, and he can see everything happening in perfect high gloss; it is all incredibly clear, incredibly obvious, incredibly slow. Alek cocks the machine gun, moves it slowly toward the two bodies writhing on the seat. Anthony can see it clearly from this angle. The bullet will pass through the man and into Spencer.

It feels like the whole of a minute for the trigger to move all the way back. Enough time for Anthony's brain to cycle through a series of ideas like a jukebox, flinging and twisting discs behind the glass.

Alek, don't do it, you'll kill Spencer too!

Alek, go, do it, kill him now because this guy is a terrorist!

Alek, don't do it because you're going to splatter that man's head on all of us and you don't want to see that and I don't want to see that either!

Anthony's brain gets all twisted; thoughts begin to intersect and blend and then the current grinds to a halt and his mind is still and silent. Alek pulls the trigger.

The gun doesn't go off. Time speeds back up, and Alek is pounding the man so violently but the muzzle hitting flesh should make blood and make sound but it does neither; still, this makes more sense to Anthony, this is right, this man needs to be administered violence but not killed. Anthony watches the man's forehead where blood should come and isn't, so Anthony looks down at the man's face. Each time a blow strikes the man, the face fizzles out of focus with the force of it, then resolves, and the man just stares at Alek.

He is hit again, he vibrates out of focus, stares at Alek again. He is not passing out. He is superhuman. He shows no signs of pain. His skin is softening with blows from the weapon, but he stares. Spencer holds him tight; it's seconds or minutes, Anthony can't be sure, but Anthony is watching the terrorist closely because he is expecting him to pass out. It lasts for an hour if it lasts a second; it is the most intense thing Anthony has ever seen. It is extreme brutality being passed between two people, but the man is not even struggling. He takes the blows, he stares.

It's haunting. He has a look on his face that is hatred, but it is a different kind of hatred from any Anthony has seen. It is not anger at what is happening right now; it is a calmer, deeper anger, deep enough that what is happening now is only disturbing the surface. It will last longer than this grasp he's in. It is deep enough that he will wait. He is saying to Alek, I'm in no rush. Eventually I will not be in this chokehold and then I will kill you and as many of your people as I can.

And then he passes out.

37.

AFTER THE CEREMONY it was time for Anthony to go home. He walked across the tarmac at Charles de Gaulle Airport toward a jet waiting just for him. *Ho-ly shit.*

An idea came to him. He dismissed it for a moment, then thought, *Why stop now?* He took out his selfie stick, extended the telescopic handle, and recorded the last of his European trip.

The interior was plush. Dark cherrywood paneling everywhere. Was it real wood? It didn't matter. Cream-colored seats that swallowed you up, trays and drawers that appeared out of nowhere with food, candy, booze, whatever you wanted, secret compartments that would magically appear to offer him snacks or juice like the whole machine was designed to anticipate his needs.

He sat back in one of the seats, the backrest collapsed and the legs extended, so that his whole six-foot-four frame was stretched out, and the seat swallowed him up. The plane was whisper quiet, the roar of the engines reduced to a soothing purr that drowned out the intensity of all that had just happened; his life arcing off in a new direction after the train, then four days during which he never came down, camera flashes and phone calls from the president, an ambassador's assistant adopting him and Spencer and Alek like they were her own children, the presidential suite, a medal he'd never heard of given by a president whose name he still wasn't sure how to pronounce, all of it pushed back into a distant corner of his thoughts by the thrum of the engine, and one final thought popped up, *We never made it to Spain,* before that too floated away and for the first time in four days, Anthony slept.

Fourteen hours later, he woke from the dead. He was in Oregon.

He rubbed his eyes, stood up, and was shown to a connecting flight to Sacramento, where he was first exposed to the maddening, funny, and more or less constant pressure of fame.

Fame. Was he famous? It was a strange thought. On the one hand, he hadn't done much to get famous. On the other, what was a bigger deal, starring in a movie, singing a pop song, putting a ball through a hoop? Or stopping a terrorist? He had sensed, during those eerily calm moments on the train, that France would go crazy. They weren't three marines like the news kept saying, but Alek and Spencer *were* military, so it still was a story of American servicemen stopping a terrorist. He wasn't surprised that France held them up and made a big deal of it. He'd seen the narrative immediately: American military saves the world!

But he didn't know *just* how big a deal it was going to be, and it hadn't occurred to him that anyone outside of France would care, or really understand, what had happened. Because *he* still didn't. It was still a small, muddled moment in his life, a brief and incomplete blip on his memory. The images that played across the screen in his mind when he closed his eyes were all things that took place on a small narrow stage, a rectangle of twenty-five square feet hemmed into the aisle of a train car. They were mostly images that involved five people. Spencer and Alek. Chris, the British man. The gunman. Mark bleeding out.

Maybe it was because it just wasn't possible to accept that hundreds of people were still alive because of him. How does one comprehend a thing like that? What does "hundreds of people" look like? How much space do they fill up? Maybe it was a matter of physiology, just a fact of science that the brain isn't equipped to visualize that much suffering. The brain needs something comprehensible. It wants familiarity.

On the short flight from Oregon back to Sacramento, Anthony saw, out of the corner of his eye, a person he thought he recognized.

Holy shit is that—? They made eye contact.

"Anthony? *Anthony!*"

Anthony was disoriented for a minute. Where was he— wait, was John Dickson on the same flight? They'd been trying to connect in Germany; now here they were in— where were they? Anthony had fallen asleep in France and woken up in Oregon and it took a beat to place himself back in America rather than somewhere in Munich or Berlin, or wherever they'd been only a week ago, a time period that now seemed impossibly long.

"John? What the hell are you doing here?" What were the odds? After trying so many times to get together in Europe, they ended up on the same tiny commuter flight from Oregon to Sacramento.

"What the hell did you guys *do* over there?"

Anthony began to ask him what it had been like playing semipro basketball in Germany, but was interrupted by a tap on his shoulder. A middle-aged woman in a power suit knelt down next to him.

"Hi, Mr. Sadler? I'm sorry to bother you, but I just noticed I happened to be on the same flight with you. I'm a reporter from a TV station in Portland." Anthony's new normal had begun. "I just saw you and scribbled down a note to you. Here's my card, just give me a call, okay? If you think you might like to go on TV."

She went back to her seat and Anthony raised an eyebrow, looked over at John, who was laughing and shaking his head. "She tried that already," John said. "She tried to give that card to *me* when we first got on. I doubt she 'just happened to notice' she was on the same flight."

So Anthony was beginning his newfound fame with a juxtaposition: he was famous enough to draw reporters onto flights just for the chance to interview him, but not famous enough to overcome the media's impressive inability to tell the difference between black people.

The small commuter jet landed and taxied, and when he walked out onto the stairs, the circus began. It was like he'd been in a hermetically sealed chamber protected from exposure to the eyes of millions of Americans, and all of a sudden the pressure had become too great, it had burst open, and now here he was, exposed. News helicopters circled overhead to capture his arrival. Three FBI agents and two policemen at the bottom of the stairs took him by the elbow and rushed him down a back entrance of the airport, before he could even properly say goodbye to John. John, meanwhile, walked into the terminal and was ambushed by dozens of camera flashes and microphones shoved in his face, "Anthony, Anthony," they yelled at John, "are you happy to be home?" While the real Anthony was being ushered into the back of a motorcade and whisked away.

His parents' house was already hemmed in by a phalanx of news trucks with satellite antennas fully extended, so Anthony's father had booked a hotel room, but Anthony wanted his own bed. "Can you just drop me off at my apartment? I'll be all right. If there's nobody out there."

Pastor Sadler rerouted the sheriffs.

Still, Anthony was having a hard time connecting himself to the experience of what was happening around him. He didn't feel in his bones that he had saved hundreds of lives. That was an almost impossible thing to accept. That was Superman, flying up to a jumbo jet and nudging it just before it crashed into a mountaintop. If he couldn't fully internalize how many lives he had saved, how, really, could all these other people? What to make of all the news trucks surrounding his house like they were guarding it? Did those reporters all understand?

Was it him they were interested in, was it the seriousness of what had happened, or was it something else? Were they like the reporter on the plane, faking (he was now certain) a chance encounter when really she wanted his face to boost her own ratings? He didn't mind it terribly, but he had no idea how long it would last, this value he now had inside him that others could extract. Soon Spencer would tell Anthony he'd gotten calls from stalkers, and from local news anchors imploring him to come on their own shows like he owed it to them, because landing one of the three heroes was a guaranteed promotion.

So Anthony had a new power now: the power to make careers.

The questions swirled in his head, more questions than answers, but the one thing he was certain of was that he was exhausted. If he was going to be any use to anyone, he needed some rest.

By some grace, none of the reporters had found his apartment yet. The complex was gated, but unguarded, and with no one watching it; the gates were always open, not keeping out undesirables so much as gently suggesting that they please, if it wasn't too much of an inconvenience, stay away. Two men in black suits got out of the SUV with him, walked him all the way up to the door. Nobody was there. "Yeah, I'll stay here," Anthony said.

Anthony was home.

Then, quiet. It was strange to be here on his own, without Alek and Spencer, who were still back in Europe being debriefed by the military, Spencer getting more medical care.

It was strange just to be back. Everything in his life was different, but everything in front of him looked the same. It felt like a minor offence that his apartment was exactly as he'd left it, after he'd just gone through ... whatever it was he'd just gone through. The colors should be brighter, the rooms bigger. Everything had been surreal, larger than life. Now he was home, and home was exactly the same, and he didn't fit it. He felt he'd been in a dream; now he was waking up to beds that needed making, an apartment decorated by a college kid rather than some Parisian interior designer, a degree that needed completing.

He didn't want to be alone. He called everyone he could think of, and soon he had twenty people over asking him to recount the story, but even with all his friends and classmates around him, there was one person he felt he really needed to talk to.

Spencer, he thought, his apartment wall to wall with bodies, *how you doing over there, brother? Spencer, how did you know the terrorist was behind us?*

38.

THERE WERE SMALL DUTIES that came with fame, Anthony was learning. He was sick with something; jet lag or maybe coming down off the high had brought on its own withdrawal, but he was groggy, exhausted, and his stomach ached. He felt pulled apart from Spencer and Alek; he wanted to talk to them, he wanted to be with them. Such a momentous thing had happened to bring them together but now he was held maddeningly apart from his partners. It made him feel incomplete, to face this country alone, as if he was the only one who'd done anything; a table with one leg.

"You have to do a press conference," his father said. "They won't leave you alone until you do. You don't want them to still be looking for you wherever you go."

The last thing Anthony wanted to do was to go out in public like this, without Spencer, without Alek, feeling exhausted and sick, but he knew his dad's house was surrounded by press, and they were starting to show up at his church. If he didn't give the press something, it wouldn't stop.

"All right," his dad said, "we'll do this. The mayor and I will do most of it, you just talk for a couple seconds and then get off. Make your appearance, and we'll say you have to go get some rest. They'll understand."

"What do I say?"

"Just think of how you feel, and say that." What would Anthony have done if his father wasn't a pastor, with years of experience and advice about public speaking? "It doesn't have to be fancy or deep. In fact, it shouldn't be. Just say what you feel, son."

"I feel like puking."

"Well, maybe don't say that."

Anthony swallowed a handful of Tums, looked in the mirror—a little pale, but otherwise you couldn't tell he was sick—and went into the city. Surrounded by police officers, he walked onto a stage outside of city hall, and then he did what he was told.

"I'd just like to thank everyone for coming out. After a crazy few days it feels good to be back on American soil, but especially in Sacramento. Um, this is my home, and I'm just glad to be back here to see everybody. It's kind of over-whelming for me. I didn't expect all this to happen, but I just appreciate you all for coming and, um, it's just good to be back home. Thank you."

And that was all he could muster. He stepped off.

When his father took the podium and agreed to take some questions, a reporter asked one that threw Anthony for a loop. Did Pastor Sadler have any concerns now, the reporter asked, that his son might be a target for terrorists?

It was a ridiculous question, and Anthony hoped his father wouldn't answer too rudely.

"Yes, I do," he said.

Anthony couldn't believe what he just heard.

"But there are no credible threats right now."

Dad thinks I'm in danger?

Anthony tried to let the thought pass. Even though the people around him were mostly press, and even though he wanted desperately to go home and collapse onto his bed, the crowd there seemed genuinely happy for him.

Later that day, he saw the local NBC affiliate report on his press conference. "Sadler spoke for less than thirty seconds," the correspondent said, "then left without taking any questions. Police closed down streets around city hall, as a motorcade whisked him away."

39.

WHEN HE FINALLY CONNECTED with Spencer, Anthony had been back in America for almost a week, which somehow felt both longer and shorter than seven days. On the one hand, it felt like just yesterday that they were all together on their reunion, all together on the train, but on the other hand, so much had happened since then. When Anthony looked back at it, the few days between then and now were dense with events that would define his life. That made it feel like more time, or at least, more *significant* time. Time itself still felt like a fluid concept, just like it had on the train. Were minutes passing, or hours?

And it felt longer also because he was experiencing it alone. This should be the three of them together, all home, all hailed as heroes together. But since those days together at the embassy in Paris, they'd been pulled in different directions. Spencer was still at Ramstein Air Base in Germany when he finally answered one of Anthony's calls, and he wasn't doing great.

"I mean, it's nice that everyone is so caring," he said, "but it's just so much. I mean it's nonstop. There are always people around, like a million people trying to take care of me. We just want to come home."

"I know, man, I wish you could be here and see what it's like back in America. They love us here."

That didn't seem to lift Spencer's spirits much. Maybe he was having his own hangover from all that had happened.

Plus, the air force had given Spencer's family a liaison to help them deal with all the strange new demands and, no bullshit, she was an alumnus of their private school. What were the odds? A school across the world with a dozen kids in a class, and she happened to be there?

"What you need," Anthony said, "is to get back here. Sacramento loves us. I'm getting into clubs for free, I've been out to eat, people just pay for me. I could get used to it."

"Well, there has been a little of that ... if you know what I mean."

"Ha! For real? What happened?"

"We snuck off the base. We had to put one of the MPs in the trunk to get past the checkpoint." They'd gone to a bar that served American servicemen from the base, run by an old American expat who for whatever reason had put down roots in Germany but must have missed American kids, because he opened a bar and did things like offer shots on the house when an American hero walked in the door. The moment Spencer put the liquor to his lips, a sound system blasted the opening synch riff to Springsteen's "Born in the USA." "Then I felt a tap on my shoulder," Spencer said, "and I swear, this girl asked me if I wanted to do a body shot. So obviously I did, and the whole place just was chanting, 'USA!! ... USA!! ... USA!!!' while I did it. Even out here, I get noticed wherever I go."

But there was something else that had hit him even harder, he told Anthony. He'd gone out for dinner off base with his and another family, and their little girl kept arguing with her siblings during the car ride about who would get to sit next to him at the table. She prevailed, but then the whole evening stared up at him like she didn't quite understand something about Spencer. After dinner she finally mustered the courage to ask him her question: "Are you a superhero?"

Anthony could hear Spencer shifting the phone.

"Then she said she wanted to hug me. But she was afraid to, because I still have the cast, and the stitches. She said she wanted to hug me, but she was afraid she would hurt me. And it just all came out. I just bawled, man. I think that's when it just all kind of hit me."

40.

IT WASN'T SERIOUS, AT FIRST. The three of them started getting media requests, then a PR manager from their hometown signed on to help them keep track of everything coming in, and produced three two-sided sheets of media requests. It was too much to do; how could one person do all of them, do even three or four or five of them? So Anthony went down the list eliminating the ones he knew he didn't want to do. Not many were easy to pass up—when fame finally comes knocking, you don't shut the door in its face—but one was an obvious "no thanks." *Dancing with the Stars*.

And then one morning a week after Anthony got home from Paris, while he (he thought) was the only one of the three back in the States, his dad told him there was an announcement on *Good Morning America* he should watch, so Anthony pulled it up. After a clip of Gary Busey riding a horse, the host teed up the ageless *Dancing with the Stars* host, Tom Bergeron.

All the final cast members had been announced but one. "Tom," one of the hosts said, "will you do us the honors and reveal the *suuuper*-secret star?"

"Yes, indeed," Tom said, sitting in a director's chair in the middle of Times Square. "I found out about this late addition to our cast last night. I'm thrilled to introduce him. He was one of three Americans who took down a terrorist on board a packed train in Paris."

Holy shit, is that Alek! In Times Square!

Or rather, Alek's shadow behind a sheer pink screen, but unmistakably him; even in monochrome silhouette, Alek had a trademark slouch. Hands in pockets, Johnny Bravo hair whipped off center. Out he walked through a beaded curtain onto national television, smiling ear to ear, then turning because the beads were clinging like tentacles to his shirt, and he had to undo himself. He broke free, walked out with a hitch in his step, and asked the sixty-five-year-old celebrity chef Paula Deen for a high five en route to his chair. Alek didn't seem shy or quiet at all. He seemed to be right in his element, sitting in Times Square in his standard jeans and running shoes, next to a handful of suits and designer T-shirts with aggressive necklines.

Anthony couldn't believe he was watching the same Alek. Was that really his friend sitting next to the Crocodile Hunter's daughter? Sitting in front of a mop-headed social media star? They beamed in a Backstreet Boy from a set where he was filming a movie. Anthony was watching his friend becoming a pop idol before his eyes.

He and Spencer would go about their more mature media requests, Anthony deciding it'd be cool to go on the shows he watched faithfully. Jimmy Fallon (which was a mistake; Jimmy Kimmel treated Spencer better); and Lester Holt for evening news, while they waited for Alek to make a fool of himself on national television.

But a crazy thing happened on the way to Alek's national embarrassment. He didn't fail.

He kept advancing.

He survived the elimination rounds.

He made it past the first half of the season.

He made it to the two-night finale, so Spencer and Anthony flew down to see him on the first night, since he'd obviously be eliminated before it got to the final three stars.

He wasn't. He made it to the final night. Alek seemed natural in the makeup, under the lights. And sure, he was the one "star" whose professional dancing partner fielded most of the questions, the producers apparently catching on quickly that Alek wasn't the most verbose contestant they'd ever had, not the best choice for a passionate anecdote, but he seemed to like the performing; he actually seemed to have this in him. Anthony had never seen that side of him, but it seemed like something that had always been there. Alek wasn't pretending; Alek never pretended. So Alek actually liked to perform. It was like he'd been hiding an artistic side all along, and it took the train to bring it out.

FOR HIS PART, Anthony chose to do his first big interview with Lester Holt. Not just because Holt anchored the highest-rated evening news broadcast, reaching almost ten million people every night. Anthony chose him because Holt was a Sacramento State alum, and he went to high school down the street from where Anthony grew up. The more globally known Anthony became, the more those local connections began to mean. It was funny, then, that though they grew up spitting distance from one another, Anthony had to go all the way to New York to meet him. Farther even, all the way to France to win the invitation.

But this was Anthony's first time in New York City, and he was without the other two. He hadn't talked to Spencer much, hardly at all except for the one call, when Spencer told him about the girl and the body shot, and the kid who made him cry.

He taped his interview in a big open room that seemed to be a swanky, modernist, minimalist loft, like the whole floor was that one room and all it had in it was a table and two glasses of water. And Lester.

By that point he'd gotten pretty good at telling the story, but there was one part that he still hadn't accepted. A question he was dodging, whenever it came up, without even realizing that's what he was doing.

"You must have played in your mind," Holt said, after they'd dispensed with pleasantries and a few minutes of small talk, "how easily this could have gone the other way."

Anthony responded by using Holt's own words as a life raft. "I've kind of laid down and thought, just how easily things could have gone . . . " but he wasn't actually thinking of how it all could have gone the other way. He was thinking about that tiny world he and Spencer and Alek had inhabited, that single train car. "He did fire at Spencer," Anthony said, "but it never went off."

When he thought about things turning out differently, he was only thinking about what could have happened to the people on the car he was on. Those memories were so powerful he hadn't yet lifted up, zoomed around the train, counted up all the souls on board. It felt like they'd saved Mark's life, and saved themselves, and that was it, and that was enough.

It turned out he was in the right place for the whole entire size of it to hit him.

41.

LEE ADLER WAS a forty-eight year-old programmer, a man with a mind that could generate ideas for computer programs without working them out on paper first. They came to him like songs came to some songwriters, already arranged in his head. It helped that he was a brilliant scientist, a PhD in nuclear chemistry, but he came across more as a teddy bear than a nerd. He coached his daughter's sports teams, spoiled his wife and his pets, gave people gifts on *his* birthday, and spent his days working high above Lower Manhattan at eSpeed, a division of the trading firm Cantor Fitzgerald.

Across the floor, a well-built thirty-three-year-old man with dark wavy hair named Anthony Perez also worked as a computer specialist for Cantor Fitzgerald. Perez had done a stint as a stockbroker that didn't go so well, so he moved to computers, and took his new passion home, building high-performing PCs for his children out of spare parts.

Other than working on computers, working for Cantor Fitzgerald, and working on the same floor of the same building, the other thing these two men had in common was that both were at work by a quarter to nine on the crystal-clear September morning when American Airlines Flight 11 crashed into the north tower of the World Trade Center. The plane struck three floors below where both men sat. Neither made it out.

Years later, when a memorial for the victims of the 9/11 attacks was being developed, planners decided to place the names of those who died in the north tower on a series of plaques surrounding a reflecting pool, and those who died in the south tower around another, and to enter their names into a specially designed algorithm that also processed requests for names to be placed together. Names of people who knew each other, or who had tried to help one another escape, or who had died together. The program told planners which names to put on which plaque, and in what order, and it told them to place two names in particular, one just above the other, on plaque N-37 on the north-facing side of the north pool.

During his brief visit to New York that day, Anthony Sadler approached the memorial from uptown, so the first panel he saw when he walked up to the pool was N-37. His eyes flitted across the bronze, scanning the names. All the letters danced and clouded together; the name ANTHONY PEREZ crossed in his vision with the name LEE ADLER, and for just an instant, a small fraction of a second, it looked like ANTHONY SADLER was inscribed on the memorial, along with all the victims.

He felt unsteady. His own name among thousands dead. For the first time he felt the weight of it, more than just him and Spencer and Alek and a few other people in a single train car.

Now he felt part of something much bigger.

Now he no longer just *knew* that all these coincidences had stopped something awful; he could feel it. He could feel how close he was. He felt what could have happened if their fates had resolved themselves just a *little* differently, if prayers had been heard or ignored or interpreted differently by whomever was up there processing prayers. He felt it as an instant of fission, static on a TV screen briefly resolving to show a different picture on the wrong channel, a glimpse of a different future.

He felt how insignificant he was. How much dumb luck, or coincidence, or God, or whatever, had conspired to keep him alive. And when he lifted his eyes, what struck him next was what he knew struck *everybody* who visited: just how *massive* it all was. The size of it bowled him over. How much physical space had changed in an instant. How much matter was removed, two huge structures gone, along with all the people occupying them. Giant skyscrapers reaching up all around, and despite the quiet, he could almost hear, and he could certainly feel, the chaos from two buildings coming down in the middle of this crowded city, the souls reaching up from the black of the reflecting pools. It was no longer something foreign that had happened across the country, a tragedy suffered by other people, running, terror-stricken people for whom he felt terrible but who could have just as easily been running from a radioactive monster in 1950s Tokyo. Now it was real. Now it was something he could understand and feel. He was tiny compared to this giant, gaping *absence*.

And his tiny role, stepping in front of something like this. *"You stopped our 9/11."* Hadn't someone in Paris said that?

He hadn't thought much of it when he was in Paris. But now he was forced to understand and see what "this could have gone the other way" really meant. What "you stopped our 9/11" actually felt like.

Before him was what uninterrupted terrorists leave behind. The 9/11 memorial at the World Trade Center changed how Anthony felt about what they'd done. It was no longer "How cool is it that we just stopped a terrorist!" It was no longer champagne and hotel robes in the ambassador's residence. Now there was a gravity that pulled him down so hard it almost paralyzed him. He began to *feel* what would have happened if they hadn't been there. *If this had gone the other way.* Not just for him and his friends, but for a whole train; a city. It became something huge and crushing. Anthony put his hands on the panel and lowered his head.

For a time he was still, listening to the low babble of water disappearing down into the pools, and leaning on the bronze panels, just thinking ... thinking, listening to the rush of wind.

THE RUSH OF WIND past the train grows quieter; Anthony realizes this only as they finish tying up the terrorist. He notices the train is slowing only now that it's almost stopped. It's a machine that runs so smoothly that moving and not moving feel almost the same. He's too busy to pay attention to extraneous senses, his sight locked in a tangle of limbs and dead weight, because even though the terrorist is no longer conscious he still seems to be resisting. *How heavy a man is,* Anthony thinks, even a skinny man like this. He's hard to move, hard to manipulate, like he has lead in his bones.

"Going to go check the other cars." Anthony doesn't know exactly what Alek is doing, but he's taken the gun with him. Alek's expression has not changed. It's just Alek.

The space is tight and awkward. They do not have the right supplies, they do not have handcuffs or rope, so they are binding him up with someone's necktie. Anthony doesn't know whose necktie. Certainly not his. And it also can't be

Spencer's or Alek's because the three of them are wearing shorts and T-shirts.

Anthony tests the knots; they seem secure. The terrorist is restrained; he will not be able to move. Anthony turns to see what's going on elsewhere in the train car.

How did he not see? Just feet away, almost close enough to reach out and touch, a man is sitting in a seat and bleeding profusely. Where did he come from? When did he get there? Anthony's vision is so tightly focused on what's in front of him that he has jettisoned his ability to recognize distractions, and some system in his brain placed disabling a gunman on a hierarchy above addressing possible victims. Now it's as if with one task accomplished, he's ratcheted on to the next and it has materialized in front of him like a hologram. A man two seats away, dying of blood loss.

Only "blood loss" does not do it justice: the man is geysering blood, a ridiculous amount of blood; his shirt is soaked through and the blood is spurting across the aisle like a fire hose—how can a person produce that much blood? Anthony thinks this man has been stabbed, because the blood is gushing from a hole in the man's neck like in a horror movie, and Anthony does not know that in fact he's been shot, but he locks eyes with him just long enough to see the man's pupils spin up and disappear into his head and his body collapse forward out of the seat. He tumbles over his arm so that when he lands, it sticks out from under his body at a grotesque angle like it belongs to someone else, and acts as a shiv, propping his torso up just enough that Anthony can now see the pool of blood spreading in the aisle like it has intent, like the blood is trying to get out of the body and escape the train.

Deep red blood, and Anthony knows from a class four months ago that this is arterial blood, so the man is actually in even worse trouble than he looks. This man is about to die.

Anthony doesn't say anything, there is no time for conversation; if the man is not dead already he has just seconds left. How could there be any blood left in him? Anthony needs something to compress the wound with and he needs it now. He is thinking about a towel. He is not precisely sure why that's what he needs, but he knows from a TV show or class or perhaps just common sense that when there is blood loss you press the wound to stop it.

Anthony is running. He's weaving past the seats and keeping his balance like he's carving up a zone defense, he reaches a hand out to knock the handle down so the door hisses open and he barely has to slow down, he turns sideways and squeezes through the opening door without breaking stride, and explodes into the next train car, where passengers are still huddled.

"Does anybody speak English?"

"Yeah," "Me," "I speak some."

"Does anybody have a towel?"

Silence; nobody says a word, they don't know what's going on, did he say it too loudly? Did he not say it at all? Did they not understand? They are all panicked. He can see the fear etched onto their faces, and they are looking at him dumbly; he thinks these people have no idea what's going on and at just that moment their confusion fuses with his own and he thinks, *What am I going to do with a towel? A towel is not going to stop it.*

Now he is running back to the pile of limbs, he will not be able to communicate what he needs to strangers, what he needs are his friends, he has the powerful intuition that one of his friends can help him save this dying man, he is not thinking exactly that Spencer is an EMT, he is not thinking of why Spencer might know what to do, it is not such a clear thought, it is just a powerful sense that the only way he can prevent this man from dying is with the help of his friends, and when he crashes back into the car Alek is gone, but Spencer is there, still on his hands and knees over the terrorist. "Spencer, we've got to do something."

"What?"

"We gotta do something. This guy is gonna die."

"Where's he at?"

"Right there, he's right behind you. I don't know. I don't know what to fucking do."

Spencer doesn't even stand up. He turns around on all fours and crawls over to the dying man. He says, "I'm going to try and find where he's bleeding from." Spencer wipes blood from his own face, and puts his fingers into the man's neck. He feels around, then presses down hard. The bleeding stops immediately. Anthony can't believe how quickly it works. Spencer is magic.

"Don't move," Spencer is saying to the man, "or I'll lose the hole."

Anthony finds a first-aid kit in his hands, but can't remember how it got there. Is he so powerful he's summoning things to himself just by thinking about them? He dumps the kit out on the floor next to Spencer and begins rummaging through the pile, explaining to Spencer what's inside, holding things up one at a time in front of Spencer, to see if Spencer thinks any of it can help.

"Tape?"

"It won't help."

"Gauze."

"No."

"Okay. Neosporin?"

"No."

"Peroxide?"

"I'm not worried about infection right now."

"This looks like an ACE bandage."

"No."

"Scissors?"

"No. Wait—yeah, give me the scissors."

Alek takes the scissors. Alek is back from wherever Alek went. Alek is still the same monotone Alek. "I'll do a blood sweep."

He cuts the back of the man's shirt and feels around his body. Alek must have known from Afghanistan how to do that.

The man complains, "My arm, guys, guys, my arm hurts. You've got to get my arm out from underneath me."

Anthony stands watch, in case Spencer needs anything. "We're not worried about your arm right now," Spencer tells the man.

"My arm hurts. Can we move just a little?"

Why is he even thinking about his arm? Does he not feel the hole in his neck?

He groans. He complains. For ten minutes he keeps complaining about his arm being stuck, as if there was no wound in neck.

Spencer is angry now. The situation below Anthony is tenuous; he doesn't know how Spencer stopped the bleeding but however he did it, Anthony doesn't think he can count on the man on the floor surviving much longer without some kind of equipment. This man needs a hospital.

Spencer is cursing. "Why is the fucking train not moving?"

Anthony tells him that it's stopped, probably they stopped it when the attack started. Someone hears the message, their confusion is communicated, and somehow the train starts again, it picks up speed; soon it's whirring along smoothly, and Anthony is again astounded by how amazingly quiet it is. How strangely calm everyone is. The train moves on, toward some unknown station. In this train car, this strange chamber, Anthony and his friends control what they can. Other people, other forces, have decided what their destination is.

Anthony doesn't know where they're going. He just senses that bizarre calm. Did that just happen? It feels like a dream, or like being on a drug.

42.

JIMMY FALLON'S DRESSING ROOM was trippy. It was some kind of forest theme, maybe an inside joke, or a bad high. The walls looked like bark, a little fox statue stood in one corner, a mushroom-shaped stool in another. It seemed to be a room designed by people who liked to get high. Or *for* them. It was stocked with snacks and gifts for the guests, but those were weird too. All organic everything. Organic chocolates, organic nuts, organic this, organic that. The more organic, the more acutely Anthony's gag reflex activated. For a guy like him who didn't like soda in Europe because it didn't have enough artificial sweetener, the food in Fallon's dressing room was inedible.

Who liked this kind of stuff? The whole room felt like it was designed for some kind of tree-dwelling troll hippy with an aversion to corn syrup. And the gift was a pair of UGG slippers. If Anthony went back to where he was from wearing UGGs ... Fallon's sense of humor clearly didn't stop on the stage.

From the dressing room, Anthony watched Fallon tape interviews with earlier guests; he heard someone approach outside the dressing room and turned from the TV to see the no-bullshit Irish-American Hollywood fixer Ray Donovan.

Or not Ray Donovan, but the man who plays the character on the *Showtime* series, the actor Liev Schreiber. He introduced himself. A funny thing about famous people: they have to at least pretend you don't already know who they are.

"That's crazy, what you guys did," Schreiber said.

"Man, it's crazy that I'm meeting you! I was literally just watching *Ray Donovan* before I left for the trip."

"Oh, thanks, that's nice to hear." Schreiber's voice was quiet, gravelly. "But what you guys did just took balls."

It suddenly occurred to Anthony that even though he was having a conversation with a movie star, a man who'd literally played a Marvel hero on screen, it actually didn't feel unnatural. Which itself felt weird. It was somehow natural and weird at the same time; weird that it was natural. It was like he was on autopilot. He just knew what to do. He'd always planned on being famous, practicing his autograph with a star for the *A*, but always figured he'd have to get over nerves when he went out to speak in public, which he knew was a thing you had to do every once in a while if you got famous.

But he *didn't* feel nervous. During all the interviews, all the media appearances, with all the famous people he'd met so far, he never felt anxious. Performing came easy to him. Which was almost unnerving in itself. Had he been altered somehow by the train? Had he become a slightly different person?

He'd gone from interviews to media appearances, a president pinning a medal to him, everything happening in such rapid succession that there was no time and there hadn't felt like an obvious reason to think and plan. He hadn't had time to consider what was happening to him. One day he simply became famous. That was it. So from the moment he stepped off the train, everything felt halfway like being in a movie.

Maybe because it almost *was* a movie. In a few minutes he would go out onto a television set and pretend to have a natural conversation with Jimmy Fallon as if the two were best buddies, but they were going to do it with makeup, and stage lights, and hundreds of people watching, crew members and big cameras on wheels moving back and forth. It *was* like stepping into a movie. And since it all felt a little artificial, he didn't feel nervous. It wasn't real.

That changed only very briefly, and the only person who proved capable of making him nervous—to make him take a moment and think about fame—was a kid in a black T-shirt and a headset walking up to him backstage and saying, "Okay, Mr. Sadler, in ten, you're going on."

"Where do I walk?" The curtain was huge.

"Just pull it back and walk through."

"Wait, walk through where?"

"You're on in ten, nine, eight," then the kid went silent and walked away.

"Wait, hello? Where are you going?" But the kid was gone, off to prep some other guest while Anthony wondered how many seconds had gone by and how fast to count, started concentrating on counting in his head, then started to worry about tripping over the curtain on his way onstage. Or what if he couldn't even find the opening, and it was one of those slapstick situations where he gets turned around and con- fused and the audience roars with laughter at the panicked guest mummifying himself in the curtain?

Should I go? This is a pretty damn long ten seconds. It was a forced silence where Anthony couldn't say or do anything other than think, *I'm about to go on TV!* A tingle in his fingertips, his palms clammy, and then his last quiet moment was over and he had the curtain aside with an explosion of bright, blinding lights.

Anthony was back in his element. Prime time.

"THANK YOU FOR BEING ON *The Tonight Show*. I appreciate this, uh ..." Fallon didn't seem to know exactly where to begin, so Anthony bailed him out.

"It's pretty crazy, thanks for having me!" The audience laughed. This wasn't hard.

"Yeah, good, yeah, now can you just, uh, I know ... please just walk me through what happened ..."

And off they went.

He hadn't known that one of his favorite artists, the up and coming rapper Vince Staples, was the musical guest, but here he was, and Staples picked a song to perform that featured one of Anthony's celebrity crushes, the singer Jhené Aiko. She came out in matching off-white sleeveless top and calf-length skirt, exposed midriff, exposed arms so the spiderweb tattoo on her shoulder was half visible, wearing sneakers but somehow making that sexy too. Anthony felt himself get a little uncomfortable in his seat. All his dreams were coming true.

Aiko sang with her sensual, youthful voice, singing in tandem with Staples, but really, singing straight into Anthony's heart.

And if I told you that I love you would you know it was
    a lie
Pretty woman, how you function with the devil in your
    thighs?

During the breaks he shot the breeze with Fallon and David Wells, a retired Yankees pitcher. He went over to the house band, the Roots, and asked for a picture. The bandleader, Questlove, obliged, and then said, "I always have guests autograph a pair of drumsticks. Will you autograph these for me?"

"For you? *You* want *my* autograph?"

43.

HERE WAS ANOTHER THING about being famous Anthony would have to get used to: famous people had a strange fascination with boring lectures.

He and Spencer got invited to San Francisco for the big launch of the new iPhone. The night before, Spencer was doing the Jimmy Kimmel show and Anthony wanted to go down and hang in the wings. He wanted to see the city with Chris Brown, who was going to be the musical guest, and Anthony figured the singer might take them around Hollywood if Anthony could get a chance to talk to him. What better way to celebrate finally being reunited, if only briefly, with Spencer? Of course Alek wasn't there. This would become a pattern. It was rare for Spencer and Anthony to find time to get together these days, but even rarer for Alek to be there.

Anthony watched from the dressing room as Spencer sat down for his own experience with late-night TV, bobbing back and forth to try and get comfortable. *I know, it's weird, right? To try and face the audience and the host at the same time.* Kimmel stood up and gave Spencer a standing ovation, then the audience did too, and Anthony watched Spencer shifting awkwardly on his bad arm, trying to find a comfortable way to sit with his thumb in its plastic sheath.

"You look good, you look healthy," Kimmel said. "You just got back to the United States, right?"

"Yeah, just a couple days ago on the ... shoot, what was

the date?"—Spencer closed one eye, winking; Anthony recognized his friend's flustered face—"Shoot, I don't even know." Backstage Anthony laughed and shook his head. *C'mon, bruh!*

"It was like, last Tuesday . . ."

Kimmel came to the rescue. He held up a picture of the three boys on the train just before the attack, then the picture of Spencer in a wheelchair just after, X-style bandages above his right eye, on his left bicep, his left thumb wrapped in tape, and rivulets of blood streaming down his chest.

"Well, you don't have a shirt on anymore," Kimmel said, as if that were the only problem with the picture, but the audience was still *ooooing* at the sight of Spencer looking like he'd been put through a meat grinder.

"I heard that you were a big Golden State Warriors fan."

"I am, I am. You know, I didn't get to watch as many games as I wanted to because I've been on a seven-hour time difference in Portugal."

"Well, we have a visitor who wanted to say hello to you. Let's go outside right now and see—okay, you see that gentleman right there?" Behind Spencer, a giant wrap-around screen flickered to life, with a live video feed showing the glimmering front grill of a brand new convertible in an alleyway.

Backstage, Anthony's jaw dropped.

"You gotta be joking," Spencer said, "no freaking way," more to himself than to Kimmel.

"That is Klay Thompson."

"Wha . . ." Spencer popped up and spun in his seat.

"He's . . ." The headlights went off and the car stopped. An awkward silence. "Klay doesn't drive stick."

"Is he stalled-out right now?" Spencer was excited.

"Maybe Klay could walk," Kimmel said, "it's only like fifteen feet." Now the crowd began to roar as the car lurched forward in the alley behind the studio, and Kimmel ad-libbed about the basketball player's struggles. "These guys make so much money they don't drive stick."

Klay got out of the car, walked through a door, off camera, while Spencer and Kimmel stood up to go stage right, where Klay walked in, shook Kimmel's hand, and hugged Spencer as the crowd cheered. "Klay has some things for you."

Klay dutifully began handing gifts over to Spencer. First a hat: "I got plenty of them, you know." Spencer laughed. "I got a jersey for you, my man."

"He saw you had no shirt so he brought you a jersey," Kimmel said. Spencer laughed; the crowd laughed louder.

"And also, Klay, do you have the keys to that vehicle?"

"I do."

"Brand new Chevy Camaro convertible and so—we heard you didn't have a car."

Spencer still hadn't composed himself. He let out a high-pitched "What?" and he spun again toward the car.

"And we heard you were moving back to Sacramento. Do you know how to drive stick?"

"I can, I can! I learned in Portugal!" Anthony was moved by how jubilant Spencer was; he was genuinely excited, and all of a sudden Anthony didn't see the pressed air force uniform or the photo with the blood or the person people were starting to call Captain America. All of that fell away and Anthony was looking at twelve-year-old Spencer, over the moon about a new airsoft gun for Christmas.

"Well, beautiful, because that Camaro is for you . . . you never have to get on a train in your life."

AFTER SPENCER GOT HIS CAMARO, he and Anthony met up with Alek for dinner at Arnold Schwarzenegger's house. Just another day in the life.

Anthony sat out in the yard, still thinking about how surreal all of it was, how nice a house this was, how big Arnold's fireplace was, and why, by the way, you'd need a fireplace, let alone a big one, in Southern California, when he heard footsteps from somewhere off in the yard. He knew Schwarzenegger had some kind of big dog, but whatever it was moving around behind him sounded *really* heavy. The footsteps grew louder, the dog got closer, Anthony turned around and almost jumped off the patio.

"What the fuck is that?"

His host looked up.

"Sorry." Anthony tried to recover. "Pardon my—is that a *horse?*"

"Oh yes," Arnold's girlfriend said, "That's Whisky. It's a miniature horse." She smiled politely, as if it were the most normal thing in the world.

"She's a—is she like . . ." Anthony couldn't think of what to ask; this situation had never presented itself before. He'd never had to make conversation about livestock on someone's patio. "She's here like, permanently?"

"Um, yeah. She's here all the time."

That night, they had rooms at a swanky hotel in LA, and Anthony was in the lobby on the phone telling his dad that rich people in Los Angeles kept horses in their houses, when a group of what had to be at least twenty girls walked by single file to the elevator. *What the ...* Behind them was a guy Anthony recognized.

"That's A$AP Rocky—Dad, hold on. I gotta call you back."

Anthony decided to try out his new celebrity status with the famous rapper.

"A$AP! What's up!" A$AP smiled, and took the hand Anthony had offered. "Hey—"

"It's me, Anthony Sadler." A$AP's smile dimmed a little; he pursed his lips and gave a little shake of his head.

"From the train!"

Still nothing.

"The terrorist on the train; you didn't hear about the train attack in France?"

"Sorry, I don't know what you're talking about." Now he was clearly getting impatient, Anthony feeling less confident, less like a peer, more like a stalker.

"Okay, no prob, no prob. Well, where're you guys going?"

"We're going up to a penthouse party."

"Okay, I might see you up there ... ?"

"All right." No invitation came. Anthony had bungled the approach; the rapper had no idea who he was and wasn't about to let him up with his parade of girls. Anthony tried the hostesses, two girls in slip dresses standing by the elevator and flanked by security guards.

"Hey! Hello, how you girls doing? I'm one of the train heroes, you think I could get up there? Spencer Stone's with me too, he's up in his room."

The girls looked at each other. "Sorry, you're one of the whats?"

Does no one in LA read the news? He pulled out his phone, figuring he'd fight LA with LA—he'd do what people here in the land of spectacle probably did on a daily basis, he googled himself. "Look! I'm not making this up. This is CNN. It's serious!"

Finally one of the girls relented. "Okay, I might be able to let you up but not until everyone on the list is in. Come back with your friends in a couple hours." So they did. By the time they got up to the penthouse, A$AP Rocky was gone, but so be it. It was still a penthouse party in LA. They'd make do.

The next morning, they had to catch a four o'clock flight in order to make it to Northern California for the iPhone launch. Anthony still didn't get it. Why did people get so excited about going to lectures? At the launch, Spencer and Anthony walked into the hall, the lights dimmed, and they promptly fell asleep.

Next to them Al Gore, Barry Bonds, Joe Montana, and a bunch of other celebrities watched nerds talk about computers.

in line and lashed out every time someone he didn't really respect tried to show control over him, had created for himself a sense of belonging. The air force was celebrating Spencer for behaving the way Spencer always thought he should behave. For acting, rather than sitting; for thinking on his feet, thinking *for himself.* In a way, the air force was validating the person Spencer had become, independence, irreverence and all; by tackling a man with a machine gun on a train, Spencer had created for himself an institution he could belong to.

So today they would part ways, fame providing the jolt, the activation energy to send them spiraling off into their various adulthoods. They spent the morning doing press, first a shoot for *People* magazine's Sexiest Man Alive issue, during which Anthony learned that Brad Pitt and Angelina Jolie had nominated them—apparently, past winners had to nominate you—then taping their first group interview. Fox News won the sweepstakes for the first sit-down with the three train heroes together, mostly because Fox News was willing to move their whole operation to Sacramento, and the boys needed to be there for what was going to happen next.

After the morning of press ops, a car took them from the Hyatt to the Tower Bridge over the Sacramento River, where people had started to gather. Already, Anthony could tell this was going to be something special. Preparations had been under way for weeks, but he'd been only loosely aware of them; that morning a correspondent for the NBC affiliate on site told the anchors back at the bureau, "I've lived here almost eighteen years now. I don't remember anything like this in Sacramento before."

Anthony was shown to a trailer with HOMETOWN HEROES written on the side. He took a moment to marvel at it, and then he and Spencer and Alek climbed up—Spencer in his air force uniform, Alek wearing what was becoming his trademark short-sleeved shirt, jeans, and sneakers, and a pair of mirrored sunglasses. *I gotta teach these guys how to dress.*

The trailer was decked out with an archway of red and white balloons to frame them, forming a threshold in front of which they stood, as if at any moment they could turn around and disappear through a colorful passageway into another world. Anthony could see their families sitting in the back of classic cars, JFK style, feet on the seats, butts on the seat-backs, so they could see and be seen.

Their trailer was being pulled by a pickup truck, and the bed of the truck was filled with cameramen sticking out at all angles like porcupine quills, folded over one another trying to get a good line of sight to the boys, as the truck pulled out in front of the bridge and began its slow approach toward the capitol building.

Anthony felt like the pope. As he progressed through the crowd, people moved in to shout their love and hold out their hands as if seeking his grace, then filled into the wake, where they saw, behind the boys, on the other side of the colorfully festooned threshold, a gesture of symmetry: a replica of an iconic gift from the people of France to America. The Statue of Liberty, holding the torch up to all those who followed.

In front of them fire engines lined the sides of the streets, and police on motorcycles escorted them, telling well-wishers to back up. People complied only for seconds before filling back into the middle of the street to get closer, many wearing T-shirts someone had handed out with SAC HEROES PARADE written through a blue star. Way off in front, Anthony could see a marching band leading the way, and flag twirlers, drum lines, war veterans in old jeeps. Retired Sacramento Kings basketball players rode a classic fire truck in front of them, bicycle-mounted policemen holding on to the side, serving some purpose about which Anthony was unclear but right now unconcerned with.

It was a half mile from Third Street in front of the bridge down to the capitol steps, where a stage had been erected, flanked by two giant screens advertising the Jackie Green performance, and as Anthony looked up and to the sides, he was bowled over. The place was packed. The entire avenue a mass of humanity, wall to wall. It felt like a million people. These were nameless, faceless people, struggling and scrambling for a photo with them, but he didn't feel used or exploited; he felt appreciated. He felt like he'd given this town something to be proud of. He decided he loved this city, and could see himself never leaving, even though, or maybe because, it was a city with grit and not the best reputation, some storm of violent crime always a few news cycles away. A city mentioned with the kind of tongue-in-cheek derision that some backwater capitals in America are, the Albanys and the Harrisburgs, only Anthony's hometown had the violent crime to compete with a major metropolis. All these people were out here because despite all that, Anthony and his friends had given them something to be proud of.

As the parade moved forward—all the people, streamers, confetti; he didn't even know where it was coming from—it was like proceeding slowly through a fantasy in which he'd saved the day. Only here, he *had* saved the day, and the whole city had come out as if he'd saved them too.

They reached the capitol building and climbed up on a platform under a giant American flag hanging under two fire engine ladders.

The mayor took the podium and yelled, "Come on, Sacramento!!"

Anthony heard Alek whispering something to him, and then arched his eyebrows up to the roof of the capitol building. Anthony looked up and saw snipers on each corner and one in the middle, surveilling the masses of people. Every once in a while, even in the most celebratory moments, there was this: a reminder that they'd vanquished one threat, not all threats. There was still danger out there.

And that they themselves were now targets.

As if on cue, a plane roared overhead, a four-engine C-17 Globemaster out of Travis Air Force Base on a flyover, and the crowd roared to match it as the mayor began to speak.

"Ladies and gentlemen, the moment you've all been waiting for! Please get on your feet, let's welcome to the mic, the Sacramento hometown heroes, Anthony, Alek, and Spencer!" It was Anthony who happened to be standing closest to the mayor, so he was first to the mic, and though he hadn't even known he was going to have to speak and was about to address a wall of humanity as far as he could see, he didn't feel worried. Everything felt *good*. He reached for the mic, and chuckled. He scratched above his eye, and looked over at Alek. Strange, how he didn't feel nervous. Again, he felt it was all surreal. A whole city was out in front of him, waiting to hear what he had to say. He smiled a little, and the crowd reacted just to that. What power! He could control how people felt with the tiniest shift in his expression. He raised his hand to wave, and they roared louder. It was amazing, it was absurd. He felt himself smiling even bigger, he couldn't hold it, it was hilarious and amazing and the pride mixed with the absurdity, *This is us, they're here for us!* and he waved again. In his peripheral vision he saw Alek to one side, Spencer to the other. He *felt* them there. He could see that they'd felt the need to acknowledge the crowd, each doing the two-handed presidential wave, the crowd roaring somehow even louder. But Anthony was still at the mic, and sooner or later he'd have to say something. What to say? *When all else fails,* he thought of what his father said before his first press conference in America, *just say what you feel.* Anthony leaned down toward the mic.

"Um, I just want to say how overwhelming this all is." Another roar. "We've been all around the world in these last couple weeks, but I just want you all to know all the things we've received everywhere, it doesn't feel anything in comparison to being in front of our home crowd like this."

The crowd was euphoric.

"We wanna acknowledge the fact that it is September eleventh, it's kind of surreal for us 'cause we feel like our actions compared to those, all the brave people that did . . . their thing on September eleventh . . ." He could see out of the corner of his eye Alek start grinning at Anthony's loss for words, *Did I really just say 'did their thing' on September eleventh?* "And we just want to appreciate and thank everybody in Sacramento for coming out today. Thank you."

Then Alek came out. "I know it's really hot out."

It sounded like the whole country laughed.

"And, uh, that just means that much more that you guys

all showed up and we just really appreciate it and we're so grateful and, wow, like Anthony said, we've never gotten a reception like this. This has absolutely been unreal and fantastic and thank you all again." Under the podium, Anthony saw Alek's hands come together, almost like a prayer. "Thank you."

Next Spencer, who took to the podium, and just exhaled into the mic. The crowd roared.

All he has to do is breathe and people cheer! Anthony leaned forward and said, "Captain America" into his ear, and then clapped for Spencer with the rest of the crowd.

Spencer bowed toward the mic. "I don't even really know what to say. This support is amazing. And we all love you, and we love Sacramento, and we're proud to be . . . be here on this day. Thank God we could all make it back," his voice cracked a little, "in time. So."

And then Spencer ran out of things to say. Emotion overtook him. He exhaled into the mic once more, the whole city hearing him *feel*, and Anthony could tell his friend was overwhelmed.

"And like Anthony said, we don't want to forget while we're all gathered here today to . . . in remembrance of September eleventh, so . . . let's all just . . ." —Spencer was losing his way a little—"let's all just, uh, remember that." Anthony heard Alek let out a few chuckles, and it caught Anthony, so soon he was trying hard to bite down his own laughter. *Gotta teach these guys how to* speak *too!* Over at the podium, Spencer had a moment of inspiration, he turned and yelled into the mic, "Live for each other and die for each other!" And the crowd erupted.

*   *   *

AFTERWARD THEY WERE shown back into the capitol, down into its bowels, a garage underneath where the temperature dropped and they all got in cars going in different directions. Anthony watched Alek get in a car and leave for the airport, where he'd head down to LA and begin his life as a TV star.

Spencer got in another car to go in a different direction, off for a month of air force–organized media events and then back to Portugal to finish out his tour.

Anthony would stay here, to try and finish his degree.

For now, though, he was going home to nap. The city didn't have the best clubs in the world, but the ones it did have were planning some big things for the one hometown hero staying behind, so he went home, put his head on the pillow, and played the whole day in his head: the photo shoot—Brad and Angelina!—the interview, the thousands upon thousands of people cheering, the goodbyes in the garage under the capitol, the three of them peeling off in their different directions.

He wondered when he'd ever see his two friends again. And then he slept.

45.

WASHINGTON, DC, gleamed before him. How had Anthony never been here? His dad talked so much about politics and the president and everything else that it felt familiar to him, but he'd never actually visited. People never see the important sites they feel close to. And even if he'd been here in his imagination dozens, hundreds of times listening to his dad's stories, or watching *The West Wing* together, it wouldn't have felt like this.

It wasn't that it looked all that different from what he imagined—everything big, clean, and white—it was that he felt different than he thought he would.

He'd been in Europe only weeks ago, but the speed with which everything had happened since then made him feel connected to Europe as if it had been yesterday. That was the last quiet moment, the last *normal* moment he'd had, and he'd been in cities with history rising up all around him. Europe had done that to him, hit him the moment he'd landed in Italy. Maybe because he was going to see Spencer and Alek, and history was the one subject they first bonded over. Whatever it was, between all the partying and the devastating hangovers and talking to pretty girls with foreign accents, what had struck him most about Europe was how many important, somber things had happened, everywhere he went. He'd felt it all around. He'd seen it, the giant arches commemorating this leader, that war, and he'd taken enough photos to crash a computer or two. It was all around, from the ancient cobblestones in Venice that ate up his suitcase wheels, to the stones in the Berlin Holocaust memorial, to standing next to Spencer in the shadow of the Brandenburg Gate, commissioned by a king in the 1700s. Things in Europe were measured not in years but in centuries.

And yet from here, the Lincoln Memorial looked like the Brandenburg Gate back in Berlin. The residue was still with him, because as he looked up at Lincoln, a giant on a throne looking down at the Mall, Anthony thought, *We have history too*. It had taken stepping out of his own country to feel so close to it.

Now he felt not just close to it, but a part of it. By now it had become a refrain so common it sometimes felt nearly meaningless: "American heroes." But here he stood, thinking, *This is where we come from, and we just did something to make this country proud*. Anthony felt proud. In a real way—a powerful, substantive way, not just a country music song or bumper sticker kind of a way. He felt honor, he felt fulfilled. He was proud to be American, because he'd done something small that made him a part of something big. His role in history had been fleeting, but enough that he felt connected to everything that stood before him.

As he walked through the Mall, it was the World War II memorial that pulled him in the hardest. It was coming full circle, back to the war with the stories that brought him and Spencer and Alek together, and to the president Anthony idolized, whose words were inscribed on the walls. Anthony stopped in front of FDR's quote about Pearl Harbor, an inscription bigger than him, and read:

DECEMBER 7, 1941, A DATE WHICH WILL LIVE IN
INFAMY ... NO MATTER HOW LONG IT MAY TAKE US
TO OVERCOME THIS PREMEDITATED INVASION, THE
AMERICAN PEOPLE, IN THEIR RIGHTEOUS MIGHT,
WILL WIN THROUGH TO ABSOLUTE VICTORY.

And for the second time, it was a memorial that forced
him to reflect. The effect was unexpected, even though it
was exactly the effect memorials were supposed to have. He
stood, taking it in, thinking, reflecting, remembering, feeling
the whole size of what he was a part of.

HE TAKES OUT HIS PHONE and begins recording the scene.
    Did all of that just happen?
    No. No way. That was a terrorist. We just stopped a terror-
ist. My friends won't believe this. Dad won't believe this.
    He pans right.
    Spencer on the ground, a gun; he doesn't know exactly
what he should capture, he feels maybe it's important to
capture everything.
    "Where's that gun?" Alek is back, but his question doesn't
make sense. He's holding the gun.
    "What do you mean?" Anthony says. "You're holding it."
    "I mean the other gun. The pistol."
    "Huh?" There is no pistol. Anthony has seen no pistol.
    Alek's jaw is set; there's no doubt in his face. Anthony feels
unsteady.
    Alek says, "The one he tried to shoot Spencer with." Alek
ends the sentence rising in tone, as if to say, *obviously.*

Anthony feels his hand going to his forehead. Is Alek fucking with him? They were both right there for the whole fight with the terrorist; Alek saw the whole thing too, laid hands on the man, why does Alek think there was a pistol? Alek is imagining things.

"Well, then where is it?"

"It has to be in here." Alek begins looking around. Anthony helps because he's feeling the need to help; he gets on his hands and knees too, at least to humor Alek. He looks down the aisle, he looks under the seats. He looks back to where the legs of a table are bolted to the floor, right under where Spencer tried to choke the terrorist all by himself. Anthony rotates his head both ways, and sees something glint. It is dark but shiny, like an old penny, but it is small and cylindrical. He reaches for it and holds it closer. There is no mistaking it. It is a shell casing. And he knows it's too small for an AK-47 round. This is a spent shell casing from a pistol. Someone did have a pistol. Someone fired a pistol.

So where is the pistol?

He stands up and puts the shell casing on the table, with a clink. Alek looks at it and gives a nod. Anthony nods back. They look for the pistol.

Soon Anthony feels useless, going up and down looking for something that clearly isn't here, because if it was here they would have found it; it's one single, small train car. There just aren't many places it could go, and they've already looked everywhere.

He begins piling the weapons and ammo on a seat, arranging it all in one place. It feels productive, like helping a friend pack for a trip. It will save someone time, later.

He organizes it neatly.

He films it with his cell phone. The man had so much ammo.

He looks up. He looks down the train car. He experiences another stream of clarity: he is evaluating everything in front of him like he's part of a CSI team, observing each detail by itself, squinting and focusing on one thing at a time in order to unlock its meaning. He is able to disassociate things from other things, spread them out and observe each detail by itself. Everything is a stationary piece of furniture on a stage. Blood spatter on the window. Blood puddled on the floor. Spencer's head: dark red. The dying man lying down. The shell casing that he found. That he picked up—touched. It will have his fingerprints on it. What can he do about that? There is nothing he can do about that. There is not much he can do about anything. He is a small piece on this set. Maybe he can help Spencer. He goes and stands by his friend for a minute, five minutes. Spencer seems to be losing the man. Anthony can hear clearly when Spencer says, "Do you want me to say a prayer?" The man doesn't seem to respond. Anthony feels moved by something. He leans close and whispers to Spencer, "Just say one anyway."

He doesn't know if Spencer hears. Spencer doesn't reply. But he seems to bow his head.

Ten seconds go by, or maybe a minute or ten minutes, it's hard to tell, and Anthony gets up. Alek is back again. They stand together, silently. And then Anthony feels himself smiling. Alek begins to smile too. And then they are both laughing, because what else is there to do? It is a ridiculous scene in front of them, a ridiculous thing they just took part in. Spencer is on his hands and knees, bleeding out of his head and calm as can be, like it's the most normal thing in the world. The guy on the ground was gushing blood like a fire hydrant and is now talking normally. They've found themselves in the middle of the most farcical movie scene, where people gush blood out of wounds and talk quietly like they've just finished a reading at the local library.

That is what Anthony can't shake: the tranquility. It is quiet. Nobody is panicked. Everything is still. It is amazingly still. It's too still.

He walks toward the back of the car, just observing. He feels it is important to keep observing details. With his phone, with his eyes. These details will be important. Just keep observing and recording.

He moves through the train car one more time, because maybe on a second pass he will find the pistol. He can't find it but he keeps looking in the same places, because he knows it's there, it has to be, he found the bullet. Only instead of the pistol he sees something else. There is a foot sticking out from under a seat. He wills himself toward it. It is attached to a body that is trembling. He bends down and sees a human being. A girl, still hiding. How had he not seen her?

It amazes him. It is such a small space, but it keeps revealing secrets. He keeps seeing there is more in this train car than he thought.

She must have been there the whole time, under the four of them as they fought. It was all happening right over her. She lay there, in a fetal position, her body juddering, sobbing without making noise. Her face would have been inches from their feet as they fought. The man who collapsed gushing blood would have crumpled to the ground nearly on top of her. Anthony has a strange feeling; this girl was so close to where the gunman came into the train car, she would have been the first person killed if the man hadn't been stopped. Anthony is looking at a person who is alive because of him.

He has an urge to say something to her, but doesn't. He can't think of anything that would make any sense.

He is thinking about what to do when they get to a station, whenever that is. They will have to find some security guard, and try to explain what happened. That will be awkward, or dangerous. He imagines police raids in Sacramento, SWAT teams breaking down doors, he sees a scene in his mind, a battering ram and machine guns, "Everybody get the fuck down until we question everybody!" and he is anxious about being caught up in the crossfire, but as the train makes the long gentle left bank into the station, he can see out the window: they know. Men and equipment prepared for urban warfare. SWAT-style trucks, national police, dozens of people waiting, some in full combat gear. Anthony thinks, Should I get down on the ground?

But as they come in in a swarm of motion, they seem to somehow understand exactly who's who. A team of paramedics goes straight to Spencer and takes over for him. Five policemen in heavy gear move directly to the gunman, they do not even ask where he is, they do not have any ambiguity about what car he is in. It feels strange; how do they know? Someone or some agency or some entity knows much more than he does, and he feels for a moment very small, a pawn in something larger. Like someone has been watching the whole time.

The policemen do not untie the terrorist or cuff him, they simply pick him up like he is and carry him, one policeman on each limb, right off the train.

Anthony follows his face as they carry him out. He's awake

now. Anthony can see his eyes open, but the terrorist doesn't say anything. He has a stunned look, like he is thinking, *Did I really just mess that up?*

Someone is yelling in Anthony's ear. "Hey, hey! You two come with us." The authorities somehow know who he and Alek are.

Outside on the platform they begin asking him questions. "What did you guys see?" The policeman is trying to write it down, but he can't get it all straight and finally gives up. "Okay. Just come with me."

"Can we get our bags real quick?"

"Fine. Go ahead, go."

Where is Alek? Alek is gone again. Then Anthony sees him, and it's the strangest thing: Alek is just sitting by himself on a bench.

All the commotion happening around him, police on one side, paramedics on the other, and Alek just sitting there. He doesn't seem to care about any of this. He doesn't seem bothered by anything at all. Just an old man alone on a park bench. By himself, thinking.

46.

ALEK WAS OVER BY THE DEEP END. Spencer was somewhere behind him. The press was on top of them.

Literally, Anthony stood under the White House briefing room, below the place the media gathered every day to hear the press secretary and sometimes the president himself spin the day's news.

But here, underneath the briefing room, they stood in what the chief of staff explained was actually a pool. A person stricken with polio had few other ways to exercise, so Franklin Delano Roosevelt had one built in the White House. Anthony ducked under the cables and wires and servers that now occupied the place where eighty years ago, FDR went about his . . . aquacizing, or whatever it was. Anthony thought about how the three of them were all together in a pool built by their favorite president, about whom they learned in the one class they all liked, and in which they had bonded. Which was probably the reason things had turned out the way they had, and the reason they were here now, killing time before meeting the president of the United States of America.

Anthony thought about that class back in middle school, about that teacher. If he could see them now, standing in the pool that FDR exercised in! On the VIP tour, behind the velvet ropes that blocked other visitors. Being escorted into all the hidden corners of the White House.

"Hey, look at this," Alek said. "Here's where it slopes up.

This is pretty cool, this must be where the shallow end turns into the deep end."

The pool was packed with servers and cables and all the technology that powered whatever was happening above, so Anthony didn't even know he was in a pool until the chief of staff told him, and didn't quite believe it until Alek showed him an exposed part of the wall. It was a strange sensation, like a movie set collapsing around you, so what you thought was your kitchen turned out to be an airport or a grocery store. To stand somewhere, and in an instant have your whole understanding of where you stood become different.

A slope in the floor, a pattern of tile.

On one wall people had written their names, so Anthony did too: *I love you FDR—Anthony Sadler was here on 9/18/15.*

They took him to the ladies' cloakroom FDR had converted into a command center. It was like FDR didn't just have the biggest impact on the world, he had the biggest physical impact on the White House too. The room had old documents showing Hitler's advance in Europe, and Anthony thought of the *Führerbunker,* where Hitler had killed himself, and which Anthony had seen just a few weeks ago. Huge military maps hung on the wall, marked and annotated in grease pencil, which FDR had updated by *National Geographic* cartographers whose work allowed him to see, in graphic form, the spread of evil in the world.

The room had a special machine to receive and send coded messages, and a direct line to Winston Churchill. Seventy-year-old technology that somehow still seemed innovative and compelling.

"Let's see who else is around," the chief of staff said, and led them up to Cross Hall, where Anthony found himself drawn to one presidential portrait that didn't look like the others: JFK with arms crossed and head down, internally negotiating some Cold War crisis. Anthony imitated him and had Kelly snap a picture.

Then to a room where the secretary of state was waiting to greet them, along with some of the president's advisors. They talked for a while, but by then Anthony wasn't really paying attention. He was back in camera mode again, scanning his surroundings, trying to keep an itemized list in his mind so he'd be able to recall later all the things he couldn't politely photograph.

Down a hall that was much shorter than expected, in front of a door that was much closer than expected, he saw men in black suits standing a bit stiffer than everyone else. Secret Service. Did that mean the president was *right there?* He was only a few yards from the president? Everything in the White House was closer than he expected.

And then it was time. A flurry of motion over by the Secret Service men, and people started moving toward them. Before he went in, his dad pulled him aside. Anthony had expected this, some wisdom imparted from the old man before the special moment. "Son," he said, and Anthony prepared for the solemn word of advice. "One thing, before you go in there."

"What is it?"

"No matter what you do, no matter what you talk about in there, there's one thing you need to make sure you do."

"Okay. What?"

"Well . . . you need to give him my business card."

"I need to *what?*"

"Just give it to him. Tell him I know he's busy, but if he ever needs anything, he can call me."

"Dad—*what*? What's the president going to need from you?"

"Or, you know, if he just has a minute to chat. Tell him to give me a call, I'm around."

"Obama is not going to call you."

"Just give it to him."

Anthony tried to picture how he'd ever have a chance to hand the president a business card as if he was headed to some kind of freshman networking conference, rather than meeting the leader of the free world. But as ridiculous as it was, he knew how much it would mean to his father, a man who crossed the county just for the inauguration, who never thought he'd see a black president in his lifetime, let alone stand outside his office, so what choice did he have?

"Okay, Dad, all right. I'll try." He slipped the card into his pocket and walked toward the most influential office in the world.

The door opened. The president was right there. Grayer than expected, the room smaller than expected. Obama walked over to shake Anthony's hand. The president said his name—*the president knew his name*. He held out a hand and guided them all into the room, then showed Spencer to the chair next to his own.

"Sorry, guys, this is the chair for if you get injured."

"No, no," Anthony said, "he deserves it!" Anyway, Anthony and Alek were sitting where the joint chiefs sat in all press pool photos and TV shows Anthony had seen, so he was fine just where he was. He was sitting across from the president. The other butts that'd been in those seats belonged to the people who marshaled America's military might all over the world. Anthony didn't mind that at all.

And then they just chatted. As if it were the most normal thing in the world to chat with the president, in the Oval Office. Anthony let Spencer take the lead, because Anthony was contending with competing impulses: listening to the president's advice but also taking in the surroundings again. He wanted a clear mental picture of this too, everything around him, to savor later. He tried to take it all in, but to do it out of the corner of his eye so that the president wouldn't be insulted that Anthony wasn't really paying attention to him. Brighter than expected carpet. Reddish, almost rust-color drapes, not the dull yellow he expected from TV shows. A bust of Martin Luther King Jr. on the side table. Books about Martin Luther King Jr. on the shelf, which Anthony assumed came with the Obama presidency. The art, nostalgic paintings of barn houses—all the design decisions of the Obama presidency.

The conversation didn't last as long as he thought it would. Or rather, it moved so quickly, it felt so familiar, that before he could fully register it they'd spent fifteen minutes together and the press was coming in, flashes firing and signaling the end of the session.

The president got up, pressing matters of global import clearly pulling him, his attention surely drifting to the dozens of foreign crises he probably had to deal with before lunch. Anthony felt the card in his pocket, saw his father's dreams slipping away. *Shit, shit, how am I gonna say this?* He started to get nervous. He slipped his hand quickly in and out of his pocket, a gesture those close to the president don't generally love to see. Cameras rose. Anthony held the card inside his palm, hoping the president might just ask him about it and open the floor, but he didn't; instead he went and said something to Spencer, and now Anthony was stranded, a kid without a partner when the slow song comes on at a middle school dance.

I have to give it to him.

He stood awkwardly close to Obama for a moment; Obama didn't acknowledge him. But Spencer seemed to sense what was happening; he nodded at Anthony and moved away, letting his own moment with the president end, so that Anthony could make his move. Anthony patted the president on the shoulder.

The president turned, with an incredulous look on his face that said, *Did you really just tap me on the shoulder?*

"Um, sorry. But my dad, er, sorry, *sir*, but my dad"—did the president see the business card in his Anthony's hand?—"he actually really wanted to meet you, he was at the inauguration and everything and he wanted to meet you so he just gave me this and told me to—" but before he could finish Obama interrupted him.

"Is he here? Are you parents here? Tell them to come in!"

"Oh, yeah, okay!" Anthony slipped the card back into his pocket, and the moment changed from one of the few (but ever more frequent) in which he didn't know precisely what to say, to the single proudest, most selfless moment of his life. A moment in which he prioritized someone else's joy over his own composure, with the president of the United States no less, and which, in turn, became the first time he actually felt someone else's joy as if it were his own.

Because he had one more request of the president after the families came in: to take a picture with his dad. In came

Anthony's father, a man who had watched every single episode of *The West Wing* at least twice, a man who never believed he'd live to see an African American president, and who'd saved up to travel across the country just for the chance to be among two million people watching him be sworn in.

Anthony asked to move away from the president, so that his father could stand closer.

Later that day, Anthony would stand in the center of the Pentagon, feeling like the only civilian for a hundred miles, and receive the Medal of Valor from the secretary of defense while Spencer received the Airman's Medal and the Purple Heart and Alek got the Soldier's Medal. They would be honored in front of hundreds of people, including high-ranking military officials whose chests were checkerboarded with ribbons and medals. For three young men obsessed with military history, there could be no bigger thrill. But that didn't compare. It was here, in this instant, that he was proudest.

Anthony felt, at the moment he moved over so his dad could stand next to the president, that he had done something with his life. He had done something for someone. For one person, at least. He felt that the danger he faced, the family that had believed in him, and these two friends with whom he'd risked his life, had allowed him the happiest moment in his life.

He felt grateful, beloved, proud. He felt able. He felt, for the time being, like things were all right in the world.

ACKNOWLEDGMENTS

I'd like to thank God first, my baby girl, Zoe, my dad, Tony, Maria, Arissa, Naomi, Imogene, Al, Butchie, Julie, JuJu, Gary, Josh, Jordan, Justus, Renie, Champagne, Art, Breonni, Marcus, Mario, and Spencer and Alek for saving my life as well.

—*Anthony Sadler*

I'd like to thank God, my mom and dad for how they raised me, Spencer for always being there, and Anthony for stepping up when it counted most.

—*Alek Skarlatos*

I would first like to give all the credit to God. Without his wisdom, love, and strength I would not be where I am today. I would also like to thank my family for always being there and keeping me grounded throughout this past year. My friends for always having my back. The embassy staff in Paris for taking such good care of my family, friends, and me, providing everything we needed in our time of need. The Boyle family for being so generous and selfless.

The air force for providing me with the skills and opportunity to do what I do today, and the countless people who have helped refine me as a man. The first responders that came to my aid on multiple occasions. The people of Sacramento for their love and support.

Last but not least, I would like to thank all the men and women who have given their lives in the name of what's right and just.

—*Spencer Stone*

NOTES

PROLOGUE: ANTHONY SADLER, KNIGHT OF THE LEGION OF HONOR

1. *Basic and Clinical Science Course,* Chapter 6: Sensory Physiology and Pathology (San Francisco: American Academy of Ophthalmology, 2014).

PART I: AIRMAN SPENCER STONE

Chapter 10.

1. Guillermo Contreras, "Fort Sam Shooter Gets 20 Years in Prison," San Antonio Express News, September 12, 2014, http://www.expressnews.com/news/local/article/Fort-Sam-shooter-gets-20-years-in-prison-5752073.php.

Chapter 12.

1. Blimp Squadron 14, http://www.warwingsart.com/LTA/zp-14.html.
2. Ibid.

Ayoub

1. "In Madrid, he was arrested on suspicion of dealing hashish around Lavapiés, a migrant district, and was detained twice in 2009." Raphael Minder, "Scrutiny Falls on a Spanish Mosque after Failed Train Attack," *New York Times,* August 27, 2015, http://www.nytimes.com/2015/08/28/world/europe/renewed-scrutiny-for-mosque-in-spain-after-foiled-train-attack.html?_r=0.
2. "Mr. [Ayoub] Khazzani had found some part-time work, including in a Moroccan teahouse, but never a steady job—like

almost every person interviewed around his former neighborhood, El Saladillo. The unemployment rate in Algeciras is 40 percent." Ibid.

3. Isabelle Piquer and Matthieu Suc, "Attaque dans le Thalys: Ayoub El-Khazzani, itinéraire d'un routard de l'islam radical," *Le Monde*, August 24, 2015, http://www.lemonde.fr/police -justice/article/2015/08/24/ayoub-el-khazzani-itineraire-d-un-routard-de-l-islam-radical_4734995_1653578.html #5AadkiT67tRVeRwl.99.

4. Pseudo-Turpin, *History of Charles the Great and Orlando*, Thomas Rodd, trans., James Compton, printer (London, 1812), 6.

5. "Kamal Cheddad, leader of the Muslim community in El Saladillo, Algeciras, said El-Khazzani 'behaved like a normal guy for his age. He played and went to the beach with other guys; he was also looking for a job.'" John Bittermann and Bryony Jones, "France Train Attack: What We Know about Suspect Ayoub El Khazzani?" CNN, August 25, 2015, http://www.cnn.com/2015/08/24/europe/france-train-attack-what-we-know-about-suspect/.

6. "Mr. Khazzani's last drug-related arrest took place in Ceuta, a Spanish enclave in North Africa, in September 2012. A photograph of him then shows Mr. Khazzani with a beard, rather than being cleanshaven as in a police image from his arrests in Madrid." Minder, "Scrutiny Falls."

7. "He is remembered by friends here not only as devout, but also determined to stay clear of the hashish trafficking around Algeciras, a city of about 117,000 residents that is the main transit port between Spain and Morocco . . . Mr. Khazzani's apparent effort to straighten out his path, however, led to his increasing association with the Taqwa mosque, which François Molins, the chief Paris prosecutor, described at a news conference Tuesday as one 'known for its radical preaching.'" Ibid.

8. Ibid.

9. Piquer and Suc, "Attaque dans le Thalys."

10. "Taqwa mosque in the neighboring district of Moncayo, between a large supermarket and the Piñera internment

center for foreigners, with many illegal immigrants." Ibid.
(Note to the reader: This and other French article quotations
have been translated to English.)

11. "Report on immigration detention centers in Spain for
Migreurop," http://www.apdha.org/media/Report_inmig_det_
centr2011.pdf

12. "The mosque, Taqwa, was under police surveillance from
the first day work started on turning what had been an auto
repair shop into a place of worship." Minder, "Scrutiny
Falls."

13. ". . . would pray everywhere, he was seen in the six mosques
in the municipality, but it looked quite normal. In reality, Ayoub
especially frequented the radical Taqwa mosque in the
neighboring district of Moncayo, between a large supermarket
and La Piñera detention center, where it piled up illegal
immigrants. This is also where his father and brother, Imran,
prayed. According to Spanish information, the latter was the
treasurer and 'had a strong influence on the faithful.' . . . Imran
would be returned to Morocco because his papers were not in
order." Piquer and Suc, "Attaque dans le Thalys."

14. Minder, "Scrutiny Falls."

15. Google map, route from Ar-Raqqah, Syria, to Algeciras, Cádiz,
Spain, https://www.google.be/maps/dir/Raqqa,+Ar-Raqqah+
Governorate,+Syria/Algeciras,+C%C3%A1diz,+Spain/@
39.4813242,-1.701085,4z/data=!3m1!4b1!4m13!4m12!1m5!
1m1!1s0x153719cb01b7b5fb:0xc8bdaf18cf35cfe3!2m2!
1d38.9981052!2d35.9594106!1m5!1m1!1s0xd0c9496ba5d5751:
0xa626ca859cd81ce9!2m2!1d-5.456233!2d36.1407591?
hl=en.

16. "Dispelling rumors of his injury or death, the leader of the
militant group that calls itself the Islamic State issued a new
call to arms on Thursday in a 17-minute speech, belittling
President Obama's plan to send more soldiers to Iraq and
urging disciples to 'erupt volcanoes of jihad everywhere.'"
An audio recording of the speech by the leader Abu Bakr
al-Baghdadi was distributed online, along with Arabic, English,
and Russian transcripts; http://www.nytimes.com/2014/11/14/

world/middleeast/abu-bakr-baghdadi-islamic-state-leader-
calls-for-new-fight-against-west.html.

17. Scott Atran and Nafees Hamid, "Paris: The War ISIS Wants,"
    New York Review of Books, NYR Daily, November 16, 2015.
18. Ibid.
19. Ibid.
20. "Khazzani lived in the same house with his parents in
    Algeciras until he left for France in 2014." Reuters, "Spanish
    Police Search House of Train Gunman's Family," September 1,
    2015, http://af.reuters.com/article/commoditiesNews/
    idAFL5N11737K20150901.
21. "Ayoub El-Khazzani, is hired by Lycamobile, a British phone
    company 'specializing in expatriate communities.'... 'Lyca is
    well known here. It's a small seasonal job for a lot of young
    people. There is nothing else. They are given a polo shirt with
    the company logo and a cart with small gifts for distribution in
    the street,'says one of his former neighbors of Algeciras, who
    prefers to keep anonymity." Piquer and Suc, "Attaque dans le
    Thalys."
22. Karina Pallagst, Thorsten Wiechmann, Cristina Martinez-
    Fernandez, *Shrinking Cities: International Perspectives and
    Policy Implications* (New York, Routledge, 2014), 86–87.
23. "The French government has announced a plan to boost
    policing in 15 of the most crime-ridden parts of France in an
    effort to reassert state control over the country's so-called
    'no-go' zones: Muslim-dominated neighborhoods that are
    largely off limits to non-Muslims." Soeren Kern, "France Seeks
    to Reclaim 'No Go' Zones," Gatestone Institute, August 24, 2012,
    http://www.gatestoneinstitute.org/3305/france-no-go-zones.
24. "Consider Seine-Saint-Denis, a notorious northern suburb of
    Paris, and home to an estimated 500,000 Muslims ... Seine-
    Saint-Denis, which has one of the highest rates of violent
    crime in France, is now among the initial 15 ZSPs because of
    widespread drug dealing and a rampant black market.
    Because, however, the suburb also has one of the highest
    unemployment rates in France—40% of those under the age
    of 25 are jobless—it remains unlikely that a government

crackdown will succeed in bringing down the crime rate in any permanent way.'" Ibid.

25. "'He went away to France thinking that he had found a very good job, but instead they kicked him out and left him with nothing and no money,' Mr. Khazzani's father said. 'I don't know what then went wrong.'" Minder, "Scrutiny Falls."

26. "The contract, which required him to hand out pamphlets to potential customers on the outskirts of Paris, was an opportunity to make a fresh start after an untethered and jobless youth, according to his father and other residents of El Saladillo." Ibid.

27. "Ayoub El Khazanni rather left good memories. His former colleagues, faced by Europe 1, described him as a 'quiet' man and 'needy' who proudly showed his Moroccan origins. The employee came and went alone on public transport." Europe 1, "Thalys: El Khazzani, un salarié 'discret et besogneux,'" August 25, 2015, http://www.europe1.fr/faits-divers/thalys-el-khazzani-un-salarie-discret-et-besogneux-2505429.

28. "'His work, to distribute flyers and put up posters, however, was interrupted after two months,' said his former boss, the CEO of mobile operator Lycamobile." *Valeurs Actuelles,* "Attaque dans le Thalys: Ayoub El Khazanni a bien vécu en France," August 25, 2015, http://www.valeursactuelles.com/societe/attaque-dans-le-thalys-ayoub-el-khazanni-a-bien-vecu-en-france-55088.

29. "'The papers' that he presented did not allow him to work in France.' Still, 'I think I can tell you that it was going pretty good. It was promising.' said his former employer." Ibid.

30. "The suspect, who is being questioned near Paris, was flagged up to French authorities by their Spanish counterparts in February 2014."BBC, "France Train Shooting: Gunman Known to Police," BBC, August 22, 2015, http://www.bbc.com/news/world-europe-34028261.

31. "Early in 2014, fearing he could be found on French territory, they warned Paris, which established an S3 level (on a danger scale 1 to 16) in the month of February." *Valeurs Actuelles,* "Attaque dans le Thalys."

32. "... identified by the Spanish authorities to French intelligence services in February 2014." Chine Labbé and Sarah White, "France Train Gunman Identified as Islamist Militant," Reuters, August 22, 2015, http://www.reuters.com/article/us-france-train-shots-idUSKCN0QR09R20150822.

33. *Valeurs Actuelles*, "Attaque dans le Thalys."

34. "In January 2014, the company offers El-Khazzani work in France ... a six-month contract to work in Seine–Saint-Denis, confirmed a source in the Spanish Ministry of the Interior. He would be left with other young people in his neighborhood to 'sell phones to Moroccans' or more precisely rechargeable SIM cards. A month later, Madrid warns French intelligence of the possible arrival of El Khazzani in the territory. The French services place an 'S' form (for 'state security'). But it does not involve active surveillance. In an unannounced check, the police are allowed to extract maximum information on the subject." Piquer and Suc, "Attaque dans le Thalys."

35. "His father said he left for France to work for mobile phone operator Lycamobile—a claim confirmed by the head of the firm who said Khazzani stayed for two months in early 2014 and left because he did not have the right work papers." Simon Tomlinson and Tom Wyke, *Daily Mail*, "Blindfolded and Barefoot," August 25, 2015, http://www.dailymail.co.uk/news/article-3210351/Blindfolded-barefoot-French-terror-train-gunman-led-court-surrounded-bulletproof-jacket-wearing-officers-just-hours-questioning-deadline-expires.html#ixzz 3ylIj3MX3.

36. "Alain Jochimek, the French director of Lycamobile, told France Info radio that the company did not renew Mr. Khazzani's short-term contract because he did not have working papers to remain in France." Minder, "Scrutiny Falls."

37. "Lycamobile ended up separating from Ayoub El Khazzani in March 2014, a month before the end of the CSD due to a problem with his residence permit and a visibly false address." Europe 1, "Thalys."

38. "... still remembers her son and five other young Moroccans from Algeciras had been 'recruited to work in France,' in spring

2014 for 'a six-month contract' in a telecommunications company. 'But after a month, they were dismissed. They are criminals in this business of using people like that.'" "Videos. Thalys: El-Khazzani aurait travaillé un mois en Seine-Saint-Denis," *Le Parisien,* August 25, 2015, http://www.leparisien.fr/faits-divers/videos-el-khazzani-aurait-travaille-un-mois-en-seine-saint-denis-25-08-2015-5033553.php#xtref=https%3A%2F%2Fwww.google.com%2F.

39. "'What was he supposed to do? What he was supposed to eat? They are criminals in this business of using people like that,' laments his father." Piquer and Suc, "Attaque dans le Thalys."

40. Atran and Hamid, "Paris: The War ISIS Wants."

41. "He acknowledged having stayed 'five to seven months' in Aubervilliers in 2014. It was during this period that he worked for two months for a mobile operator, Lycamobile. His former employer had said Monday it had terminated its contract 'as the papers he had submitted did not allow him to work in France.'" Piquer and Suc, "Attaque dans le Thalys."

PART II: SPECIALIST ALEK SKARLATOS

Ayoub

1. "Still, the ISB have traced him on May 10, 2015, according to *Libération.* He was spotted because of the S form at the Berlin airport, boarding a GermanWings flight to Istanbul. This information is transmitted to the Spanish intelligence services on 11 May and it takes ten days to inform their counterparts that the young Moroccan is now in Belgium." *Valeurs Actuelles,* "Attaque dans le Thalys."

2. "Cazeneuve did not give a name, but . . . said he was believed to have flown from Berlin to Istanbul on May 10 this year." Labbé and White, "France Train Gunman." "German police had also flagged the gunman as a risk to French security services after he aroused suspicion while waiting to take a flight from Berlin to Turkey en route to Syria. 'The security services lost track of him after he arrived in Istanbul,' sources told *Le Parisien*

newspaper." Robert Mendick, David Chazan, and Gregory Walton, "Paris train gunman's links to Syria," August 22, 2015, http://www.telegraph.co.uk/news/worldnews/islamic-state/11818772/Paris-train-gunmans-links-to-Syria.html.

3. "According to François Molins, it would be back on European soil on June 4 by a flight from Antakya, a city near the Syrian border." Piquer and Suc, "Attaque dans le Thalys."

4. *Valeurs Actuelles*, "Attaque dans le Thalys."

5. "Molenbeek is the source of the highest concentration in Europe of jihadi foreign fighters going to fight in Syria and Iraq and returning battle-hardened and determined to take their fight to the capitals of Europe." Ian Traynor, "Molenbeek: The Brussels Borough Becoming Known as Europe's Jihadi Central," *Guardian*, November 15, 2015, http://www.the guardian.com/world/2015/nov/15/molenbeek-the-brussels-borough-in-the-spotlight-after-paris-attacks.

6. "Raids conducted Monday in Sint-Jans-Molenbeek, near Brussels, have established that he stayed 'very recently' with his sister, said François Molins. The Belgian public prosecutor confirmed to the world that the young woman came spontaneously to the Police." "Thalys: El-Khazzani mis en examen et écroué pour une attaque «ciblée et préméditée»," *Le Monde*, August 25, 2015, http://www.lemonde.fr/police-justice/article/2015/08/25/attaque-du-thalys-suivez-en-direct-la-conference-de-presse-du-procureur_4736412_1653578.html.

7. "Molenbeek-Saint-Jean is a densely-packed district where unemployment is high and disengagement rife. Children play on green open spaces framed by graffitied walls, and behind the colourful shop facades there are pockets of poverty." Alex Forsyth, "Paris Attacks: Is Molenbeek a Haven for Belgian Jihadis?" BBC, November 17, 2015, http://www.bbc.com/news/world-europe-34839403.

8. Atran and Hamid, "Paris: The War ISIS Wants."

9. "During his detention, El-Khazzani reportedly admitted to have traveled in the past six months in Belgium, Germany, Austria, France and Andorra, trips made each time by train." Piquer and Suc, "Attaque dans le Thalys."

10. "Reportedly, El-Khazzani, who has a Spanish residence card, would have been recognized in custody to have traveled in the past six months in Belgium, in Germany, in Austria, in France and Andorra, the trips made each time by train." *Le Monde,* August 25, 2015.

11. "He said he had not spoken to his son since he left Algeciras in 2014 although his wife, named in the article as Zahara, had spoken to him by phone about a month earlier, it said." Reuters, "Spanish Police Search House."

12. Weather history for Melsbroek, Belgium, August 2015, https://www.wunderground.com/history/airport/EBBR/2015/8/21/DailyHistory.html?req_city=Brussels&req_state=&req_state name=Belgium&reqdb.zip=00000&reqdb.magic=1&reqdb.wmo=06451.

13. "Ayoub al-Khazzani was also in possession of a mobile phone 'clearly dedicated to the commission of the offense.' The telephone line was activated the same day and the suspect had watched a video from this unit call for jihad." Miguel Medina, "Ce qu'a révélé le procureur de Paris sur l'attaque d'Ayoub el-Khazzani," France 24, August 25, 2015, http://www.france24.com/fr/20152508-thalys-attaque-ayoub-el-khazzani-terrorisme-procureur-francois-molins.

14. "Coulibaly reportedly purchased the weapons near the Gare du Midi train station in Brussels for less than 5,000 euros ($5,876), reported the Telegraph. The area around the station, which serves as the Eurostar's Belgian terminus, is known as a hub for illegal weapons sales." Lora Moftah, "Belgian Arms Dealer Supplied Paris Gunmen with Weapons," *International Business Times,* January 14, 2015, http://www.ibtimes.com/belgian-arms-dealer-supplied-paris-gunmen-weapons-assault-rifles-used-charlie-hebdo-1783432.

15. "What Belgium adds to the mix, analysts say, is a long, troubled history of lax gun laws and a pedigree of gun manufacturing, led by FN Herstal in the Wallonia region. The country has an unusually high number of people with technical and commercial expertise in guns." Christian Oliver and Duncan Robinson, "Paris Attacks: Belgium's Arms Bazaar," *Big Read,* November 19,

2015, http://www.ft.com/cms/s/0/33a2d592-8dde-11e5-a549-
b89a1dfede9b.html#axzz40jF7DzO1.

16. "The flow of illegal guns into Belgium began in earnest in the
1990s amid the Balkan wars and the fall of the Soviet Union.
Mr Moniquet says a large Balkan community built up during
those years, when guns circulated freely around the fragmen-
ting Yugoslavia, and former communist officials took to
trafficking their states' vast and often mothballed munitions
reserves. . . . Mr Moniquet estimates that 90 per cent of the
arms circulating in Belgium probably originate from the
Balkans. 'You have mountains of Kalashnikovs in Bosnia,
Serbia and Croatia,' he says. When you take in people, you
take in their luggage. Smuggling is a living tradition for these
guys." Ibid.

17. "Nils Duquet, an arms expert at the Flemish Peace Institute,
notes that until 2006, purchasers could buy guns simply by
showing an ID card. The government only tightened its rules
after 18-year-old skinhead Hans Van Themsche went on a
racially motivated shooting rampage in Antwerp that year,
killing two people and injuring one. By that stage, however,
a large pool of guns had built up in Belgium. 'We had got a
reputation,' says Mr Duquet. 'People knew Belgium was a place
to go to buy guns.'" Ibid.

18. Thalys terminal, https://foursquare.com/v/thalys-terminal/4bf
b9014d2b720a13d22336a.

19. Thalys terminal timetable, https://www.thalys.com/be/en/
timetables-correpondances?gare_dep=Amsterdam&gare_arr=
Paris&date_aller=2016 -06-10&plage_horaire_aller=00-
24&plage_horaire_retour=00-24&as=y.

20. "Q: He was suspicious so walked over to see what was going on?
A: Exactly.
Q: What happened next?
A: Well, when the person came out of the bathroom, my
   husband saw him coming out with a gun, and there was a
   young guy who wants to remain anonymous so far that had
   grabbed him from the back, and my husband was able to
   take the AK from the shooter, and unfortunately he didn't

know that the bad guy had another gun, a hand gun, so he shot him in the back.

Q: You were just feet away as I understand it.

A: Yeah, yeah. I was about a foot, or maybe a foot in a half. He told me, "I'm hit." He said it twice, "I'm hit, I'm hit, it's over." Isabelle Risacher-Moogalian on *Today*, http://www.today.com/video/wife-of-french-american-train-hero-he-said-im-hit-514941507836.

21. "Mr Moogalian, 51, and wife were seated facing each other on the high-speed train when she saw only his expression and the urgent 'Get out, this is serious.' Then, Isabelle Risacher Moogalian said, she ducked behind some seats as he lunged to grab the assault rifle from the gunman's hands." "French-American Mark Moogalian Is New High-Speed Train Attack Hero," News.com.au, August 26, 2015, http://www.news.com.au/world/frenchamerican-mark-moogalian-is-new-highspeed-train-attack-hero/news-story/146d22a604bb3ba0ae37f600d3 ada203.

22. "The bullet traveled through his shoulder-blade and through his collarbone. It also pierced his left lung. 'I saw my husband through the chairs . . . and he told me, 'I'm hit, I'm hit, it's over.'" Savannah Guthrie, Kelly Cobiella, and Nancy Ing, "Mark Moogalian Thanks Airman Spencer Stone for Saving Life on Train." August 28, 2015, http://www.nbcnews.com/storyline/french-train-attack/mark-moogalian-thanks-airman-spencer-stone-saving-life-train-n417591.

23. Link to photos of Spencer Stone, https://www.google.com/search?q=spencer+stone&source=lnms&tbm=isch&sa=X&ved=0ahUKEwiB_-SD7onLAhVDWh4KHZKBD8QQ_AUICCgC&biw=1149&bih=626#imgrc=MGtydTZYg9j2nM%3A.

PART III: ANTHONY SADLER, KNIGHT OF THE LEGION OF HONOR
Chapter 35.

1. "More Than 100 Killed," CNN, http://www.pastpages.org/screenshot/2609665/.
2. Soren Seelow, "Abdelhamid Abaaoud, l'instigateur présumé des attentats tué à Saint-Denis," *Le Monde,* November 16, 2015, http://www.lemonde.fr/attaques-a-paris/article/2015/11/16/qui-est-abdelhamid-abaaoud-le-commanditaire-presume-des-attaques-de-paris_4811009_4809495.html.